Source pg 7
argument ⊕ 11

RELATED LIVES

RELATED LIVES

Confessors and Their Female Penitents, 1450–1750

Jodi Bilinkoff

CORNELL

UNIVERSITY

PRESS

ITHACA & NEW YORK

First published 2005 by Cornell University Press

Printed in the United States of America

Library of Congress Cataloging-in-Publication Data

Bilinkoff, Jodi, 1955–
    Related lives : confessors and their female penitents, 1450–1750 / Jodi Bilinkoff.
        p. cm.
    Includes bibliographical references and index.
    ISBN-13: 978-0-8014-4251-3 (cloth : alk. paper)
    ISBN-10: 0-8014-4251-6 (cloth : alk. paper)
        1. Confession—Catholic Church—History.   2. Monastic and religious life of
women—History.   3. Confessors—History.   4. Spiritual directors—History.
5. Penitents—History.   6. Christian hagiography—History.   I. Title.
    BX2262.B55   2005
    282'.09'03—dc22   2005013287

Cornell University Press strives to use environmentally responsible suppliers
and materials to the fullest extent possible in the publishing of its books. Such
materials include vegetable-based, low-VOC inks and acid-free papers that are
recycled, totally chlorine-free, or partly composed of nonwood fibers. For further
information, visit our website at www.cornellpress.cornell.edu.

Cloth printing   10 9 8 7 6 5 4 3 2 1

✣ CONTENTS

❧ ILLUSTRATIONS

Some fifteen years ago, when I was invited to present an essay at a conference in honor of my dissertation advisor and mentor Natalie Zemon Davis, I proposed to write a piece on five holy women, nuns and *beatas*, from the diocese of Avila in the sixteenth and seventeenth centuries. As I began to examine the documents relating to these women and their religious experience, however, I noticed a striking commonality. Despite differences of social class, age, religious order, and origin in rural or urban settings, all five women maintained close relationships with male confessors or spiritual directors. In three out of five cases, the confessors wrote pious biographies, or hagiographies, of their exemplary penitents after the women's deaths.

These hagiographical texts proved fascinating reading. The confessor-penitent relationship, I had thought, was a rather simple and fundamentally repressive one in which confessors exercised complete authority while penitents responded with total obedience. Control and censorship would be the dominant elements in clerics' treatment of women, my previous studies had led me to believe. However, close examination revealed that in practice relations between confessors and female penitents were frequently more complex, more nuanced, and more reciprocal than I had expected. And I found that not only did clerical authors narrate the lives of their saintly subjects, but they also revealed much about themselves: their lives, their motivations for writing, and especially their relationships with women they regarded as Servants of God.

Encountering these texts completely changed my orientation. The resulting essay ("Confessors, Penitents, and the Construction of Identities in Early Modern Avila") went from being about women to being about men—men whose identities had been profoundly affected by their interactions with women. As I began to read more broadly and discuss my findings on Avila with other scholars, I came to realize that these five cases from one diocese in central Castile represented a very small part of a much larger whole. The phenomenon of clerics and pious women developing close relationships, followed by the writing of exemplary lives, was in fact ubiquitous throughout Catholic Europe and its colonies in the early-modern period. I began to speculate that the study of these relationships and the resulting literatures of spiritual autobiography and hagiography could prove a remarkably fruitful way of studying gender, that is, the roles, expectations, and self-definitions of both men and women. And I began to wonder what impact experiencing—or at least reading about—these sorts of relationships might have had on both clerics and women.

This book, then, explores both the ways in which clerics related to female penitents they determined were spiritually gifted and how they related the lives of these women for others to read and emulate. I offer my reflections on a pivotal, if not always sufficiently appreciated, aspect of early-modern Catholicism: the emergence of the confessor or spiritual director as biographer and the composition of hagiographical accounts by confessors as a recognized—indeed, popular—form of life-writing. In many ways this is a book about texts, as well as their authors, readers, structures, themes, circumstances of production, and multiple uses. In reading dozens of these texts, from several parts of Europe and both sides of the Atlantic, I have come to believe that the enterprise of establishing relationships and relating lives had a significant impact on religious faith, identity formation, and the construction of models of behavior. I have become convinced that this represents a particularly rich episode in the alliance between women and clerics that has periodically animated the history of Christianity and may help to account for the preservation and expansion of Catholic culture during a conflictive age. This is how, and why, a brief examination of five cases from Avila evolved into a book-length project of fifteen years' duration.

This book has taken a long time to write, and I have incurred many debts of gratitude. My earliest thinking on relationships between male confessors and female penitents was stimulated during an undergraduate course that I audited from Natalie Zemon Davis at Princeton University around 1980. She asked whether there were circumstances in which early-modern women could have meaningful friendships with men outside the institution of marriage. This book is, in part, an attempt to answer that question. It is as well a tribute to Natalie, extraordinary mentor and friend. Researching this book also gave me an opportunity to reestablish contact with a teacher who had inspired and supported me as an undergraduate student at the University of Michigan. I thank Thomas Tentler for his unparalleled erudition and now his friendship.

Several friends and colleagues have read and commented on all or most of this book while it was still in manuscript form. Barbara Diefendorf and John Coakley proved exemplary readers, both informally and in an official capacity. Allan Greer offered invaluable advice on this book, and kept us both sane during our collaboration on *Colonial Saints*. I would like to especially recognize Alison Weber, who was indefatigable in making helpful comments, offering moral support, and correcting commas. I am truly fortunate to have her as a soul mate.

Many others have helped me with suggestions, references, linguistic assistance, and encouragement of all sorts: Daniel Bornstein, Kathryn Burns (who inspired the title of chapter 5), María Cruz de Carlos, Simon Ditchfield, Lurdes Fernandes, Colleen Gray, Daniella Kostroun, Susan Laningham, William Link, John O'Malley, Moshe Sluhovsky, Ronald Surtz, Nancy van Deusen, Cordula van Wyhe, Christopher Wilson, Marjorie Woods, and Gabriella Zarri. I am especially grateful to James Amelang for his good-humored and timely intercession. I have presented material from this book at many talks and conferences over the years; I offer my sincere thanks to members of those audiences for their thoughtful questions and remarks.

Generous financial assistance for this project came from the National Endowment for the Humanities (Summer Stipend FT-37279), the Mellon Foundation, the American Association of University Women, and the University of North Carolina at Greensboro. I spent the 1999–2000 academic year as a Fellow at the National Humanities Center, an experience I will never forget. I am deeply grateful to the Center's staff and to my fellow fellows for their help, stimulation, and companionship. My thanks also to John Ackerman, Sheri Englund, Jamie Fuller, Karen Laun, and others at Cornell University Press for their efforts in moving this from project to book.

For years Rich Haney has offered indispensable help, technical and otherwise, and demonstrated patience worthy of the saints. Amanda Bilinkoff Haney has made me as interested in the present and the future as I have always been in the past. I dedicate this book to them.

RELATED LIVES

INTRODUCTION

The notion that weak and fallible human beings commit sins or wrongdoings of some sort and consequently need to expiate those sins in a ritual or regularized way can undoubtedly be found in many religions. It is, however, a salient feature of Christianity. From its earliest centuries the faithful were exhorted to confess sins they had committed against God and their neighbors and perform some sort of public act of recompense. By the twelfth century penance had come to be codified by the Catholic Church as one of the seven sacraments, rites understood as outward signs of inner spiritual grace. After examining his conscience a sinner was to undergo a multistaged process: first acknowledging remorse or contrition for his transgressions, then making a formal confession to a priest, who subsequently granted absolution and assigned an act of penance as satisfaction. This basic system for the forgiveness of sins would persist into modern times, even as its circumstances and relative significance would change according to time, place, and historical context.[1]

My purpose here is not to provide a narrative history of confession and penance in the Christian tradition nor to examine the innumerable theological debates about its meanings and role in salvation carried out over the centuries.[2] I likewise do not discuss in any detail confessors' manuals or other forms of prescriptive literature that attempted to mandate how believers should make their confessions and how priests should listen and assign appropriate penances. These fascinating topics have been thoroughly studied by other scholars, to whom I acknowledge my debt.[3]

In this book, rather, I focus upon the practice of confession in late-medieval and early-modern Europe, with special attention to the interpersonal relationships involved as well as to the inner change of heart at least hoped for in each individual repenting sinner. I mention here two aspects of confession that had far-reaching implications for the forging of sacramental and social relationships: the fact that it was oral and was to be kept confidential. A turning point in the history of oral confession occurred with the famous decree of the Fourth Lateran Council of 1215, which required that "All believers of both sexes who have attained the age of discretion must faithfully confess their sins in person at least once a year to their own priest, and must make the effort to carry out the imposed penance according to their ability."[4] Here confession is defined as a sacrament that involves not only the repenting of sins but also a direct encounter with a priest at least once a year. As we will see, by the late Middle Ages many Catholics desired to unload their consciences—and have a talk with a priest—much more frequently than this.

Another important historical development is the notion that confession to a priest should be irrevocably confidential. By the time of the Fourth Lateran Council the concept of a binding "seal of confession" was already in place. The edict urges that a priest should "exercise the greatest precaution that he does not in any degree by word, sign, or any other manner make known the sinner . . ." Sternly, the papal authorities warn that "He who dares to reveal a sin confided to him in the tribunal of penance . . . [shall] be not only deposed from the sacerdotal office but also relegated to a monastery of strict observance to do penance for the remainder of this life."[5]

This legislation, however, says nothing about maintaining the seal of confession after the sinner's death. Moreover, what if information learned during confession reveals to the priest that the penitent is not an ordinary sinner but rather a person of extraordinary spiritual grace? Given his apostolic responsibilities, should he not broadcast this life of signal holiness and hold it up for emulation? Many late-medieval and early-modern clerics were intensely interested in both safeguarding the privacy of the confessional experience and promoting saintly exemplars.[6] In the case of extraordinary female penitents, the latter imperative often trumped the former. The Jesuit Paul Ragueneau, for example, readily accepted a commission to write the life of his penitent, the Hospital Sister Catherine de Saint Augustin, shortly after her death in 1668. He could not refuse an opportunity to present "for the edification of the public and the consolation of pious souls the example of a life and death so pure and so precious before God," and share with readers "the communications that she gave me herself of all that happened in the most secret [recesses] of her soul . . ."[7] These interlocking issues of oral communication, intimacy, and exemplarity would continue to inform the confessional process and its expression in women's spiritual autobiographies and biographies of female penitents written by confessors throughout the early-modern period.

In this study I use the terms "confessor" and "penitent" somewhat generically, although I recognize that there are more technical, theological meanings as well.[8] In many ways the definition of a confessor derives from the intersection of two sacraments: penance and ordination. During the Middle Ages the power to "bind and loose"—that is, hear confessions, impose penances, and offer absolution for sins—became an integral part of what it meant to be a Catholic priest. As we have seen, the 1215 edict spelled out the duties and responsibilities of priests as well as parishioners. In this book I refer to ordained clerics, both diocesan priests and members of religious orders, as confessors when they are carrying out this duty, so critical to their sacerdotal and personal identities.

By penitent I mean, simply, anyone who came under the sacramental care of a confessor—men and women, laypersons, and members of religious orders. I do not limit the term to tertiaries or members of third orders of penitence, as was, for example, Catherine of Siena.[9] I do focus, however, upon individuals who confessed to a priest on a regular basis, going well beyond the minimum annual requirement.

Finally, a word about the term "hagiography." This is commonly defined as "lives of the saints." I follow in the paths of scholars such as André Vauchez, who suggests a broader definition of a literary genre that remained extraordinarily popular throughout the Christian centuries. This would include biographical accounts of persons regarded as holy or exemplary in their own time, even if they were not formally canonized as saints. By the late Middle Ages, Catholic culture boasted thousands of "saints," official and unofficial.[10] In this book I examine the hagiographical treatment of "modern saints," as opposed to "saints of old," that is, texts written by authors who were exact or near contemporaries of their exemplary subjects. Usually these hagiographers were personally and often well acquainted with their subjects.

The boundaries of this study—geographical, linguistic, and chronological—deserve explication as well. I examine here cases and texts from Spain, Italy, France, Portugal, Spanish America, and French Canada—in many ways the "heartland" of Catholicism in the early-modern period. Scholars typically choose to study writings from, say, Spain or the Hispanic world, or Italy or France. This line of research has resulted in many important studies, to which I acknowledge my debt. It can, however, perhaps inadvertently lead to the conclusion that a whole range of issues relating to religious authority, gender

relations, constructions of identity, and the uses of exemplarity were some-
how unique or exclusive to a particular group or region.

For this reason I attempt a comparative or cross-national approach, blur-
ring as it were geographical and linguistic borders in order to explore this
body of literature within a broad, trans-Atlantic Catholic culture of the early-
modern period. I recognize, of course, that there are always specific local circumstances involved in the production and reception of texts; indeed, I try to
closely attend to them. But my reading of hagiographical narratives from different parts of Europe and its colonies has convinced me of the need to consider the similarities as well as the particularities. My encounters with these
texts have compelled me to think about the big story of which all these individual life stories constitute a part.[11]

The chronological reach is quite broad, too, from roughly 1450 to 1750.
There are several justifications for beginning in the mid-fifteenth century. One
is historiographical. Medievalists have produced numerous studies of hagiographical texts and the construction of sanctity; most of these studies end
around 1400. This has given rise to a common assumption that hagiography
was a purely "medieval" genre. Yet, as Thomas Heffernan points out, this literary form has one of the longest continuous histories, "beginning with St.
Luke's rendering of St. Stephen's martyrdom in Acts and having no de facto
end . . ."[12]

Certainly the writing of saintly lives did not end at the close of the Middle
Ages. Indeed, the advent of printing around 1450 had the effect of proliferat-
ing texts of all sorts. As we will see, hundreds of religious life-narratives, including biographies of saintly women written by their confessors, were
published, translated, and distributed throughout Catholic Europe and its
colonies in the first three hundred years after the invention of the printing
press. In terms of sheer numbers of texts produced, it is the early-modern period that should be considered the "Golden Age" of hagiography! In any case,
it seems indisputable that the age of printing serves as a critical watershed in
European cultural history generally and thus an appropriate point of departure for this study.

Beyond possessing the technological means to produce more texts than
ever, from the fifteenth century on confessors had a number of compelling
reasons to record the lives of exemplary female penitents. From earliest Christian times there had been women who reported visions, voices, and other supernatural gifts and male clerical authorities who had questioned these claims.
But as many scholars have shown, by 1400 the issue of women's charismatic

authority had become especially fraught. In an age of schism, political insta-
bility, and growing anxieties about heresy and witchcraft, women's behavior
and spiritual status came under special scrutiny. Theologians such as Jean Gerson warned of women's physical and moral weakness, their vulnerability to
deception by the devil, and their willingness to make fraudulent claims of
sanctity in order to gain attention.[13]

During the middle decades of the fifteenth century this atmosphere of increased suspicion and surveillance may have made some priests reluctant to
promote holy women, but this pause did not last long. By the 1480s, nuns, tertiaries, and pious laywomen such as Battista da Varano and María de Ajofrín
were once again being lauded as pious exemplars, especially in northern Italy
and Iberia.[14] The need for clerical authorization, however, had become more
crucial than ever. Confessors now routinely ordered their female penitents to
write accounts of their lives and spiritual experiences. They carefully checked
these autobiographies for theological errors, often correcting or even remov-
ing material before granting their approval.[15] Even more commonly, confessors composed their own biographical accounts, a strategy that offered an
extremely effective way of certifying spiritual daughters as orthodox as well
as narrating the details of saintly lives. This legitimizing impulse, I suggest,
goes a long way toward explaining the high incidence of life-writing in the
early-modern period, as well as the prickly tone sometimes adopted by authors who were as determined to defend their penitents as they were anxious
to establish their own credentials as spiritual guides.

The outbreak of the Protestant Reformation in the early decades of the sixteenth century only intensified concerns about orthodoxy and authenticity.
The writing of saintly lives could now be deployed as a polemical tool in the
struggle against Protestantism. The French priest André Duval, for example,
expressed hope that works such as his 1621 biography of Barbe Acarie would
command attention in his homeland, "because in so many places there are
great numbers of heretics."[16] Hagiographers, of course, insisted upon the va-
lidity and efficacy of the cult of the saints, which had been challenged or even
rejected by reformers such as Luther and Calvin. Highlighting the salutary effects of the confessor-penitent relationship, these clerical authors launched a
spirited defense of key Catholic sacraments and institutions. In their accounts,
penance, communion, ordination, and the embrace of the religious life bring
innumerable spiritual benefits to individuals and communities.[17]

Two other developments during the sixteenth and seventeenth centuries
inspired priests to write hagiographical texts. One was the formalizing of

canonization procedures. For centuries the faithful would simply acclaim certain men and women as saints, and, perhaps with the support of the local ecclesiastical hierarchy, a cult would form after their deaths. By the end of the Middle Ages efforts were under way to regularize practices and reserve canonization as a papal prerogative. Procedures established first at the Council of Trent (1545–63) and then under the pontificate of Urban VIII (1623–44) required, among other things, the amassing of information as to the Servant of God's holy life, heroic virtues, and postmortem miracles.[18] Hagiography could now function as documentation, and hagiographers as informants or even witnesses in processes of beatification and canonization. As we shall see, the desire to prove that a spiritual daughter was not just exemplary but an actual saint could serve as a strong impetus for a confessor to turn biographer and could influence the content and structure of his hagiographical text.

As Europeans discovered, conquered, and colonized the lands of the New World, they brought their religious sensibilities with them. From the late-sixteenth through the eighteenth centuries settlers in Spanish America and French Canada recognized women as pious exemplars, and confessors and other clerical promoters busily recorded their lives for posterity. The mere presence of traditional "holy women" such as Catherine de Saint Augustin and Rose of Lima on American soil, as well as the textual memory recorded in hagiographies, contributed to the massive enterprise of transmitting and consolidating Catholic culture across the Atlantic.[19]

The phenomenon of priests and pious women forming relationships and the resulting literary genres of spiritual autobiography and hagiography were, of course, not new to the early-modern period; both had important precedents in the early Christian and medieval eras. Between the mid-fifteenth and the mid-eighteenth century, however, printing, Protestantism, and colonial expansion, along with other historical changes, profoundly altered the meanings ascribed to relationships and the quantity and reception of texts. By the second half of the eighteenth century the religious landscape had changed once again. I end my study around 1750, when theological and political challenges to church unity and greater value placed on "useful" service in the world, rather than ascetic and contemplative sacrifice, would lead many Catholics to consider new models of saintly behavior.

It remains for me to discuss the sources I have used in writing this book and assess their relative strengths and weaknesses. At the core are life-writings that derive from the confessor-penitent relationship, hagiographies of exemplary women written by male promoters, and autobiographies composed by the women themselves at the prompting or even command of their confessors. There were, as we shall see, hundreds of such texts produced in Catholic lands in the early-modern period; clearly no one scholar could look at all of them. In examining approximately fifty cases I have made certain choices. I have concentrated on printed books. There are more examples from Spain represented here than from any other geographical region, nearly half of the total, a reflection of my years of research in this field before embarking upon a more broadly based study. This is not, therefore, a "random sample" in a technical statistical sense. It is, however, a selection that is large enough and diverse enough to give the reader a good sense of the sorts of texts composed and read during the fifteenth through eighteenth centuries.

I have looked at forty-two life-narratives in which the subject is a woman, with the following geographical and linguistic distribution: from Spain, twenty; Spanish America, six; Italy, six; France, four; French Canada, four; and Portugal, two. Generically, these texts are sometimes hard to characterize: approximately eighteen are hagiographies, and another eighteen are autobiographies. However, in many cases these are really hybrid texts: autobiographies with biographies appended at the end, biographies with long excerpts from women's memoirs, or some other combination. In chapter 3 I explore the collaborative processes responsible for such endeavors. In several cases I have gleaned biographical information on women and their confessors from other sorts of sources: trial records, letters, convent chronicles, urban histories, and the like. For purposes of comparison I have looked at seven cases in which the subject of the life-narrative is male: six hagiographies and one autobiography. Three of these texts come from Spain, with one apiece from Spanish America, France, and Portugal.

What was the religious status of women who wrote spiritual autobiographies or became the subject of admiring hagiographical accounts? Here, too, the categories are not always crystal clear. Of the forty-two women studied here, twenty-seven, or somewhat more than half, had formal religious vocations. However, of these, at least eight spent significant periods of their lives as wives and widows, entering convents as nuns or lay sisters after the deaths of their husbands, as was the case with Barbe Acarie. Fifteen of the women I studied gained renown as pious laywomen (in Spain usually known as *beatas*; in Italy, *pinzochere*) and never experienced enclosure at all. This observation confirms current research that points to the wide range of religious styles practiced by Catholic women, even after the Council of Trent would seem to have prohibited anything but the cloister.[20]

Women who decided to profess as nuns or make nonbinding vows as tertiaries had many different religious orders from which to choose. No one order predominates in this study, from which the following approximate
distribution emerges: Franciscan, or Poor Clares, eight; Discalced Carmelite,
five; Augustinian, especially in its reformed Recollect branch, four; Dominican, 3; Ursuline, three; Carmelite, two; Visitandines, two; and one apiece for
the Mercedarians, Cistercians, and the Hospital Sisters. Here too, however,
counting and classification are made difficult by the fact that women sometimes had affiliations with different orders at different times in their lives. A
case such as that of the Castilian Juana Rodríguez (1574–c. 1640), who became a Discalced Carmelite tertiary while still married but professed as a Poor
Clare after being widowed, is not terribly unusual.[21]

The religious affiliations of the male promoters of holy women show more
marked trends, however. Most were secular priests rather than members of religious orders. Of the forty-three men whose status can be traced, fifteen, or
nearly a third of the total, were Jesuits, a striking statistic that no doubt reflects
the Society's strong mission as spiritual directors. Another eleven were members of the diocesan clergy, including four bishops and cathedral canons or
prebendaries. Confessor-biographers who belonged to religious orders could
be found among the Discalced Carmelites (four), Dominicans (four), Augus-
tinians (three), Franciscans (three), and the Benedictines, Carmelites and
Mercedarians (one apiece). It is worth noting that many women had more than
one confessor during the course of their lives, and these came from various
orders and affiliations. The Spanish Cistercian María Vela, for example, had
at least five spiritual directors during the course of her tumultuous life: two
Jesuits, one Discalced Carmelite friar, and two members of the local diocesan
clergy.[22] Thus one does not necessarily find a one-to-one correlation between,
say, a Dominican nun and a Dominican confessor.

Some interesting patterns emerge from examining the chronological distribution of lives and life-narratives and factoring in geographical origin. In
my sample of forty-two cases of women who maintained close relationships
with confessors, three—two Italians and one Spaniard—lived during the end
of the fifteenth and beginning of the sixteenth century, in the period of
roughly 1450–1520. During the sixteenth century, between 1500 and 1620, the
number rises to twelve, seven of whom were from Spain and Spanish America, three from Italy, and one each from Portugal and France. A similar cohort
of ten lived in the late sixteenth and early seventeenth century, between 1550
and 1640—eight from the Hispanic world and one each from France and New

France, but none from Italy. The largest number of cases and texts (seventeen) come from the period between 1650 and 1740. Again, Spain and its colonies predominate, with ten cases, followed by France and French Canada (five) and one case each from Italy and Portugal. Thus one is more likely to find examples from the seventeenth century and from Iberia or the New World colonies than from other times and places. Based, admittedly, on a small sample, these observations nevertheless raise some intriguing suggestions about the changing contours of Catholic piety during the transition to the modern age.[23]

Perhaps a more serious question relates to the usefulness of religious lifewriting, especially hagiographies, as historical sources. This is a point much debated by scholars. These texts, many would argue, do not tell us what their subjects were "really like." They are so formulaic, so filled with moralistic and literary commonplaces, so heavily based upon earlier models that they offer nothing new to the reader. The goal of the hagiographer, after all, is the edification of the faithful, not "truth" in some objective, journalistic sense.[24]

It is hard to dispute these points entirely. Certainly one needs to read these, and all literary and polemical texts, with care and a certain critical eye. I suggest, however, that for all its limitations and pitfalls, hagiography has a great deal to offer the historian. One compelling feature is the sheer number and wide distribution of these texts, surely significant for anyone interested in the production and diffusion of cultural values. The biographies of the "modern saints" studied here are nearly all firsthand accounts by authors who personally knew their subjects, a relative rarity in the premodern period.

Some ask, aren't all hagiographies alike, stamped out of the same mold? There are, to be sure, many formulaic elements in pious biographies, as there are in, say, legal documents. In more than a decade of reading these texts, however, I have never found one that did not have its own unique features, some detail not found in any other account. Confessor-biographers highlighted the inner spiritual experiences of their exemplary penitents but also provided a wealth of data about everyday life. In the process of reading about a nun's heroic virtues we may also learn about convent factions, urban politics, family disputes over property, the difficulty of travel, and other fascinating items that place that account in the context of this particular nun's life and times. Moreover, even textual similarities can be significant. I have tried to be attentive to patterns of thought and behavior gleaned from these biographical accounts, considering that common experience is just as likely to give rise to literary topoi as the reverse. Finally, as I stress throughout this book, in the process of promoting their spiritual daughters, clerical authors such as Paul

Ragueneau and André Duval invariably revealed details about themselves. The texts they produced were sometimes as autobiographical in nature as they were biographical, and thus they provide a window into the lives and aspirations of that most neglected of social groups, Catholic priests.

If pious biographies are not transparent descriptions of reality, then, neither are they so opaque that close readings go unrewarded. They are also an unprecedented source for understanding the meanings and values a society ascribes to persons regarded as holy and worthy of emulation. In this study I use these texts above all to explore the ways in which clerics presented female penitents as exemplary and how they constructed their own identities around their interactions with exceptional women.

This is a book, then, about both lives and the writing of *Lives*. Chapter 1 sets the stage by tracing the formation of a penitential culture during the last two centuries of the Middle Ages. In the fourteenth and fifteenth centuries, as penitential confraternities and sermons grew in popularity, influential churchmen also began to advocate more frequent confession and communion. Catholics in great numbers, especially women, responded to this call to examine and expiate their sins. The devout longed for lives of greater spiritual perfection but required guides to show them the path of virtue and divert them from the path of error. I examine the emergence of spiritual direction as a recognized social institution and of the spiritual director as a role increasingly demanded of priests and male religious. I also reflect upon the connections between these habits of self-reflection and narration and the biographical urge to record exemplary lives. Finally, I consider the towering figures of Catherine of Siena (1347–80) and Raymond of Capua (1330–99). Their personal relationship, Raymond's extraordinarily influential hagiography of his penitent, and Catherine's rapid promotion to sainthood all served as powerful precedents for later generations of priests and pious women.

By the start of the sixteenth century clerics acting as spiritual directors to devout women had become a familiar feature of Catholic life. Nevertheless, only certain priests wrote the lives of saintly penitents. In Chapter 2 I look at those priests who made this literary as well as pastoral decision. I explore their motivations for becoming hagiographers and analyze the techniques they used in documenting exemplary lives for the benefit of a reading public and for posterity.

The next two chapters move from authors to texts, focusing upon the memoirs written by pious women and the hagiographical accounts composed by their clerical promoters. These texts do not always conform to simple classification as "biography" or "autobiography." In Chapter 3 I offer close readings of five case studies from Spain, France, and New France to investigate some of the collaborative strategies that resulted in texts in which the voices of authors and subjects are intricately interwoven. Chapter 4 highlights one of the most prominent themes in the religious life narratives of the early-modern period, that of spiritual friendship between priests and women. I examine these stories of personal bonding and speculate on their rhetorical uses in an age in which adherence to the Catholic faith could no longer be taken for granted.

In Chapter 5 I ask the critical question, how do we know anyone actually read these books? After surveying the numbers of hagiographies printed, translated, and distributed throughout Catholic Europe and its colonies I turn to women's autobiographies for what they reveal about reading patterns and preferences. I also assess the influence of hagiographical literature on women's identities, religious vocations, and creative expression.

Examining the interactions between confessors and their female penitents reveals a fascinating set of interpersonal dynamics and provides a way of exploring relationships that were frequently reciprocal, if not equal in power. The literatures of spiritual autobiography and hagiography offer compelling accounts of individuals caught up in the pursuit of holiness and the effort to construct models of behavior for others to admire and emulate. These related lives, I suggest, provide a key to understanding the persistence and perpetuation of Catholic culture throughout the early-modern period. This is a conclusion I could not have predicted when I first looked at five cases from one Spanish diocese.

CHAPTER ONE

SPIRITUAL DIRECTIONS

Few readers of his classic biography of Martin Luther can forget Roland Bainton's vivid account of his protagonist's struggle with the sacrament of penance. The sensitive young Augustinian, overcome with his own sinful nature, "endeavored unremittingly to avail himself of this signal mercy," confessing "frequently, often daily, and for as long as six hours on a single occasion." For Luther, the question was not the relative gravity of individual sins but whether he had recalled them all. He was terrified that after confessing for hours "he could still go out and think of something else which had eluded his most conscientious scrutiny." All this anxiety left the monk in a pitiable state:

> Panic invaded his spirit. The conscience became so disquieted as to start and tremble at the stirring of a wind-blown leaf. The horror of a nightmare gripped his soul, the dread of one waking in the dusk to look into the eyes of him who has come to take his life. The heavenly champions all withdrew; the fiend beckoned with leering summons to the impotent soul. These were the torments which Luther repeatedly testified were far worse than any physical ailment that he had ever endured.

Eventually Luther would recover, but in the process he formulated a whole new theology of grace. He came to reject the sacrament of penance as well as many other Catholic doctrines and traditions. Thus, the advent of the Protestant Reformation in 1517 was due, in large part, to what Bainton called "the failure of confession."[1]

The practice of confession and penance may have failed Martin Luther but not because it was moribund or irrelevant. Indeed, his dramatic story illustrates the extraordinary importance that confession held in the lives of late-medieval and early-modern Christians. One could argue that it was precisely because the pursuit of penance had become such an integral part of European society that Luther's disappointment in its ability to assuage his guilt was so palpable, his bitterness so keenly felt. He would not have reacted with such pain and passion if confession and penance had not mattered. In this he was a typical Christian of his time, if exceptional in the depth of his emotions and the brilliance of his theological response. Luther's experience, compelling and consequential though it was, must be understood within the context of the religious culture in which he was raised.

The Formation of a Penitential Culture

Many scholars have noted the increased participation of the laity in the religious life of western Europe during the last two centuries of the Middle Ages—or perhaps more precisely, in forms of piety that fostered a greater degree of interaction between laypeople and members of the clergy than had previously been the case. This late-medieval lay piety had many manifestations: attendance at sermons, membership in confraternities and third orders affiliated with religious houses, pilgrimages, the purchase of indulgences, and a marked increase in eucharistic devotion, just to name a few of the most important. A common thread that connected all these religious practices, however, was an intense interest in penance. In this period, it seems, many Christians felt a particularly strong impulse to examine their consciences, confess their failings, and perform acts of penance. Some went even further, renouncing sin and resolving to change the direction of their lives. For the pious penitence was not just an annual ritual but, in the words of André Vauchez, "a condition, virtually a way of life."[2]

Let us take preaching, for example. In this period sermons became increasingly frequent and popular, especially in urban settings. Laypeople gathered for the routine preaching they would hear from their parish priest on Sundays and feast days but also for those special occasions when itinerant preachers came through their town. Charismatic figures such as Vincent Ferrer (1350–1419) and Bernardino of Siena (1380–1444), famous for their dramatic oratorical styles, could attract immense crowds. Cities found that they had to enlarge the public spaces in front of their churches in order to accommodate the people who came for entertainment, news, and gossip as well as edifying spiritual messages. The sermons of well-known preachers were also recorded and circulated in written form. Eventually printed sermon collections, in both Latin and vernacular languages, would find a wide audience.[3]

Preaching, then, was pervasive throughout late medieval and early modern Europe, and the need for penitence was one of the most prominent topics. As an Italian preacher reminded his fellow Christian orators, this "most noble and necessary theme" was the one that "Christ first preached."[4] Accordingly, preachers exhorted their listeners to confess their sins and make proper restitution. "Neither the greatness nor the magnitude of one's sins . . . can keep one from the possibility of remission, pardon, and divine compassion if the sinner repents of his sins and corrects them according to the will of God," one French preacher insisted. Another proclaimed, "A man confessing his sin is washed inwardly in his conscience, and is made new in the sight of God."[5] Preachers often brought along priests to hear confessions or heard confessions themselves, effectively linking sermon and sacrament.[6]

As early as the twelfth century laymen and laywomen began to organize themselves into groups such as confraternities, where they could pray and carry out works of piety together. This longing for a collective religious experience would continue into the late-medieval and early-modern periods. During the fourteenth and fifteenth centuries, for example, third orders, usually affiliated with the mendicant orders, grew in number and popularity. By joining a third order (or becoming a tertiary) laypeople could experience some aspects of monastic life but without taking binding vows or completely abandoning the world of business and family. These organizations of the pious were often dedicated to a particular devotion—the eucharist or the Virgin Mary, for example—or to distributing charity to the poor. For a great many, however, the central theme was penitence.[7]

In fact one of the most important groups came to be known precisely as the Order of Penitence (Ordo Poenitentiae). It first emerged in Italian towns and cities in the thirteenth century, and its members' most dramatic (although not their only) activity was public flagellation. Motivated by the desire to imitate Christ and a strong belief in the redemptive value of physical suffering, they whipped themselves in order to expiate sin and forestall the wrath of God. These lay penitents brought an ascetic spirituality long associated with the monastic cloister into the churches and streets of western Europe. Dressing in distinctive habits and performing public acts of mortification and reconciliation, the members of the Order of Penitence and numerous similar groups signaled to their contemporaries their willingness to do penance for their own sins, and for those of their communities.[8]

Thus we see a widening circle of aspirations and expectations during the final centuries of the medieval era. Lifestyles and religious devotions that in earlier times one would have expected to find only in monastic settings were now being practiced by growing numbers of lay Christians. Given this climate of religious fervor and innovation, it is not surprising that priests would begin to advocate that laypeople participate in the sacraments of confession and communion on a much more frequent basis than ever before. Recall that legislation at the Fourth Lateran Council of 1215 had mandated that the faithful confess their sins to a priest once a year. While there is no way to gauge compliance with any precision, scholars agree that the majority of Christians made this one, annual confession, usually during the Easter season, and no others. As confession was by then considered a necessary prelude to receiving the eucharist, average Christians probably took communion only once a year as well.⁹

For those who made vows and lived in monastic communities, however, both communion and confession were more common occurrences. Gradually this idea spread to devout laypersons as well; members of the Order of Penitence were expected to confess and receive the host three times a year, for example. By the early fifteenth century theologians were urging more frequent confession for most Christians. The influential Jean Gerson (1363–1429), who trumpeted confession as "the most efficacious way to Christ," recommended that laypeople avail themselves of the sacrament four times a year, or every month or even every week on feast-days.¹⁰

Christians responded to this call, sometimes demanding confession and communion with a degree of enthusiasm that fairly overwhelmed the clerics responsible for administering the sacraments. This wave of piety among the laity has long captured the attention of scholars. Less commented upon, however, is the significance of this sea change for priests. Increased frequency of confession and communion meant, by definition, increased frequency of contact between priests and penitents. As we shall see, these changing expectations regarding access and attention contributed to a whole new definition of what it meant to be a priest.

Another crucial aspect of this evolving penitential culture was that it was a highly gendered one. Contemporaries noted the prominence of women among the faithful now hastening to sermons, absorbing devotional literature, joining third orders. "There are indeed women who in many things are more devout than men, whether it be praying, visiting holy places, or taking the sacraments," insisted the French preacher Guillaume Pepin (c. 1465–1533).

The Dominican observed that women "confess often and take communion on the principal feast days, while few men do so."[11] This female piety may have earned the admiration of clerics, but husbands and fathers sometimes expressed resentment, grumbling that by attending so many sermons and masses women were neglecting their household duties. In a satire written in the early sixteenth century the Italian poet Ariosto commented that if his wife "wished to attend more than one mass a day I should be displeased, and I would have it suffice if she confessed herself once or twice a year." He added petulantly, "I should not wish her . . . to be making tarts and repasts every day for her confessor."[12]

Why did women participate so actively in late medieval religious life, especially in those institutions and rituals related to penitence? Some, to be sure, simply seized an opportunity to get out of the house. As Corrie Norman comments, attending sermons was "one of the few permissible reasons for women to enter public space." An Italian moralist railed against those "vain women" who went to mass only to "greet all the merchants, their neighbors, their family and friends in the house of God . . ."[13]

Other women, however, took their religious duties much more seriously, having perhaps assimilated widely held notions of female carnality and disobedience. If a woman, Eve, had been responsible for the fall, and women were by nature more sinful than men, so the reasoning went, then women had an even greater need to do penance than men and would have to perform even more intense acts of penitence. But another cultural construct held sway as well—that women were more pious, more compassionate, more humble than prideful men. Here the preeminent exemplar was Mary Magdalene, the woman who had been a sinner yet through a profound change of heart had come to symbolize perfect penitence.[14] The various penitential devotions available in late-medieval Europe offered the sorts of emotional and experiential forms of spirituality open to all Christians, unlike those that required the academic training accessible to male clerics alone. Finally, during the later Middle Ages a significant number of women—nuns, tertiaries, and laywomen—gained fame as saintly ascetics, prophetesses, healers, and the like. The rise of the holy woman can be seen as both a cause and an effect of the broader women's religious movement we have been tracing.[15] With models from both sacred history and their own times to emulate, many women now began to seek their own individual paths to holiness. For this they would need personal guides.

From Confession to Spiritual Direction

After the death of her husband in 1391, Dorothea of Montau aspired to a life of greater Christian perfection. She asked her current confessor for the name of a specialist who might help her find her way and then sought the "advice of the man who had been recommended to her." This was the priest John Marienwerder, to whom she consequently "opened her heart." For the next three years, until her own death in 1394, Dorothea confided in John, "always revealing to him as the Lord inspired and ordered her to say."[16]

The case of Dorothea of Montau and John Marienwerder presents a number of fascinating features. Dorothea clearly desired something more than confession and absolution. Any ordained priest could have administered the sacrament to her. She also wanted "advice" and to be able to "open her heart" to a particular kind of priest, one with an already established reputation. John, for his part, was willing to serve as both confessor and confidant (and eventually, biographer) to a woman of exceptional piety, perhaps even saintliness.

The relationship between Dorothea and John is a relatively early example of a phenomenon that would become familiar to Catholics during the fifteenth through eighteenth centuries. In the hagiography he composed after Dorothea's death John referred to himself simply as the holy woman's "confessor." It is apparent, however, that he provided more than his priestly office required. In subsequent decades clerics such as John would be explicitly labeled "spiritual directors" (or "spiritual fathers," "spiritual guides") and the service they offered recognized as "spiritual direction." The desire of individuals to talk with and receive personal instruction from a spiritual master or teacher was, of course, not new to the late-medieval and early-modern period and can be traced far back in Christian history, especially in monastic circles. But as scholars such as Patricia Ranft, John Coakley, and Gabriella Zarri have suggested, the fifteenth century proved a crucial transition period, in which the traditions of confession and spiritual direction were effectively fused, resulting in new expectations on the part of penitents and new responsibilities for priests.[17] My purpose here is not to provide a comprehensive history of spiritual direction. I explore, rather, an emerging interpersonal dynamic that compelled some women to "open their hearts" to priests and some priests to open their ears to the words of women.

Women had a number of reasons for placing themselves under the guidance of spiritual directors. Doing so ensured regular personal contact with a priest in a way that attending sermons, masses, or confraternal activities did not. Women such as Dorothea of Montau, who claimed to receive visions or other manifestations of divine grace, were always vulnerable to accusations of fraud, demonic possession, and the like, as well as to devastating bouts of self-doubt. For them a spiritual director could provide protection and authorization as well as helpful advice. In subsequent chapters I discuss several cases of women whose shaky reputations improved dramatically once they were directed, and endorsed, by respected clerics.

Spiritual direction, moreover, offered something that may have been quite rare for women in premodern society: sustained and serious conversation with a member of the opposite sex. In autobiographies and hagiographical accounts both pious women and their confessors described the process of spiritual direction as involving, above all, the exchange of words. Cattaneo Marabotto recalled how "whenever God worked anything within [Catherine of Genoa], which [affected] her much in soul or body, she would confer about it all" with him.[18] Writing about his first encounter with the Spanish Cistercian María Vela, Miguel González Vaquero recalled "her way of speaking, so humble and sincere, so full of the love of God, and of such prudent virtue." María, for her part, remembered how "the first day I spoke with [Vaquero] . . . I was left with such satisfaction and delight of the heart that I hardly knew myself for having found that which I so long desired, which was to meet a person who had experience of this sort of spiritual direction [or conversation]."[19] Unlike fathers, husbands, or male civic authorities, then, spiritual directors were obliged to truly listen and talk to women. The writers of confessors' manuals warned of individuals whose overly tender consciences drove them to constantly confess even minor faults. In the case of female penitents, however, the desire for attention from and conversation with priests may also have been a contributing factor. Recognizing the interpersonal exchange and potential validation involved in receiving spiritual direction at least provides some perspective on behavior conventionally understood as "excessive scrupulosity."[20]

What about priests? What inspired them to take on the role of spiritual director, especially to women? Providing personalized spiritual guidance was not a required part of clerics' pastoral and sacramental duties and even entailed some risks. In a misogynistic age writers warned of women's intellectual and moral weaknesses. To some monastic and diocesan authorities, all women, no matter how saintly, represented sexual temptation, and priests did well to limit their contacts with them to the minimum required by their office.

Jean Gerson, for example, cautioned "for even the most deeply religious men, no matter how great their sanctity, a common life and familiarity with women are not safe."[21]

Despite the warnings, late-medieval and early-modern priests persisted in serving as directors to women, especially ones they identified as spiritually gifted or advanced. Some even came to be recognized as specialists in this field, which actually had a long pedigree in the Christian tradition. Priests, and their female penitents, looked back to the relationship of St. Jerome with the pious Roman widow Paula and her daughter Eustochium in the fourth century. In a series of letters Jerome offered instruction and advice to the women but also expressed deep gratitude for the inspiration and insights they gave to him. This early example of male-female spiritual friendship, as well as spiritual direction, was frequently evoked by writers and artists during the fifteenth through eighteenth centuries.[22]

The later Middle Ages would not seem, at first, a promising time for the sort of male-female relationships represented by Jerome and Paula. In this age of plague, schism, and political upheaval throughout much of western Europe, fears of heresy and witchcraft were on the rise, and women's spirituality in particular came under intense scrutiny. As suspicions of women grew, so did the perceived need for surveillance and control. Some priests became experts in the "discernment of spirits," a complex process of examination that required a firm grasp of theology as well as an ability to judge character and gauge the human heart.[23] Ironically, in order to make considered assessments priests had to spend more time with women than would normally be the case, checking their written and spoken words for signs of heterodox beliefs, monitoring their behavior for indications of fraud or diabolical magic. Often the judgments of priests upon women were negative, an outcome that could mean severe punishment, even the stake. But other times the examiners of women became convinced that they were genuinely pious, perhaps even holy exemplars. This decision, too, could have profound consequences for both women and clerics.

In any case, a perceived talent for discerning true from false spirits and guiding souls toward greater perfection could bring a priest considerable notoriety and prestige. During the early-modern period, this ability was increasingly regarded as not only a skill but also a charisma, evidence of divine grace.[24] From its foundation in 1540, spiritual direction was an integral part of the mission of the Society of Jesus, and its membership undoubtedly selected for men who had an interest in and aptitude for interacting with penitents in

this way. In hagiographies and other devotional literature Jesuits actively promoted this vision of a gifted priesthood. One biographer celebrated Baltasar
Alvarez for his special skill (*maña*) as a confessor as well as for being the recipient of "a great gift of God . . . in guiding souls."[25] Paul Ragueneau, a
younger French Jesuit insisted, "displayed that rare talent for direction with
which God had endowed him."[26] His mastery of spiritual direction, more than
any other activity or virtue, was responsible for Claude de la Colombière's
reputation during his life and eventual elevation to the altar in modern times.
Of this his most famous penitent, the visionary Margaret Mary Alacoque, had
no doubt, the Lord having told her directly in prayer: "Father Colombière's
talent is to lead souls to God."[27] With this sort of endorsement as a possibility, no wonder so many priests were willing to undertake the spiritual direction of women.

Confession and Spiritual Direction in Practice

For many clerics in early-modern Europe, then, hearing confessions and
offering spiritual direction to the pious became a crucial component of their
personal and professional identities. It remains now to explore the varied circumstances in which priests and penitents, especially female penitents, interacted in this sacramental and social relationship. Some might assume that
confession then, as in more modern times, took place once a week and in an
enclosed box or confessional. In fact, written and visual evidence suggests an
extraordinarily wide array of customs and practices, at least well into the eighteenth century.

Exactly how frequently Christians should make confession was a much-
debated question. Around 1400 some clergymen began urging laypeople to
receive the eucharist once every eight days. They further insisted that the
faithful confess prior to communion in order to "receive the Sacred Eucharist
worthily," as the Council of Trent later proclaimed.[28]

This marked increase in sacramental activity created something of a
quandary for many ecclesiastical authorities. On the one hand, greater frequency and intensity of confession and communion helped stimulate devotion
and foster the dignity due to priests as purveyors of both absolution and the
consecrated host. Some clerics objected, however, fearing that overuse and
routinization would diminish a desired sense of awe and mystery toward the
body of Christ. Frequent communion (and confession), of course, required
frequent interaction with a priest and often, in the case of a devout woman,

FIGURE ONE

Confession in a church. Illuminated manuscript, Flanders, c. 1492.
Courtesy of the British Library.

the same priest who had agreed to be her spiritual director. A priest's willingness to service a female penitent in this way meant not only that he was constantly exposed to sexual temptation but also that he might be distracted from
broader pastoral responsibilities.[29] Nevertheless, by the sixteenth century
confessors and spiritual directors throughout Europe were acquiescing to the
demands of women to receive confession and communion once or several
times a week and even, more exceptionally, on a daily basis. That such frequency had become fairly common is indicated by the biography of a pious
noblewoman composed around 1606. Its author, Pedro de Ribadeneyra,
praised Doña Estefanía Manrique de Castilla for her exemplary humility, citing as evidence the fact that she requested communion no more than twice a
week.[30]

The spatial arrangements under which confession and spiritual direction took place also proved remarkably fluid. During the late Middle Ages, confession of laypersons was a fundamentally public enterprise. A late-fifteenth-century illustration shows a typical situation. The faithful have come to a church, in which a priest sits on a raised chair. A penitent makes his confession, kneeling beside the chair. There is no effort to screen this activity; indeed all takes place in a central part of the church, in plain view of (and one imagines, clearly audible to) the other churchgoers. If confessing certain sins caused embarrassment to the penitent, Jean Gerson remarked, the priest should simply avert his eyes. Another writer advised clerics to pull their hoods over their eyes while hearing confessions and warned them never to look at the faces of female penitents. Well into the sixteenth century artists would continue to depict the act of confession as occurring in this quite open manner.[31]

Maintaining confession as a very conspicuous and public event was, in fact, a deliberate policy, especially with regard to female penitents. Gerson and other late-medieval authors insisted that confession should always take place in view of others ("coram oculis omnium") in order to avoid possible scandal. This sentiment was echoed in the 1306 synodal laws of Fiesole, which mandated that priests hear the confessions of women "in the open" ("in loco patenti") so that both clerics and penitents could be seen by others. They also prohibited priests from looking into the faces of female penitents. This regulation was perhaps motivated by fears about women's seductive powers over priests as well as a desire to foster frank and complete confessions, a concern cited frequently in confessors' manuals.[32]

A hagiographical account provides another insight into this preference for public forms of confession. According to Alonso Fernández de Madrid, Hernando de Talavera, during his tenure as Archbishop of Granada (1493–99), made it his custom when his duties allowed to seat himself in "el confesionario público." This term connoted an open space for the purpose of hearing confessions, not a confessional box, as it would come to be used in more modern times. Talavera would sit between the afternoon dinner hour and nightfall and "hear the confessions of anyone who wanted to come and confess to him." The prelate's biographer characterized this gesture of generosity and accessibility to a wide Christian community as "a signal act of charity."[33]

The sixteenth century saw the beginnings of an evolution in values and logistics that would reconfigure confession as a much more private experience. Some clerics now voiced concerns that doubts about confidentiality or sheer embarrassment would keep penitents from making sincere and thorough confessions. Priests began to place barriers such as veils, curtains, or screens between themselves, their penitents, and bystanders.[34] These arrangements could be quite informal, and rather flimsy, however. In the spring of 1527, Doña Sancha Carrillo, the fifteen-year-old daughter of a Spanish noble family, resolved to make a full confession to the noted preacher and spiritual director Juan de Avila. As his biographer, Luis de Granada, later recounted, Sancha entered Juan's "confesionario," a term whose precise meaning is once again unclear. The priest may not have been able to see the young woman, but he could plainly hear her rustling the taffeta shawl she was wearing. He "bitterly reprimanded her because, coming to confess and weep over her sins, she came in such luxury."[35] Although sturdy, wooden confessional boxes, complete with doors, did come to be used in some parts of Europe during the sixteenth century—Milan under Charles Borromeo is a notable example—they were not widely adopted until the late seventeenth or even eighteenth century.[36] And ironically, as confession became more private and priests and female penitents hidden from the view of others, anxieties about sexual misconduct resurfaced. During the seventeenth and eighteenth centuries authorities throughout Catholic Europe and its colonies were compelled to investigate and prosecute clerics charged with soliciting sexual favors in the confessional. Thus arrangements designed to solve certain problems inadvertently caused others to arise.[37]

Being a confessor or spiritual director in early-modern Europe required considerable mobility because these activities occurred in many locations besides one's own church. As we have seen, itinerant preachers would listen to confessions after delivering their sermons, whether in indoor or outdoor venues. Priests also routinely accompanied pilgrimages and made visits to shrines to hear the confessions of the faithful gathered at these places. Confession and devout conversation frequently took place in private homes. Many aristocratic penitents, for example, had their own oratories or chapels. Clerics had long been expected to provide confession and communion to the sick in their own homes, especially when their recovery was in doubt.[38] By the sixteenth century, however, some expressed the same urgency about giving spiritual guidance at the homes of penitents "whenever it was necessary for the good of their souls."[39] Pedro de Ribadeneyra recounted a case of rather aggressive spiritual direction. Ignatius Loyola had worked long and hard to persuade a "dissolute and profane" priest he knew in Paris to change his ways. Frustrated by the man's resistance to his efforts, one Sunday morning the future saint walked into the priest's house and roused him from his bed, ostensibly to have him listen to Loyola's own confession. In the course of their interaction, however, the two effectively changed roles, the sinful priest at last coming to "abhor his present life and desire to amend it." He also resolved to take Loyola as the "master and father of his soul," undoubtedly the true purpose behind this early-morning house call.[40]

There was one class of penitents for whom in-house confession and spiritual direction was an absolute necessity: cloistered nuns and lay sisters. In some cases female religious could make their confessions to priests in the convent's parlor or chapel. Artists continued to depict clerics on chairs, with nuns kneeling at their feet, well into the seventeenth century, although it is possible that idealization or nostalgia played some role in their creative decisions. In the mid-sixteenth century, the Council of Trent (1545–63), secular and diocesan authorities, and reformers such as Teresa of Avila demanded a much stricter understanding of enclosure than had previously been the case. New regulations required convents to erect walls, grilles, and other physical barriers, although implementation was often slow and enforcement somewhat sporadic.[41] These measures, designed to curtail nuns' interactions with (and interference from) laypersons, surely affected the ways they confessed and conversed with priests. They did not, however, prevent nuns and clerics from establishing close sacramental and personal relationships, as we shall see in chapter 4. In fact, limiting the senses of touch and sight may have only heightened the power of voice, ear, and imagination in the forging of spiritual friendships.

Moreover, spiritual direction could take place even when priests and penitents were apart, by way of letter. Indeed, some priests became renowned for their ability to advise, console, and edify via the written word. By the seventeenth century, as Michel de Certeau has observed, letters of spiritual direction had gained new respect as a literary genre, as well as a medium of pastoral care. Popular devotional writers such as Jean-Joseph Surin addressed letters not only to individuals but also to circles of devout readers, who then circulated them among themselves.[42] In the case of cloistered nuns, corresponding with their spiritual directors may have in some way compensated for the physical proximity now forbidden in the post-Tridentine convent. Unlike personal visits, letters transcended space and time. And unlike speech acts, they could be read, reread, shared, copied, and preserved for posterity.

Thus in churches, homes, and convents, in person and by letter, priests in early-modern Catholic Europe heard confessions and dispensed advice to penitents. Many responded to the growing demands of women, lay and religious, for instruction and guidance in achieving greater spiritual perfection. What sorts of relationships resulted from this personal as well as pastoral decision? In theory, priests—male, formally educated, imbued with the power of office—directed penitents, male or female, who then blindly obeyed their dictates. This view, expressed in some confessors' manuals and other prescriptive literature, has sometimes been taken at face value. Scholars have accordingly stressed the exclusively repressive aspects of the Catholic confessional system, especially after the Council of Trent.[43]

Moving from theory to practice, however, reveals a much more varied and complex picture, especially with respect to women regarded as exceptional for their piety and spiritual gifts. There were indeed cases in which clerics manipulated and controlled their exemplary female penitents. This sort of relationship of domination-submission could take extreme, even—at least to modern sensibilities—sadistic forms. For example, in 1661 Catalina García Fernández, a Castilian widow, entered a community of Franciscan tertiaries, adopting the religious name Catalina de Jesús y San Francisco. At this house she received a confessor who decided to subject his new charge to the most rigorous of penitential practices. Perhaps betraying a certain anxiety about her previous class and sexual status as a comfortable married woman, the priest assigned two and sometimes three women to strip her from the waist up and administer the discipline, that is, whip her. He compelled her to sleep on the floor, with only a block of wood for a pillow, and made her fast on bread and water. Most disturbing was the way in which Catalina's confessor publicly humiliated her, ordering her to walk the streets of Madrid as if she were a heretic being punished by the Inquisition. She reportedly obeyed all these commands without question; such was her fervent desire to imitate the sufferings of Christ. Catalina de Jesús y San Francisco, who, in the words of her biographer, epitomized the very "idea of perfection and virtues," died in 1677, at the age of 38.[44]

There were also cases in which priests submitted themselves to the direction of charismatic women. In 1698 a woman friend became so suspicious, or jealous, of the relationship between the Bolognese seamstress and Ursuline tertiary Angela Mellini and their common confessor, the Franciscan friar Giovanni Battista Ruggieri, that she denounced them both to the Inquisition. During the subsequent investigation, the inquisitors ascertained that Angela had not only revealed to Ruggieri the extraordinary mystical gifts bestowed upon her by God but also her knowledge of his own secret sins. Angela recalled that once, while conversing with Ruggieri, she had received a clear message that he regularly fell into mortal sin. In prayer Christ commanded the seamstress to tell her spiritual director what she knew and to help him to overcome this "sin against chastity," masturbation perhaps. The priest, after recovering from his initial surprise and shame ("You are a gypsy!"), also came to believe that the Lord "wanted to show now and on other occasions that [Angela] was graced by him."[45]

Friar Giovanni Battista tried hard but had trouble resisting temptation and turned to his female penitent for help. Gradually they developed a ritual. After he heard Angela's confession and gave her his blessing, she would in turn bless him, "her hand raised moving it in the manner of the priests." One day Angela felt "inspired internally" to let her confessor call her "mother," as the priest repeatedly requested of her. They effectively exchanged roles. Angela recalled, "One evening . . . I felt something in my heart as if the said Father Ruggieri was saying there, 'Good evening, mamma or mother' and I with my mouth answered him, 'Good evening, my son, be good.'" The inquisitors, anxious to uphold the principle of male clerical authority, imposed penances on Angela Mellini. They severely reprimanded Giovanni Battista Ruggieri for having dared to confide in a woman, especially on such a delicate matter as his own chastity, and sent him away.[46]

Much more common in discourse and, one suspects, in practice were relationships that fell somewhere between these two extremes. Most interactions between confessors and female penitents were quite nuanced and reciprocal, if not equal in nature. Take, for example, the case of the Madrid *beata* Mariana de Jesús. In 1598, at the age of thirty-three, Mariana's life changed when she met and took as her spiritual director the Mercedarian friar Juan Bautista del Santísimo Sacramento. The priest who had previously guided her had brusquely "turned her away, saying 'go look for a teacher [or master] who has more leisure time, and less to attend to.'" Small wonder, then, that Mariana regarded Juan Bautista's arrival in Madrid as providential. God, she was certain, had given her a new spiritual director "so that he might help and guide me in those most interior matters to which I had been called." She added, with evident relief and gratitude, that "in a very brief time he greatly benefited my soul . . ." Mariana went on to attain considerable prestige as an urban holy woman during the first two decades of the seventeenth century. Without clerical support and promotion she might have suffered the same fate as many other *beatas* in Madrid, suppressed by the Inquisition in this same period.[47]

When he met Mariana de Jesús and took her as his penitent, Juan Bautista's life changed significantly as well. He had harbored from his earliest days as a Mercedarian a strong desire to reform his order. For all his piety and zeal, however, he never received divine confirmation of this plan. Juan Bautista now turned to his visionary penitent. Mariana provided him with a revelation about the advent of the Mercedarian reform, which "filled his soul with joy." And she offered her confessor more than moral support in this venture. With strategic connections to elites at the royal court and on Madrid's city council, as well as a citywide reputation for intercessory prayer and healing, the *beata* proved instrumental to the establishment of a discalced or reformed friary in the capital in 1606.[48]

Clearly, spiritually inclined women such as Mariana de Jesús needed the authorization of priests such as Juan Bautista del Santísimo Sacramento more than the priests needed the women, but, as this case shows, clerics could certainly benefit from these confessional relationships as well. Moreover, once confessors became convinced of the holiness of their female penitents, many responded to another imperative of their priestly office: to promote saintly lives and hold them up as models for emulation. To accomplish this goal they turned to sermons and, increasingly in the early-modern period, to the written word.

Confession and Life-Writing

At the heart of the confessor-penitent dynamic was the experience of narrating details of one's personal and religious life to another. Some priests and penitents would take this biographical impulse one step further, recording aspirations and revealed confidences in writing. Habits of self-reflection and recollection acquired through frequent confession and spiritual conversation no doubt eased the transition from verbal to written expression. Two broad literary forms resulted from the confessional process; both would contribute to the forging of identities and religious values.

The first, spiritual autobiography, has a venerable history in the western Christian tradition. St. Augustine's riveting account of his life and sins, his difficult conversion and eventual resolution to serve God and his church, has served as both a source of inspiration and a model for imitation for Christian writers since its composition at the turn of the fifth century.[49] However, only in the late Middle Ages does one see significant numbers of spiritual autobiographies written by women, a trend that greatly accelerated in the sixteenth through eighteenth centuries.[50]

"[M]y confessors commanded me and gave me plenty of leeway to write about the favors and the kind of prayer the Lord has granted me . . ."[51] So begins arguably the most famous spiritual autobiography by a woman, the *Life* of Teresa of Avila (1515–82). Here the Spanish nun identified her ostensible reason for writing this book: because she was so ordered by her confessors. This was, in fact, a common phenomenon in the late Middle Ages and early-modern period. Anxious to gauge the orthodoxy and authenticity of their spiritual daughters, confessors would order them to compose accounts of their lives and inner spiritual experiences and submit them for their scrutiny and approval. Pious women, for their part, frequently protested that they never had any intentions of writing and that they merely wrote out of obedience. Recent feminist literary analysis has placed this humility topos and the entire question of obedience under careful examination. Scholars have pointed out that the confessor-ordered autobiography, which certainly served as an instrument of clerical surveillance, also gave women an unparalleled opportunity for self-expression and a convenient excuse for taking up the pen.[52] Obedience can be understood as authorization or affirmation, not merely blind acquiescence to demands. Nevertheless, confessors played an undeniably critical role in instigating the autobiographical process. They often intervened or collaborated in the production of women's texts and were instrumental in editing, publishing, and promoting them, as we shall see in chapter 3.

Much more numerous are the hagiographies or pious biographies of exemplary female penitents written by their confessors after the women's deaths. As far back as Jerome and Paula clerics celebrated the lives of holy women. Beginning around 1200, priests began to compose full-length biographies, or *vitae,* of saintly women, relating their lives but also detailing their spiritual gifts as ascetics, visionaries, and prophetesses. However, as John Coakley has observed, medieval clerical authors did not necessarily characterize themselves (or indeed, serve as) the confessors of the subjects of their hagiographical accounts or link the composition of edifying *vitae* to the confessional enterprise. The biography-by-confessor as an identifiable genre would emerge only at the end of the Middle Ages.[53] This development was closely linked to the evolution of spiritual direction as a practice and of the spiritual director as a distinct role for priests. One particular confessor-penitent relationship and its textual expression would serve as the precedent that inspired and authorized women and priests throughout the early-modern period.

This was the one shared by Catherine of Siena and Raymond of Capua. The two met in the summer of 1374. Catherine had by this time gained fame as a holy woman in her native Tuscan city and beyond. Born in 1347 to a family of artisans, she reported having visions and other mystical experiences at a very early age. As a young woman Catherine joined the *mantellate,* also known as the Sisters of Penance, one of the many penitential groups for pious laypeople flourishing in the period and in this case affiliated with the Do-

FIGURE TWO

Raymond of Capua writing the life of Catherine of Siena. From *La vida de
la bienaventurada sancta Caterina de Sena* (Alcalá de Henares, 1511).
Courtesy of the Biblioteca Nacional, Madrid.

minican order. She spent several years praying and fasting in the isolation of
her father's home. By 1374 she had embarked on a remarkable public mission,
or apostolate. Inspired by God's commands, Catherine began preaching peace
and charity, urging Christians to unite in a new Crusade to the Holy Land, and
attempting to reconcile conflicts and reform the papacy. She traveled constantly, talked to whoever would listen, and dictated hundreds of letters to
popes, nobles, city councilors, and ordinary townspeople. Suspected by some,
revered by many, Catherine was perhaps the most controversial—and charismatic—figure of her day.[54]

In 1374 Raymond of Capua was a well-established and respected Dominican in his mid-forties. He had already held several important positions within his order, served as chaplain to a community of nuns, and written the *vita* of a saintly woman. That summer his order's master general charged Raymond with a delicate task, to serve as the "director" ("magister") of Catherine of Siena. For the next three and half years, until his transfer to another position in Rome, he worked closely with Catherine, aiding her in her many missions. The friar would continue to correspond with his famous spiritual daughter until her death in 1380. Five years later Raymond, now himself Dominican master general, began to compose a lengthy biography of Catherine. This Latin text, which came to be known as the *Legenda Maior,* would, he hoped, ensure her legacy and achieve her recognition as a saint.

The fascinating story of Catherine of Siena and Raymond of Capua brings together many of the historical trends we have been tracing in this chapter and anticipates future developments in the relating of lives and *Lives.* As we have seen, Raymond's monastic superiors appointed him to serve as Catherine's spiritual director, or "master," suggesting that by the 1370s this was a recognized role, at least for some clerics. Catherine also made this identification, referring to the friar as her "spiritual father" and the "father of my soul." Perhaps most important was Raymond's own self-presentation in the *Legenda,* in which he cast himself as Catherine's confessor in a more explicit and extensive way than did earlier hagiographers of exemplary women. He described the many occasions in which he heard the holy woman's confessions and/or gave her communion. In building the case for Catherine's holiness he made ample use of information he gleaned from her confessions, often sharing with readers "the secrets she revealed to me." He described their many conversations on spiritual matters, communications carried out both in person and by letter.

And as would be the case with so many priests and female penitents, the relationship that emerges from the *Legenda* and Catherine's own letters is a highly complex and reciprocal one. Raymond played an indispensable role in certifying Catherine's supernatural experiences and, even more critically, in defending her unusual public ministry. She certainly never seems to have questioned his clerical authority. Yet as Coakly has suggested, Raymond often acted more like Catherine's "companion and collaborator" than her director, and he intimated the existence of a genuine partnership, with "male priesthood and female apostolate complementing each other."[55] In her letters, moreover, Catherine did not hesitate to advise, exhort, and even chide her confessor. Raymond recalled how he had once attempted to downplay the seriousness of one of her youthful failings. Catherine, he reported, cried out, "Oh my Lord God! What sort of spiritual father have I got, who excuses my sins?" and proceeded to lecture him on the true significance of her transgression. Raymond highlighted incidents of role reversal of this sort throughout the *Legenda* but also used them to illustrate central points about Catherine's saintliness, in this case her virtual absence of sin.[56]

This anecdote points to another striking feature of Raymond's biographical account: the extent to which he included or inserted himself into the text. This sort of authorial initiative would become common during the early-modern period. His primary motivation for composing the *Legenda*, after all, was to promote Catherine's canonization as a saint. To this end Raymond offered himself as not only her biographer but also the main source of information and frequent eyewitness to extraordinary events and spiritual gifts. His goal was providing evidence of Catherine's saintliness, but in the process he revealed a good deal about himself as well. Raymond's agenda also accounts for the highly defensive tone he often adopted in describing his penitent's words and activities, as if anticipating criticism from would-be detractors, another feature commonly found in the texts of early-modern confessor-biographers.

The efforts of Raymond of Capua and other Dominican promoters eventually bore fruit. Catherine of Siena was canonized in 1460, a mere eighty years after her death. Significantly, this date coincides with the invention of the printing press. Within a few decades the *Legenda* had been published and quickly translated into Italian and other vernacular languages. From the sixteenth century on it would enjoy numerous editions, becoming a hagiographical "bestseller" on both sides of the Atlantic.[57] It was through Raymond's compelling biography that countless women would learn of the extraordinary life of Catherine of Siena. Some would attempt to emulate her virtues and perhaps also duplicate her fame. Clerics, too, could find a powerful model in Raymond of Capua. Confessor, confidant, arbiter of orthodoxy, director, disciple, promoter, biographer: many priests would seek to take on these roles with respect to exemplary female penitents. Their relationships with these women and the texts they would produce are the subjects of the following chapters.

CHAPTER TWO

HOW TO BE A COUNTER-REFORMATION HAGIOGRAPHER

In a brief but influential essay published in 1984, Peter Burke examined the fifty or so cases of men and women formally canonized as saints in the period following the Council of Trent. Burke asked, among other questions, "What kind of person had the best chance, during the Counter-Reformation, of achieving this particular form of upward mobility?"[1] He identified certain factors such as sex, class, national origin, and affiliation with a particular religious order as important in constructing a "prosopography of the saints." Burke ended his essay by calling for "further study" of the "process of negotiation" between ordinary Christians and elites by which certain individuals came to be certified as possessing heroic virtues and deserving of veneration by the culture at large.[2]

In this chapter I take up Burke's call but change the focus of inquiry from saints to saint-makers.[3] In early-modern Catholic Europe and its colonies, priests frequently developed relationships with penitents, especially female penitents, whom they regarded as spiritually gifted. Many confessors felt further compelled to record the lives of these exemplary penitents and to publish or circulate them after the women had died. What inspired priests to become hagiographers? And once they had made this literary, as well as pastoral, decision, how did they go about the process of documenting the lives of their saintly penitents? In examining the extensive hagiographical literature of the early-modern period, one can often catch a glimpse of the hagiographer at work and gauge something of his objectives, his techniques, and his sense of vocation as an author.

From Confessor to Author

In 1609 the Jesuit Vincenzo Puccini published the life of his penitent and fellow Florentine Maria Maddalena de' Pazzi, two years after the death of the Carmelite nun. Puccini began his book with a statement of conviction and purpose. "The Eternal God always showed and does continually show himself wonderful in his Saints . . . that in every age some may be found. . . ." As "in these days of ours he has appeared wonderful in Suor Maria Maddalena," Puccini declared,

> I will therefore describe her life and death . . . in a plain manner, to the end that . . . everyone might (by looking into that glass of Goodness) be inflamed with the heavenly fire which was ever burning and feeding upon her purest heart.[4]

For Puccini, the primary motivation for writing was apostolic: to edify believers and provide them with models of pious behavior. This had been, after all, the goal of moralists and preachers since the beginning of the Christian era. Printed books, available since the late fifteenth century, were highly effective as supplements to sermons, the traditional medium for admonishing, teaching, and consoling the faithful. José Esteban Noriega, who had guided María Quintana, a *beata* from Segovia, adopted a pastoral tone as he informed readers of his motives for "bringing this *Life* before the public" in 1737. He wanted to broadcast María's story of sin, repentance, and redemption for the benefit of despairing sinners, "so that no one lose confidence in [God's] mercy, no matter how numerous, grave and heinous his own afflictions may be."[5] Often the same clerics who published the lives of exemplary penitents also extolled their virtues in sermons.[6]

Puccini's insistence upon the universality and efficacy of saints took on an extra edge in an age in which Protestants criticized and rejected this devotion. The effort to use exemplary lives to reaffirm the cult of the saints and other aspects of Catholic doctrine may have been especially intense in France, with its significant Huguenot minority. In the introduction to his biography of his penitent, Barbe Acarie, the founder of the Discalced Carmelite order in France (d. 1618), André Duval spoke of the fruits to be gained from reading the lives of saintly persons. "It would seem," he stated, "that France has more interest in [this type of reading matter] than the rest of Christendom, because in so many places there are great numbers of heretics." Duval expressed hope that after hearing about this Servant of God, honored by so

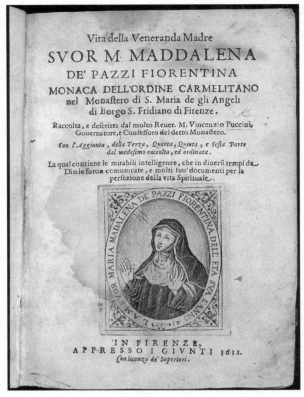

FIGURE THREE

Maria Maddalena de' Pazzi. Frontispiece to Vincenzio Puccini, *Vita della Veneranda Madre Suor M. Maddalena de' Pazzi Fiorentina* (Florence, 1611). *Courtesy of the British Library.*

many miraculous graces in a way that none of their fellows had been, "some among [the heretics] will be able to place themselves under the teachings of the Church . . ."[7]

Sometimes confessor-hagiographers targeted particular segments of the population for their moralizing messages. Pedro de Ribadeneyra singled out upper-class women in Toledo, his hometown and that of his subject, the pious laywoman Doña Estefanía Manrique de Castilla (d. 1606). The Jesuit explained that he had decided to write her life in order to "arouse by her example those *señoras* who are entranced by the baubles and unedifying things of this life."[8] Only five years after Doña Estefanía's death Isabel de Sosa was born in the same Castilian city. This Carmelite tertiary and visionary, known in religion as Isabel de Jesús, died in 1682. Three years later, when her confessor Manuel de Paredes published Isabel's spiritual autobiography, along with his own reminiscences and glosses, "for the instruction of the faithful," he also made references to certain "devout and well-known women" in Toledo.[9]

Confessors were thus eager to publicize the pious lives and divinely endowed gifts of their spiritual daughters and offer them as models for emulation. Few failed, however, to highlight their own roles in bringing to the attention of the public previously unknown figures. This was especially true in the case of cloistered nuns. For example, because Maria Maddalena de' Pazzi "remain[ed] shut up in a Monastery, they were few who saw the wonderful things which our Lord wrought in her," Vincenzo Puccini lamented. This regrettable state of affairs had now, of course, been rectified, thanks to his biographical efforts.[10] Manuel de Paredes built his entire exposition of the life of Isabel de Jesús around the metaphor of a "hidden treasure" ("tesoro escondido") at last "brought to light" by the holy woman's trusted confessor and confidant.[11] In 1677, the French Benedictine Claude Martin published the spiritual autobiography, with extensive commentary, of the Ursuline Marie de l'Incarnation, who also happened to be Martin's mother. He introduced his exemplary subject to readers in a way that underscored his contribution as well as hers, insisting that "the *Life* of this excellent nun that I give to the public is rare and extraordinary."[12]

This last case shows how hagiographers often had their own, personal reasons for relating lives. Other clerical authors expressed the filial obligation to celebrate family members or mentors. Composing the biography of a person who had played a significant role in his own life allowed a priest to repay a debt of gratitude while at the same time constructing an exemplary role model for public consumption.

Sons who grew up to be the "spiritual fathers" of their biological mothers acknowledged that this unique relationship contributed to their impulse to write the lives of these widowed Servants of God. The Jesuit Marcos Torres, son of the pious and charitable Doña María de Pol (d. 1659), recognized that some people would greet his hagiographical account with skepticism, as when " biased parents praise their child." He likened the situation to someone who keeps his treasure hidden under his bed, but, he assured his readers, "my priestly status [*sacerdocio*] is the key that unlocks it." Moreover, Torres had been ordered to compose this account. The Bishop of Málaga charged him to

FIGURE FOUR

Doña María de Pol. Frontispiece to Marcos Torres, *[N]oticias . . . de la vida
y virtudes . . . de Doña María de Pol, su Madre* (Málaga? 1660).
Courtesy of the Biblioteca Nacional, Madrid.

write in order to "satisfy the obligation of your blood," reminding him that as
both María's son and confessor "you have more intimate knowledge [of the
subject] than anyone else."[13] Juan Bernique shared with his readers "the reasons that motivated [him] to bring to light" the story of his mother, Catalina
de Jesús y San Francisco, citing the strict obligation of children "to honor and
venerate their parents." "The light of reason dictates it, human laws promote
it, and divine precepts confirm it," the Franciscan friar concluded.[14]

A fascinating web of family loyalties, biological and symbolic, informs the
complex process by which the *Life* and "works" of the renowned holy woman
Caterina Fieschi Adorna, better known as St. Catherine of Genoa, came to
be recorded. From the 1470s until her death in 1510, Catherine served as the

spiritual leader of a coterie of laypersons and clerics devoted to serving the poor and sick in Genoa. Two of her closest collaborators were her confessor, Cattaneo Marabotto, and a pious lawyer named Ettore Vernazza, twenty-three years her junior. Catherine regarded and addressed Vernazza as her "son"; he in turn called her his "mother." After Catherine's death Marabotto and Vernazza continued to collaborate, compiling and distributing her many sayings and teachings. Manuscript versions of what came to be known as Catherine's *Vita e Dottrina* circulated during the first decades of the sixteenth century; a preface to the edition eventually published in 1551 explained that the text had been "gathered together by two of her devout followers (her confessor and a spiritual son of hers)."[15] Vernazza had asked Catherine to stand as godmother to his first daughter, Battista, born in 1497. Battista, who became an Augustinian canoness at the precocious age of thirteen, would later write the life of her exemplary father and prove instrumental in the composition of her godmother's most famous treatises, *Purgation and Purgatory* and *The Spiritual Dialogue*.[16] Priestly father and daughter in confession, spiritual mother and son, godparent and godchild, biological father and daughter: all these relationships came into play in the construction of Catherine of Genoa as saintly model, mystic, and teacher.

The same bonds of "filial" loyalty and gratitude could inspire clerics to write the life-narratives of beloved teachers or mentors. A fascinating case involved three "generations" of French Jesuits during the course of the seventeenth century. Between 1628 and 1631 Louis Lallemant (1587–1635) presented a series of lectures. His "disciples," especially Jean Rigoleuc (1595–1658) and Jean-Joseph Surin (1600–65), took careful notes. Rigoleuc later gave his notes to his colleague or student Vincent Huby (1625–93). Pierre Champion (1632–1701) at last published this collection, known as Lallemant's *Spiritual Doctrine*, along with a biographical account, in Paris in 1694. In a preface Champion explained that he had acceded to the wishes of his own teacher, Huby, "another holy man whom we are bound in gratitude to mention . . . under whose influence it was that I undertook [these] little works . . ." At Huby's request Champion also compiled the life and writings of Rigoleuc in 1686.[17]

Writing the lives of exemplary penitents also offered priests the opportunity to pay tribute to their native cities or regions. The title page of a hagiography first published in 1618 identifies its subject as "Doña María Vela, Cistercian nun of the Convent of Santa Ana of Avila," and its author as "Doctor Miguel González Vaquero, her Confessor, native of the same city." While the book's opening chapter treats the holy woman's "origins and birth," Dr. Vaquero, as he was known, devoted the first two folio pages to extolling her (and his) hometown. Surely, he proclaimed, "divine Providence" had wanted to "authorize and honor this city of Avila" by sending generations of noble lineages, valiant warriors, and saintly women. His penitent, María Vela, represented only the most recent chapter in Avila's long and distinguished sacred history.[18] Failure to publicize the life of Barbe Acarie, André Duval insisted, would "deprive France of a very great honor and debase it, placing it below the other nations that have in our time been favored by Heaven by such illustrious Saints" as Italy's Charles Borromeo and Spain's Ignatius Loyola and Teresa of Avila.[19]

This sense of devotion to place could be especially intense among hagiographers from Europe's New World colonies, intent as they were upon establishing the Christian credentials of both the land and its people. The case of Mariana Paredes y Flores, born in Quito, in modern-day Ecuador, in 1618, offers just one example among many. When epidemics broke out and an earthquake threatened in the spring of 1645, the deeply pious and ascetic *beata*, who had taken the religious name Mariana de Jesús, offered her own life as expiation for the sins of her countrymen. She died two months later, at the age of twenty-seven. Her confessor, Alonso de Rojas, preached a sermon at her packed funeral, publishing it the following year. *Quiteños*, he proclaimed, ought to "be glad that this Servant of God blessed [the city] with her assistance," thankful that she offered herself as a "holy sacrifice" for the well-being of the *patria*.[20]

This effort to forge a connection between holy woman and homeland was later taken even further by Jacinto Morán de Butrón, a Jesuit and native of the region. In composing an exuberant hagiography of Mariana, he used the occasion to sing the praises of Quito: its mineral wealth, its agricultural products, its architecture, its many learned and devout citizens. Celebrating Mariana de Jesús as "The Lily of Quito" allowed a Creole priest like Morán to express pride in his American roots while performing his pastoral duty to promote a saintly exemplar.[21]

The ultimate goal of many confessors, however, was the formal recognition of their penitents as saints, and they fashioned their biographical accounts accordingly. Indeed, sometimes clerics were ordered to write by monastic or clerical superiors anxious to add another Servant of God to the roster of saints produced by their religious order or diocese. Anticipating beatification or canonization, many hagiographers carefully marshaled the testimonies of

witnesses, as we shall see. Sometimes they testified at hearings themselves, participating in yet another way in the saint-making process.[22]

Thus confessors had a variety of motivations—personal, traditional, institutional—for making public the lives of exemplary penitents, but only a small number became authors. I suggest that the ones who did had genuine literary, as well as religious, vocations. Indeed, their very sense of their missions as priests and their impulses to express themselves in writing may have been closely related, the one put to the service of the other.

One indication of a distinct literary bent on the part of certain clerics was the sheer size of their literary output. Far from representing a chance, one-time occurrence, many authors wrote more than one hagiographical text; some were prolific writers generally.

In a preface to the *Life* of his mentor Ignatius Loyola, first published in 1572, Pedro de Ribadeneyra protested that he lacked sufficient strength or talent to produce this work but that he had bowed to the requests of his superiors in the Society of Jesus. Despite this recourse to a humility topos, typical of his time and humanistic training, Ribadeneyra had a long and productive career as a writer on a wide range of topics and in a variety of genres: political treatises, devotional works, translations of Latin texts. And he was especially active as a hagiographer, recording the lives of several early Jesuit leaders, including Loyola, and of two pious lay noblewomen, as well as authoring a popular compilation of traditional saints' lives, or *Flos Sanctorum*.[23] Serafino Razzi wrote the *Vita* of Caterina de' Ricci (d. 1590) but also composed hagiographies of at least seven other figures, male and female, and published two collections of biographical sketches lauding exemplary members of the Dominican order, of which he was himself a friar.[24]

Many of these active clerical authors knew one another and referred to one another's works. Virgilio Cepari and Vincenzo Puccini both directed Maria Maddalena de' Pazzi, conferred together on occasion, and published accounts of her life. In his 1609 biography Puccini recounted how nine years earlier the nun had been granted a vision of the recently deceased Luigi (Alyosius) Gonzaga in heaven, and ecstatically exclaimed, "Luigi is a great Saint." Interestingly, one year earlier, in 1608, Cepari had published a life of Gonzaga. In reporting this incident Puccini underscored the mystical holiness of his penitent Maria Maddalena but also succeeded in affirming the presence of saints among the members of the Society of Jesus, the group to which he, Cepari, and Gonzaga all belonged. And he may well have been calling his readers' attention to his colleague's book.[25]

Like authors of all sorts, hagiographers sought precedents for their literary efforts. Scholars have noted how Catherine of Siena, the fourteenth-century Dominican tertiary, church reformer, and mystic, came to function as a powerful role model for aspiring holy women throughout Catholic Europe and, later, its colonies. In like manner, Raymond of Capua, Catherine's confessor and the author of the popular and influential Latin account of her life and miracles, could serve as an authorizing precedent for aspiring confessor-hagiographers. When the Mercedarian friar Juan Bautista del Santísimo Sacramento set down the life of Mariana de Jesús around 1616, he located himself within a genealogy of zealous and *writing* confessors. Juan Bautista explained that he fashioned a written record of his penitent's spoken confidences "in the same way as did Father Friar Raymond of Capua," and insisted that "the same thing can be seen and read about in many other chronicles and histories."[26] How many clerical promoters, as they proclaimed their spiritual daughters "new" Catherines of Siena, imagined themselves "new" Raymonds of Capua?[27]

Finally, some clerics wrote because they felt compelled by a sense of destiny or divine calling. Juan Bernique recalled a childhood spent with his mother, the future Franciscan tertiary Catalina de Jesús y San Francisco. When he was nine or ten years old

> she ordered me to read in the presence of my sisters the life of Doña María de Pol, written by Father Marcos de Torres, SJ, her son, and when I marveled at the mystery by which a son could be the author of the virtues of his [own] mother, she replied that the same was going to happen to [me], jokingly calling me several times "her historian," and whenever she noticed me lukewarm in my studies, she would coax me out of my laziness, saying to me, "There's a good plan in store for you, to be my chronicler . . ."

While Bernique may have succumbed to his mother's forceful personality, he represented the hagiographical account he published in 1693 as due to the workings of "Heaven" and the fulfillment of the "prophecy" that had helped to determine the course of his life.[28]

Another example of how both autobiographical and hagiographical expression could be understood as divinely inspired comes from the Castilian city of Segovia during the first decades of the eighteenth century. In 1727 María Quintana, a one-time "sinner" who had become an extreme ascetic and mystic, heard God issue a direct command: "'Daughter, tell your confessor to write your life.'" María duly reported this to her confessor at the time, the somewhat timid and elderly Pedro de Arias, but he balked at the idea. The priest hesitated in part because he was unsure whether María's voices were celestial or diabolical, the classic theological dilemma of the period. But he also gave personal reasons for his unwillingness, citing his "lack of talent and of time and the great difficulty he had in writing." Pedro de Arias was not, it would seem, cut out to be a hagiographer.[29]

This role would fall to the man who directed María during the two years leading up to her death in 1734, José Esteban Noriega. In the biography he published three years later, the priest protested his deficiencies as well, stating "I am well aware of my ignorance, lack of passion [*tibieza*, literally, luke-warmness], and lack of experience, especially in these matters." He managed to overcome these stated feelings of inadequacy, however, as he went on to produce 675 pages of densely packed prose.[30] The sense that he was the un-named confessor designated by God to record María's life no doubt helped to propel José Esteban Noriega from confessor to author.

Watching the Hagiographer in Action

Inspired, then, by one or more motivating factors and compelled by a vocation for the written word, many confessors resolved to record the lives of their exemplary penitents. Biographers now, as well as spiritual directors, they embarked upon the process of collecting data, documenting the miraculous and the mundane, even while their penitents were still alive. What methods did they employ?

Like modern-day journalists they made every effort to interview and observe their subjects, and their positions as confessors often gave them ample opportunity. The Mercedarian Juan Bautista del Santísimo Sacramento added his own reminiscences to the spiritual autobiography of the Madrid *beata* Mariana de Jesús. "I record and refer here [to the things] that I remember the Servant of God said to me," he explained, "I as her confessor having asked her about certain matters for the glory of God." Miguel González Vaquero recalled the "many times [he] used to watch" the Cistercian nun and mystic Doña María Vela during the fifteen years that he served as her spiritual guide.[31]

Describing the gift of prophecy bestowed upon his penitent Isabel de Jesús, Manuel de Paredes mentioned a prediction she "told and warned [him] about" on 1 January 1676. Nine years later he assured his readers that all these things had come to pass just as Isabel had foretold "down to the last detail" ("al pie de la letra"), a comment that suggests that he took notes on the earlier occasion. María Quintana also "dictated" many of her supernatural experiences to José Esteban Noriega, although, the priest ruefully admitted, there was probably "much more that even she herself did not know how to put into words."[32]

The somewhat unusual case of a priest and an exemplary male penitent vividly illustrates the data collection involved in the hagiographical enterprise. Francisco Losa emigrated to New Spain from Castile around 1566. In 1578, after more than twenty years as curate and almoner at the Cathedral of Mexico City, Losa was sent to investigate a strange wandering hermit named Gregorio López. While many admired López's life of intense prayer and ascetic denial, others suspected the Madrid native of holding heterodox beliefs.[33]

Losa met and conversed with López and became convinced not only that the layman was entirely orthodox but that he was endowed with divine graces, that he was a saint. By 1589 the priest had resigned his curacy, renounced his benefice, and moved with López to a hermitage. The two spent the next seven years "living in the same house, eating at the same table, and sleeping in the same chamber," until the holy man's death in 1596.[34]

During those years Losa busied himself preparing the biography of Gregorio López. For example, he carried out numerous interviews. During their frequent "chats" (*pláticas*) he asked the hermit questions about his family origins, his decision to emigrate to the New World, his preferred reading and penitential exercises, and many other topics. He also listened in as López gave counsel to his numerous devotees. The hagiographer could be as persistent as he was precise in his record keeping. Once, Losa remembered, he "importune[d] him very much" to speak of his sufferings. "After many days" López finally consented, going on to "utter somewhat of that which did inwardly pass between God and him." This unexpected revelation left the priest so "amazed" that "presently [he] wrote down these words which he has said, being March in the year 1591."[35]

When priests could not query penitents directly, they sometimes turned to surrogates or helpers. The well-known Jesuit Luis de la Puente sent a young girl to take down the testimony of the Valladolid holy woman Doña Marina de Escobar (d. 1633), information he later used to construct her biography. The divinely sent "gifts" and "spiritual affects" ("regalos e sentimientos espirituales") penned by the Poor Clare Ana de la Cruz, the widowed Countess of Féria, were first read and approved by one confessor, then passed on to another, Martín de Roa, who transcribed them and incorporated them into the hagiography he published in Córdoba in 1604. Timoteo de' Ricci, chaplain to the Dominican nuns of San Vincenzo in Prato, worked closely with the

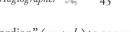

sister designated as Caterina de' Ricci's "guardian" (*custode*) to ensure that the ecstatic nun wrote down "the many marvelous and truly holy things" she experienced. This spiritual diary was later utilized by Friar Timoteo's colleague—and Caterina's first biographer—Serafino Razzi.[36]

Hagiographers also frequently consulted with their penitent's previous confessors or, if this was not possible, perused their notes. We have already seen how Martín de Roa and Serafino Razzi used transcriptions prepared by their predecessors in preparing their biographies of Ana de la Cruz and Caterina de' Ricci, respectively. Juan Bernique carefully described his sources for memorializing his mother Catalina de Jesús y San Francisco. The Franciscan singled out for special mention the written responses to his queries he had received from Friar Damián Cornejo, "who treated [Catalina] for many years, confessed her at the end of her life, and in whose care ("en cuyos manos") she died . . ." Another biological son turned priestly biographer, Marcos Torres, also acknowledged his debt to the insights that "some of her confessors communicated to [him]" when composing the life of Doña María de Pol.[37]

Miguel González Vaquero depended heavily on the advice of one of his predecessors in directing María Vela and on the writings of others in constructing her hagiography. He described how the Jesuit Francisco Salcedo had ordered María to record all the "supernatural gifts" she had received and then kept these "mercies" among his papers. Salcedo's notes later came into Vaquero's possession, and, as he explained to his readers, he "drew from them in order to [write] this history."[38] In his 1621 *Life* of Barbe Acarie, André Duval cited the pious laywoman's first vision of St. Teresa of Avila, which she experienced while confessing to a Dom Beaucousin. Duval lamented his inability to detail the precise nature of this vision "since on account of the death of the director there is no way of finding out." His remark suggests that, had his predecessor still been alive, Duval would have certainly pressed him for information about their exemplary penitent.[39]

Indeed, priestly authors surveyed acquaintances and witnesses of all sorts in their quest for information and authorization. Juan Bernique, who, as the son of Catalina de Jesús y San Francisco, could not have had firsthand knowledge of her early life, diligently sought out "the testimony of those who saw and heard her."[40] Information about Gregorio López that Francisco Losa could not glean directly from his subject he set about compiling from other sources. He talked to priests and others who had known the hermit during his first years in New Spain. He solicited López's letters and other examples of his writing. The dozens of anecdotes about the holy man he collected, Losa later assured readers, came on good authority, from "so many witnesses, so worthy of credit, and such as none can [object to] . . ."[41]

In one of the most fascinating—and thorough—instances of this sort, confessors of Maria Maddalena de' Pazzi polled all sixty nuns of the convent of Santa Maria degli Angeli regarding the nature and veracity of her "raptures and revelations" ("ratti ed intelligentie"). The Jesuit Virgilio Cepari oversaw the depositions (*attestazioni*) taken in September, 1601, six years before the mystic's death, and his colleague Vincenzo Puccini oversaw those of August 1607, three months after. On both occasions the testimonies were carefully witnessed, notarized, and signed by each sister "in [her] own hand," ("di mia propia mano"). Many swore further that they had been present during Maria Maddalena's ecstasies and apprehended these marvels "with their own eyes and ears" ("con i propri occhi visto e sentito con i propri orecchi").[42]

Later both Cepari and Puccini wrote hagiographies of their extraordinary spiritual daughter. In a preface to the *Life* he published in 1609 Puccini insisted upon the accuracy of the details he narrated, for, he pointed out, they had been "verified, and that upon oath, by these other religious women who lived with her, in [the] presence of their spiritual magistrates who had authority to take full information thereof." The Jesuit also apparently interviewed Maria Maddalena's convent sisters about miraculous cures effected by the Servant of God. Puccini related numerous accounts of thaumaturgic intervention, often concluding with phrases such as "This she herself who is yet living has testified upon her oath."[43]

Finally, confessor-hagiographers made extensive, and sometimes exclusive, use of the writings of the exemplary penitents themselves. The same spiritual directors who ordered their female penitents to record their autobiographies or memoirs were frequently the ones responsible for publishing them after the women's deaths. Often priests would append their own reminiscences to these autobiographies or compose biographies that featured lengthy excerpts from the women's accounts; in the next chapter I consider some of these hybrid texts.

But many priestly biographers zealously collected everything written by their exemplary subjects—documents that could serve as source material for hagiographies, as testimony in beatification and canonization proceedings, and as cherished relics. Francisco Losa quoted from at least three letters written by Gregorio López in his *Life*. The priest lauded the hermit for his prudent use of language, so different from that of the gaudy and verbose courtiers of his day. López, his hagiographer proclaimed, "did not only keep silence in speaking but also in writing, for he . . . did not return an answer unless charity or necessity did require it . . . and then he did only use those words which were necessary for the business." Losa could speak with authority on this point, assuring his readers, "I have many of his letters in my hands . . ."[44]

This question of possession or access was apparently an important one for these clerical authors, a way of underscoring their positions as trusted confidants of the Servants of God during their lives, and guardians of their legacies after their deaths. Thus Juan Bernique explained how, in presenting the life of Catalina de Jesús y San Francisco, he "made faithful transcriptions of the papers and letters that she wrote out of obedience, and that have ended up in my possession" ("que en mi poder paran"). Marcos Torres likewise described how he had kept all the letters he had received from his mother, Doña María de Pol, "among [his] papers" ("entre mis papeles"), a quantity large enough, he asserted, to be published separately as a book of spiritual advice.[45]

After the death of Doña Estefanía Manrique de Castilla, Pedro de Ribadeneyra obtained access to a collection of prayers, spiritual reflections, and the like that the pious noblewoman had guarded so closely that not even her confessors had been aware of its existence. The noted Jesuit then made extensive use of "her private papers" ("sus papeles secretos") in composing the narrative of her life. Manuel de Paredes also seems to have systematically mined the papers of his penitent Isabel de Jesús; he cited some poems or songs (*canciones*) penned by the Carmelite tertiary that he "ran across among her papers" ("las topé entre sus papeles").[46]

Like modern-day biographers or journalists, then, early modern hagiographers used a variety of methods in documenting the lives of their spiritually gifted penitents. They observed, interviewed, and queried their subjects during their lives and their acquaintances after their deaths. They consulted, when possible, with former confessors. They took the testimony of witnesses, sometimes informally, sometimes in a very systematic and legalistic fashion. And they collected—some might say, appropriated—letters, memoirs, and other papers produced by their penitents, a process often begun while the subject was still alive and accelerated after her or his death. Motivated to write and equipped with plenty of biographical data, these confessors were now ready to become hagiographers, memorializing the lives of the women (and sometimes men) whom they had directed and who had touched their own lives in such profound ways. In the next chapter I examine some of the texts confessors and penitents would produce together.

CHAPTER THREE

WHOSE LIFE *IS THIS ANYWAY?*

We have seen how, as a result of developing close relationships with extraordinary penitents, many clerics came to redefine and expand their priestly vocations. No longer would they merely direct the spiritual lives of these penitents; they would also record them for the edification of others. They would become hagiographers.

The end product of this intense biographical urge was, of course, texts—hundreds of texts produced in the Catholic lands of Europe and their colonies in the sixteenth through eighteenth centuries. But what sorts of texts are these? They often defy easy categorization as "biography" or "autobiography." These narratives of exemplary lives make fascinating reading indeed, but prove rather untidy when it comes to making conventional generic distinctions.

A book published in Paris in 1677 illustrates this dilemma. On the title page to the *Life of the Venerable Mother Marie of the Incarnation, First Superior of the Ursulines of New France* (*La Vie de la Venerable Mere Marie de l'Incarnation Premiere Superieure des Ursulines de la Nouvelle France*) no author is listed. One cannot tell whether this is a narrative written by Marie herself before her death in 1672 or by someone else.

This ambiguity of authorship is, as it turns out, intentional. The preface makes an intriguing statement:

> There is not one Author to this work; there are two and both are necessary to its completion. This great Servant of God did the work herself, and her son has put in the final touches, nevertheless he speaks as an echo that responds to that which she says with her own words. . . .[1]

The reader is given to expect that Marie is the primary author and that she has a coauthor, who is her son. However, an additional thirty pages or so of preface and transcribed letters go by without mention of his name. When it finally does appear, on page thirty-four, its placement seems significant: in an approval given by a learned theologian of the Sorbonne to the book "*composed by* the Reverend Father Claude Martin, Benedictine Monk of the Congregation of Saint Maur." He was also, as we shall see, Marie's biological son. On the very first page of the preface Martin extols "the *Life* of this excellent nun *that I give to the public.*"[2] How, then, to characterize the role of Claude Martin: faithful echo or primary author? And is this an autobiographical or a biographical account of Marie's life?

While there certainly were texts produced in the late-medieval and early-modern periods that clearly fall into one category or the other (a well-known example is that of Teresa of Avila's self-authored autobiography),[3] cases such as the *Life* of Marie de l'Incarnation abound. Literary scholars and historians who have worked on these life narratives, in which two or even more voices are blended in various ways, have struggled to come up with a descriptive language with which to discuss them. They have used expressions such as "mixtures," "cooperative ventures," "auto-biographical combination[s]," and (my personal favorite) "cut-and-paste jobs," all of which point to the conceptual difficulties involved.[4] In this chapter I examine several of the forms of collaboration utilized by early-modern authors, preferring to focus upon process rather than to attempt generic definition.

Forms of Collaboration: Adding "That Which Is Lacking"

During the late Middle Ages and early-modern period many religious women wrote or dictated spiritual autobiographies or memoirs of some sort. And behind these self-revelations almost invariably stood a male cleric, usually the woman's confessor. Women wrote because so ordered by their confessors. Many protested that if not for the express command of their spiritual directors, to whom they were bound by vows of obedience, they would never have taken up the pen. Sometimes these protestations of literary disinclination seem merely formulaic and ring a bit hollow. Recent scholarship on Teresa of Avila (1515–82), for example, concludes that she had a strong sense of literary vocation and that the obedience to confessors she consistently maintained is more properly understood as authorization or affirmation than as blind submission to demands.[5] Some women, however, may have been genuinely reluctant to write and reveal themselves in this way. The Chilean Poor Clare Ursula Suárez (1666–1749) described the obligation to write as a form of "torture." She begged her confessor to "remove this penance and give me any other," a plea that went unheeded.[6]

In any case, confessors played a critical role in the production of female-authored texts, often serving as the instigators of the autobiographical process. They were, as we have seen, frequently the ones responsible for making the writings of their spiritual daughters available to a larger public after the women had died.

Confessors also intervened directly in the texts of their female penitents, however, and the results bear the imprint of both authors. For example, it was not uncommon for a woman to write or dictate her life and afterwards for her confessor to add to the same text his own reflections, reminiscences, moralizing observations, and prayers. Usually this male authorial intervention comes appended at the end of the woman's narrative. Often the priest's addition includes an account of the holy woman's exemplary death—clearly an impossibility in a "purely" autobiographical text! For example, Isabel de Jesús (1586–1648) dictated her life to a fellow Augustinian sister between 1645 and 1648. When some twenty-five years later her confessor Francisco Ignacio had her account published, he "added that which was lacking of her blessed death."[7] In order to explore in greater detail the ways in which clerics appended their own writings to the writings of their exemplary penitents—and revealed their own preoccupations and personalities—let us examine a few case studies.

Mariana de Jesús and Juan Bautista del Santísimo Sacramento

Mariana Navarro Romero was born to a family of artisans in Madrid in 1565. From a young age she spent hours listening to sermons and engaging in acts of charity. She heard preachers describe the life of Catherine of Siena and resolved to adopt the Italian saint as her "companion and guide" ("compañera y guía"). By her early twenties Mariana had made a private vow of chastity, cut her hair, dressed herself in the simple garb of a tertiary, and taken the religious name Mariana de Jesús. Over the years she developed a reputation within her neighborhood for piety and sage advice; she was regarded as a holy woman (*beata*).[8]

Born in the province of Cuenca in 1553, Juan Bautista González followed the example of an older brother and joined the Iberian-based Mercedarian order. In 1573, at the age of twenty, he received ordination as a priest, his friar's habit, and a name in religion: Juan Bautista del Santísimo Sacramento. The young friar immersed himself in the abundant spiritual literature of his day and, like his future penitent Mariana de Jesús, was greatly influenced by the

FIGURE FIVE

Mariana de Jesús. Portrait by Vicente Carducho, 1625. Reproduced in
Diego Angulo Iñiguez and A.E. Pérez Sánchez, *Pintura madrileña
del primer tercio del siglo XVII* (Madrid: CSIC, 1969).
Courtesy of the Biblioteca Nacional, Madrid.

lives of saintly persons. According to one account, after reading the life of an
esteemed contemporary, the Valencian Dominican Diego Anadón (1540–
1602), Juan Bautista was inspired with a longing for a more ascetic life and a
desire to reform his order. During a long career as a missionary in Peru,
monastic administrator, and chaplain to several female religious houses in
Spain Juan Bautista gained considerable respect, especially for his skill as a
spiritual director.[9]

In 1598, now in his mid-forties, Juan Bautista was appointed to a prestigious
position in Madrid, the seat of Spain's royal government. It was there that he
met the thirty-three-year-old Mariana de Jesús and agreed to take her on as a

FIGURE SIX

Juan Bautista del Santísimo Sacramento. Portrait at far left. Frontispiece
to Pedro de San Cecilio, *Anales del Orden de Descalzos de Nuestra
Señora de la Merced* . . . (Barcelona, 1669).
Courtesy of the Biblioteca Nacional, Madrid.

penitent. This encounter would prove highly significant for both priest and *beata*. For eighteen years, until Juan Bautista's death in 1616, the two main-tained an extremely close personal and working relationship. Mariana, re-lieved to finally have a confessor sympathetic to her mystical experiences, soon became affiliated with the Mercedarians as a tertiary. Thanks to her growing reputation for efficacious prayer and thaumaturgic healing—and extensive connections to elites on Madrid's city council and at court—she proved in-strumental in the establishment of a new friary in the capital in 1606. This was to be one of the first houses in the reformed (or Discalced) Mercedarian or-der of which Juan Bautista had been dreaming for some twenty years.[10]

Mariana de Jesús and Juan Bautista del Santísimo Sacramento also collab-orated textually, recording the holy woman's life. Around 1613 Juan Bautista's superiors requested that he acquire a written record of the *beata*'s spiritual ex-periences, or what she referred to as "tidbits of the mercies from God" ("cosi-tas de las misericordias de Dios"). Over a two-year period, roughly 1614–15, Mariana dictated an account that gave a few details of her early life among family and neighbors but concentrated on her many intimate encounters with the divine. Juan Bautista served as her amanuensis, at least in the early phases of transcription. He was well aware that by engaging in this partnership not only was Mariana joining a long line of holy women and autobiographers, but he was entering the ranks of famous confessors, biographers, and scribes. A prologue begins with these words:

> The whole history of the Blessed Angela of Foligno was known to her con-fessor, he having heard it from her own mouth, in the same way as did Father Friar Raymond of Capua, who was the confessor of the Blessed Catherine of Siena, and also this is how was written the life and miracles and revelations of the Blessed Mother Teresa de Jesús [Teresa of Avila] . . . and the same could be said about many other lives and revelations, especially the account that of her holy life the Venerable Mother Battista Vernazza of Genoa gave to her confessor . . . and the same thing can be seen and read about in many other chronicles and histories.[11]

Because he was writing in an atmosphere in which some clerics were in-tensely suspicious of women who claimed supernatural experiences, Juan Bautista's tone of edgy defensiveness seems to be anticipating objections from some quarters. But his words indicate a pride of pedigree, too, both for his ex-emplary penitent and for himself.[12]

Juan Bautista's death in 1616 cut short his and Mariana's life-writing activities, although the *beata* lived on for another eight years. The textual result of their joint efforts remained unedited, untitled, and unpublished for some forty years. Around 1660 the Discalced Mercedarian Juan de la Presentación, who had known Mariana in his youth, incorporated her spiritual memoir—and Juan Bautista's added reminiscences—into his documentary history of the order, once again combining genres. This manuscript version circulated within Mercedarian circles and served as the basis for later published biographies of Mariana and beatification proceedings for both Mariana (successful) and Juan Bautista (unsuccessful).[13]

It was Juan de la Presentación who first divided the text into chapters. Mariana's account takes up the first ten chapters, Juan Bautista's the final eight. In this particular case of collaboration the contributions made by holy woman and confessor are virtually equal in length. As I have already examined Mariana's autobiographical writings,[14] I turn now to her confessor and what he added to her self-revelations.

Juan Bautista does not offer a systematic, chronological account of Mariana's life but rather a series of more or less random recollections. The effect is, as he himself recognizes, a rather disjointed piece, "not set out with much order" ("no va puesto con mucho orden").[15] One indication of this lack of order is that he states his motivations for writing not in a preface, as was most common for hagiographers, or even at the end of the text, as in some cases, but right in the middle. "I took on this task of writing here something of the life and divinely bestowed gifts [*mercedes*] of this Servant of God," Juan Bautista explains, "with the holy goal of the glory of Our Lord and also because I am her confessor." He seems to have accepted this biographical and authorial charge as part of the responsibility of being a confessor, at least in the case of "servants of God."[16] Moreover, he claims that he did not want to put off this obligation any longer, recognizing that because of Mariana's many illnesses and advancing age (just under fifty) and his even more advanced age (about sixty) they soon will not be around to make known to others the wondrous gifts of God's mercy.[17] He cautions readers that he touches only briefly on matters of profound spiritual significance because of his "poor health and poor abilities" ("por mi poca salud y poca suficiencia"). The fact that the text ends very abruptly and that Juan Bautista died shortly after the transcription was completed suggests that this was more than just a standard humility topos.[18]

The priest thus endeavors to set down memorable episodes in Mariana's relationship with the divine, based upon his own recollections, responses she made to questions he asked her in his capacity as confessor, and anecdotes passed along to him by others. These were all, as we have seen, methods commonly used by spiritual directors once they had determined that they had a truly exemplary penitent, worthy of record for posterity.[19] Many of the sorts of experiences he mentions are also discussed by Mariana herself. However, there are some issues that receive greater emphasis in the appendix written by the confessor than in the testimony of the *beata*.

Most notably, Juan Bautista highlights the services that the holy woman rendered to others, either to individuals or the community at large, whereas Mariana speaks almost exclusively of the graces God granted to her. This may be due to an expected humility on her part, as well as a general reluctance to talk about herself; Mariana's entire memoir takes up less than thirty pages in a modern printed edition. The *beata* makes very brief, and rather oblique, references to people seeking her prayers or words of advice, but her confessor cites more specific instances. For example, he relates how the spirit of a dead woman once came seeking Mariana's aid to have masses said for the release of her soul from purgatory. During her life this woman had helped the *beata* with alms and before she died had arranged for a certain number of masses to be recited for her soul. But now she desired more. Mariana arranged for the additional masses, thereby bringing some ease to this perturbed soul in purgatory. Juan Bautista succeeds here in illustrating Mariana's gift as intermediary between this world and the realm of the divine, a theme that would be stressed in subsequent beatification hearings and biographies. At the same time he reinforces the doctrinal imperative of chanting masses for the souls of the dead, a task reserved for priests such as himself.[20]

Mariana's confessor marvels at her ability to divine the future and to find lost objects. He also recalls occasions when her efficacious prayers brought relief to the drought-stricken city. This image of the holy woman as bringer of rain and as thaumaturge generally would become one of the most salient features of the urban cult that developed in Madrid after her death.[21]

Finally, Juan Bautista takes pains to identify Mariana not only as holy but as a Mercedarian. Both the *beata* and her confessor discuss how she was cured from a protracted illness by the intercession of Nuestra Señora de los Remedios. This highly venerated Marian image was located in Madrid's oldest Mercedarian friary. At the time of the miracle Juan Bautista was serving as the shrine's custodian, and it was here that the two met and began a relationship as confessor and penitent. Mariana narrates the incident in a way that links receiving a divinely sent cure with receiving a divinely sent "spiritual father," but she does not make a particular institutional connection. She likewise makes only fleeting reference to events in the fledgling Mercedarian reform movement and never mentions the order by name. Perhaps most significant, she does not discuss her own eventual affiliation with the order.[22]

Thus, it is left to her confessor, a friar of forty years' standing, to describe in some detail the process by which Mariana obtained permission to become a Mercedarian tertiary. Juan Bautista relates with pride how the Master General traveled from Valencia to Madrid to personally bestow the habit upon the humble *beata*. The ceremony, carried out "with great solemnity" and attended by "many people of high quality and standing," took place at the new discalced friary of Santa Bárbara, whose establishment both Mariana and Juan Bautista had worked so hard to bring about.[23] For Juan Bautista del Santísimo Sacramento, adding his own account to the autobiography of Mariana de Jesús served several purposes. It gave him an opportunity to sing the praises of his exemplary penitent and to render service to "the glory of God" but also to promote the Mercedarian order that had provided him with a career, an identity, and an institutional home for his entire adult life.

Isabel de Jesús and Francisco Ignacio

Like Mariana, Isabel Sánchez Jiménez was a woman of modest origins who first became a lay *beata* and eventually established an affiliation with a religious order. But Isabel was as rural in background and orientation as Mariana was urban. She was born around 1586 in the tiny village of Navalcán, in the Gredos Mountains south of Avila. Isabel frequently recalled her early years in a family of impoverished agricultural workers, describing herself as a "rustic shepherdess" and a "poor farm woman" ("rústica pastora" or "pastorcilla," "pobre labradora").[24] Married at the age of fourteen, she bore three children only to watch them all die. At the death of her husband in 1624, the thirty-eight-year-old widow moved to another village to avoid remarriage. Over the next two years, Isabel traveled around the region taking on various menial jobs simply to survive, but her longing for a religious vocation steadily grew. She had already begun to relate her many visions to her neighbors, gaining the admiration of some and arousing the suspicions of others. After many vicissitudes Isabel was finally able to enter, as a lay sister, the convent of San Juan Bautista of Augustinian Recollects in the town of Arenas in 1626. Now known by her religious name, Isabel de Jesús, she would remain in this community until her death in 1648.[25]

In stark contrast to the abundant—and gripping—details of Isabel's nar-

RETRATO DE LA V. M. YSABEL
DE IESVS RECOLETA
AGVSTINA.

Orozco Presbyter

FIGURE SEVEN

Isabel de Jesús. From *Vida de la Venerable Madre . . .
Isabel de Iesus . . .* (Madrid, 1675).
Courtesy of the Biblioteca Nacional, Madrid.

rative, we know almost nothing about the man responsible for making them known to a general public. On the title page of the book he published in 1675 Francisco Ignacio identified himself as a "preacher of the Order of Saint Augustine," and "her confessor." He had become Isabel's spiritual director in 1640, upon assuming the post of chaplain to the Arenas nuns. The friar received orders from the bishop of Avila to investigate and preserve in writing the inner spiritual life of the lay sister; he appears to have been quite well connected with local ecclesiastical authorities.[26] I speculate that he was himself a native of this mountainous region, but this is a guess. What we do know is that

Francisco Ignacio played a pivotal role in transmitting the life of Isabel de Jesús from oral account to written record to published hagiographical text.

During her first fifteen years or so at San Juan Bautista, Isabel suffered a fate common to many women with charismatic claims: an extremely hostile confessor. The house's chaplain had, as the *beata* recalled, "a poor opinion of her spirit" ("mal concepto de su espiritu"), and tried to persuade her that her visions and raptures were either merely imaginary or sent by the devil. She later ruefully recalled this period "when my confessor so oppressed me" ("cuando me tenía tan oprimida mi confesor") but insisted that God had continued to comfort her.[27]

One of the divine favors Isabel received at this difficult time was a vision of Catherine of Siena, to whom she had long been devoted. The fourteenth-century Italian saint, who had served as a role model for Mariana de Jesús as well, was a mystic and a lay holy woman affiliated with a religious order as a tertiary, as were the two Spanish *beatas*. Catherine had maintained a long and intimate relationship with her confessor, Raymond of Capua, who later recorded her life. Significantly, in Isabel's narrative, her account of the vision of Catherine is followed immediately by the arrival of a sympathetic confessor. Although unnamed, this was Francisco Ignacio. The convent's new chaplain quickly indicated his support, referring to another saintly female precedent in order to reassure Isabel that her "spirit [was] as good as that of the holy mother Teresa of Jesus." Soon afterwards, she was rewarded with an apt vision of deliverance and hope, finding herself transported before the gates of the heavenly Jerusalem.[28]

Ignacio's assumption of the role of spiritual director to Isabel de Jesús around 1641 in fact seems to have marked a general shift of opinion toward the former shepherdess. A number of constituencies were now anxious to learn about her life and elaborate visionary experiences. Isabel may have understood her impulse toward self-revelation strictly in terms of obedience to God's commands, but the bishop of Avila, the prioress of San Juan Bautista, the parish priest of Arenas, and, of course, her confessor all had roles to play in the unfolding biographical enterprise.[29] Between late 1645 and her death in 1648, the illiterate Isabel was ordered by various authorities to dictate her memoir to a fellow nun named Inés del Sacramento, who had been appointed to serve as her secretary in this undertaking.[30] Nearly thirty years later, in 1675, Francisco Ignacio published his penitent's autobiography, appending his own account at the end.

His main goal, Ignacio assures his readers, is to make known the exemplary life of Isabel, as stated in her own words. He declares that he has merely presented her own testimony "without a single word having been added to or deleted from her writings." Moreover, he claims, it would not have been "decent" to have added fancy flourishes to her simple style, or to have introduced "clauses, glosses or explanatory notes to that which God dictated to a rustic shepherdess."[31] The technique to which Ignacio refers, glossing the language of an inspired if unpolished subject, was in fact employed by other hagiographers, as we shall see.

Nonetheless, Isabel's confessor still felt compelled to add to her four hundred-page account some contributions of his own relating to "her blessed death, the things she prophesied during her life, and the miracles that Our Lord has worked through her."[32] Francisco Ignacio carefully catalogs the saintly virtues of his penitent but also takes pains to situate her within a specific institutional and regional context, factors that may have held more significance for the priest than for the holy woman.

For example, Ignacio emphasizes Isabel's gift of prophecy, something she does not mention at all. The friar calls particular attention to her prediction that a new convent of Augustinian Recollect nuns would someday be founded in the town of Serradilla, just south of Plasencia.[33]

A bit of institutional background is helpful here. When she entered the convent of San Juan Bautista in 1626, Isabel was joining one of Spain's newest religious orders. The reformed (or "Recollected") branch of the venerable Augustinian order had only been established in 1588, that is, when Isabel was about two years old. The convent in Arenas was founded in 1623, just three years before Isabel's arrival as a lay sister. Isabel had actually wanted to enter another religious house in Arenas, that of the Discalced Franciscans, but had been turned away three times. That the Augustinian Recollects would accept an impoverished and controversial, if intensely pious, country woman may have been due, in part, to the newness of the convent and the relatively fluid situation in which this nascent order found itself.[34]

Nevertheless, Francisco Ignacio identifies Isabel de Jesús as a devoted daughter of Saint Augustine: "Recoleta Agustina." He details the "mercies and gifts that Our Lord made to her *in her holy house* [of San Juan Bautista]." For him, Isabel's association with this convent signals its favored position with God; her presence there can be understood as both a cause and an effect of its exemplary status. The mutual endorsement of convent and holy woman was not lost on the nuns of San Juan Bautista, who, after her death, jealously guarded her bones as relics. And Isabel's prophecy, predicting the foundation of a new Augustinian Recollect community, which actually occurred in 1660, certified as divinely ordained the success and growth of the fledgling order.[35]

Ignacio highlights aspects of Isabel's life and afterlife that promote not only the Augustinian family of which they were both members but also the geographical region of which they were both natives or at least longtime residents. Nearly all the events narrated by Isabel and her confessor take place in an area roughly defined by a triangle with points in Avila, Toledo, and Plasencia, tracing the western fringe of Castile and the northeast edge of Extremadura. Publishing the *Life* of Isabel de Jesús gave Ignacio an opportunity to write local sacred history as well.

For example, when Isabel died in June of 1648, she was buried in her convent among the other deceased sisters. But six years later, in 1652, Bishop José de Argáiz of Avila, under whose diocesan jurisdiction Arenas lay, ordered her remains moved to the chapel's high altar so that they could receive greater exposure and respect. Francisco Ignacio recalls that very few people attended the reburial ceremonies because the nuns of San Juan Bautista, with "the anguish and pain they felt at losing such a great Servant of God [from the cloistered part of the house] . . . did not announce this to anyone, not even to the friars of the Augustinian monastery in the same town," a group that presumably included Ignacio himself. But in the following days God provided "recompense" because "many people came, not only from the town [of Arenas] but from the whole region" (la Comarca).[36]

For Bishop Argáiz, acknowledging and associating himself with a local holy person helped to enhance his own personal authority and to extend centralized episcopal control in one of the more remote corners of his diocese; this method had been utilized by a number of prelates in Avila before him.[37] One of the eventual outcomes was the promotion of a regional cult around the figure of a previously obscure *beata*, a process with which Francisco Ignacio was of course intimately involved.

Isabel had also reportedly received a vision of "el Santo Fray Pedro de Alcántara." Pedro, an austere Franciscan from Extremadura, was born in 1499. After a number of travels he settled in Arenas, where he instituted the order of reformed or Discalced Franciscans in 1540 and died in 1562. Recall that it was among the Discalced Franciscans that Isabel had first aspired to live. In 1669 Pedro de Alcántara was indeed canonized as a saint, as Isabel seems to have predicted.[38] His adopted town quickly changed its name to "Arenas de San Pedro," as this figure, too, became integrated into the region's sacred landscape.

Why did Ignacio wait nearly thirty years to publish this collaborative life-narrative? We will probably never know his exact motivations, but a consideration of these institutional and regional commitments may at least offer some perspective. While there is no evidence that the friar deliberately delayed publication, waiting this long did enable him to point out that many of the prodigious events Isabel had predicted had actually come to pass. In his seventy-page appendix to the autobiography of Isabel de Jesús Francisco Ignacio strove to validate not only his pious penitent but also his religious order and his native or adopted homeland as truly graced by God.

Marie de l'Incarnation and Claude Martin

In April of 1672 an aged nun suffered through her final illness. Some five years later her biographer related that

[o]ne hour before her death she shed three or four large tears . . . a short time afterwards she gently opened her eyes, which she had kept closed for several hours, so as to be able to make a final farewell to her beloved Sisters . . . then she closed her eyes again and never opened them again to this world and its creatures. Finally at six in the evening . . . giving out only two small sighs, she relinquished her blessed soul into the arms of him for whom she had sighed her whole life . . .[39]

This excerpt from a rather lengthy account of the death of the Ursuline sister and missionary to Canada, Marie de l'Incarnation, is so precise, so vivid, and so painstaking in its rendering of physical detail that one would never guess that it was written not by an eyewitness but rather by someone living in France, many thousands of miles away. This paradox, of two people intimately connected yet separated by great distance, animates the fascinating personal and authorial relationship between Marie de l'Incarnation and her biological son, Claude Martin, whom we have already met at the beginning of this chapter.

Unlike those of the Spanish holy women discussed above, the life of Marie Guyart is quite well known. She was born in 1599 in Tours and raised in the mercantile milieu of this provincial French city. Married at seventeen, Marie was left a widow with an infant son by the age of twenty. She joined the household of a sister and brother-in-law and for some ten years efficiently contributed to their family business. But an ardent piety and series of visionary experiences left Marie with a longing for a religious vocation. Facing intense

La Venerable Mere Marie de L'Incarnation Premiere Superieure des Ursulines de la
Nouuelle France; qui apres auoir passe trente deux Ans dans le Siecle, en des penitences extra-
ordinaires; huict ans au Monastere des Ursulines de Tours, dans la pratique d'one tres exacte
Observance; et trente trois ans en Canada, dans vm Zele incroyable pour la Conuersion des
Sauuages, est decedee a Quebec en odeur de Saintete le dernier d'Auril 1672, agee de 72 Ans
Six mois, 13 Iours.
I. Edelinck fecit.   P.Marette ex.

FIGURE EIGHT

Marie de l'Incarnation. From *La Vie de la Venerable
Mere Marie de l'Incarnation* . . . (Paris, 1677).
Courtesy of the British Library.

opposition from kin but supported by a Jesuit spiritual director, the young
widow entered the convent of Ursuline nuns in Tours in 1631, adopting the religious name Marie de l'Incarnation. She left her distraught eleven-year-old
son, Claude, in the care of his aunt and uncle. Eight years later, in 1639, Marie
and several other French nuns and laywomen set sail for New France (Canada)
to found a religious house and aid in the effort to missionize the native peoples.
During a remarkable thirty-four-year career as a convent administrator,
teacher, and writer Marie de l'Incarnation mastered several Amerindian languages and gained renown as a mystic and spiritual guide to the young Catholic
community of French Canada. She never returned to her native land.[40]

Marie's son, Claude Martin, born in 1619, for years fought feelings of bitterness at having been abandoned by his mother. He began university studies in his late teens but had some difficulty in choosing a vocation. In 1641, at the age of twenty-one, he joined the French Benedictines of the Congregation of St. Maur, a decision that delighted Marie; he eventually received ordination as a priest as well. The two corresponded regularly over the years, exchanging religious advice and counsel as well as news. Ironically, as a priest the son could now assume the role of spiritual "father" to his own mother, at least by way of the written word. Martin had a distinguished career as a monk and scholar, holding a succession of administrative posts within his order and writing many theological treatises, editions of patristic texts, and books of prayer and devotion before his death in 1696. However, he is best known for publishing the life and works of his exceptional mother.[41]

Claude Martin contributed to the production of Marie de l'Incarnation's life-narrative in several crucial ways. One was that of instigator. As in so many cases of spiritually gifted women, Marie recorded the events of her exterior life and abundant mystical experiences of her inner life in response to commands from confessors, first in France and then in Canada. But she also received many letters asking for an account of her "secrets" from Dom Claude Martin, her son/priestly father/brother in religion. Whether out of deference to him as a cleric, a desire to share her insights as a way of guiding his own spiritual path, or capitulation to the "emotional blackmail" wielded by the child she had once left behind—or a combination of all these motivations—Marie finally acquiesced to Martin's request and sent him her autobiographical *Relation* in 1654.[42]

In 1677, five years after his mother's death, the Benedictine set out to publish Marie's memoir, piously ignoring her stated desire that only her son and a niece who had become an Ursuline should ever see the manuscript. The text is divided into sixteen chapters; each contains Marie's testimony, followed by an "Addition" (this is the French term) composed by Martin. The learned monk's commentaries are quite extensive, often much longer than the chapter they are meant to explicate. Some indication of the sheer mass of Claude Martin's authorial intervention can be gauged by the fact that an English translation of Marie's autobiography, which does not include the Additions (and also somewhat abridges Marie's own text), runs to 182 pages of small print. The original French edition ends on page 757![43]

A number of scholars—notably Guy-Marie Oury, Jacques Lonsagne, and, most recently, Natalie Zemon Davis—have examined the ways in which Claude Martin glossed, corrected, and, in some cases, subtly censored Marie's words in his Additions. Davis, analyzing Martin's modes of interacting with his mother's writing, points to his concern as a theologian to establish the doctrinal accuracy and authenticity of Marie's pronouncements and visions and his anxiousness as a man of letters to "polish" her rough frontier prose.[44]

I thus focus here on the last four chapters (approximately thirty pages) of the *Life* of Marie de l'Incarnation. This final section was written exclusively by Claude Martin, who, like his Spanish contemporary Francisco Ignacio, appended to an autobiography an account of his subject's exemplary death, an excerpt of which has already been cited. The French Benedictine signals this change of voice right in the first sentence of chapter 17, advising his readers: "This is no longer Mother [Marie] de l'Incarnation who speaks: death, which imposes silence on even the greatest Saints, has closed her mouth . . ."[45] How, then, does Claude Martin speak?

For one thing, he provides a plethora of detail. Perhaps to compensate for the fact that he was never an eyewitness to events in her life in New France, he writes in a way that emphasizes the concrete and the visual, such as the exact number of tears that flowed down the Ursuline's cheek at a precise moment. "I must report here more particuliars," Martin states at one point, repeating a sentiment found throughout his text. This sort of dense description gives the distinct impression that the author was actually there at Marie's bedside and makes the reader feel as if he or she had been there too.[46]

How did Martin, who had never visited Canada, acquire such a wealth of information about Marie? Sometimes he is very explicit about his sources. For example, he reproduces in its entirety a letter of condolence that the Ursulines in New France wrote to him after Marie's death, offering it "for the consolation and example of anyone who would like to read it." He acknowledges the remarks of "those who were in attendance" at a particular event and cites the *Relations,* the yearly chronicle of the Canadian mission maintained by the Jesuits.[47]

However, most of the time the monk is more vague, simply reporting the words of "a certain nun," quoting from letters sent to others, utilizing a memoir that "fell into my hands."[48] What Martin does not usually specify, but one suspects, is that he actively solicited written or oral data from a great range of individuals who had known his exemplary subject. In this rather special case, moreover, people may have honored his requests for material out of respect for his status as Mère Marie's biological son as well as his position as a priest. One of his mother's Ursuline sisters wrote, "I account you blessed to be he who you are."[49] The fact that Martin was, in effect, writing family history as well as hagiography may have helped him in his efforts to gather information and overcome obstacles of time and distance that most confessor-biographers did not have to face. He lamented that when his mother's close friend and collaborator Madame de la Peltrie died before she could send Martin a promised memoir of Marie's life, he "was deprived of this great source of assistance" ("ce grand secours").[50] He may well have been referring to help in reconstructing his mother's *Life*, as well as in recovering from the grief of her death.

Although Claude Martin likened himself to an echo of Marie de l'Incarnation's inspired words, he was acclaimed in his time as a scholar, teacher, and theologian. Accordingly he makes some effort to impress his readers with his erudition and eloquence. He offers Latin quotations from the Old and New Testaments.[51] Like many hagiographers before him, he places Marie within a genealogy of distinguished female predecessors, citing the by-then usual precedents of Catherine of Siena and Teresa of Avila. Martin, however, also lists some less commonly mentioned figures—notably Thecla, the protaganist of the second-century apocryphal "Acts of Paul and Thecla," who exhibited great "zeal for the faith and for the conversion of the infidels," and Monica, the mother of St. Augustine, who struggled mightily "to win for God a misguided son." Steeped as he was in scriptural and patristic studies, Claude Martin understood perfectly the relevance of these heroines of the early Christian past to a modern-day woman missionary and mother who had fervently prayed for the religious vocation of her son.[52]

Unlike Juan Bautista del Santísimo Sacramento, who apologized for the disorderly nature of his writing, Martin fairly dazzles his audience with his command of the elegant French prose of the Grand Siècle. His style features lengthy and complex sentences, repetition, and metaphor, in addition to the detailed and highly visual description mentioned above. Demonstrating his flair for classical rhetoric, Martin frequently makes use of the device of *occupatio*, in which the writer first denies he is about to say something and then says it. Thus, a long catalog of Marie's virtues and gifts is punctuated with the following disclaimers: "I pass over in silence her extreme penitences and mortifications . . . I will likewise not speak with any precision about her communications and intimate unions with the divine Majesty . . . I decline to speak in detail of her freely given graces . . ." The resulting effect is, of course, to provide the reader with more information, not less.[53]

Unlike Francisco Ignacio, who thought it "indecent" to meddle with the words of the unlearned but enlightened Isabel de Jesús, Claude Martin cannot resist glossing some of the documents he transcribes in the closing section of the *Life* of Marie de l'Incarnation. For example, sentiments expressed in a letter from the Québec nuns compel him to offer "a small reflection" ("une petite réflexion"). The nuns had referred to the recently deceased Marie as a "saint," and while her son finds their use of this term perfectly understandable, as a theologian he feels obliged to explain that "only the Vicar of Christ" can bestow this title "through a solemn and authentic declaration called canonization" before a figure can receive "the public veneration of the faithful."[54]

I suggest that Claude Martin, like so many clerical authors, had precisely this issue of sainthood in mind when he composed his appendix to his mother's autobiography, especially the last two chapters. This section, in fact, resembles (in small scale) a process of canonization, a procedure with which he was evidently quite familiar. Perhaps he also recognized that his situation in France, close to the centers of publishing, political influence, and ecclesiastical authority, provided a strategic advantage over residency in Canada.

He thus marshals and reproduces the testimony of witnesses (*témoignages*) as to the heroic virtues of Marie de l'Incarnation. He organizes these testimonies in the manner of many canonization processes, beginning with those who knew Marie the most intimately and could observe her most closely: her Mother Superior, her convent sisters in Canada, Madame de la Peltre, nuns who knew her back in France, and her Jesuit confessor. He then moves to more general reminiscences and ends with accounts of her miraculous postmortem apparitions.[55] Claude Martin closes this book with these confident words:

> If it is permitted to judge her [future] glory by the virtues that she practiced and . . . the services that she rendered to God, one cannot doubt that she will be elevated to a very high degree . . . and given the measure [of reward] of the greatest Saints . . . [for] it will be difficult to find a moment in her life that was devoid of merit.[56]

It is equally difficult to find a moment in this text devoid of the presence of Claude Martin. Having added his commentary to every chapter of Marie de l'Incarnation's autobiographical account, he further appended a narrative of her final illness and death as vivid as any eyewitness report and laid the foundation for future canonization processes. Religious vocation and distance separated Claude Martin from his mother during most of his life, but becoming Marie's hagiographer offered him a most effective way of integrating himself into her *Life*.

Forms of Collaboration: "It Is Necessary to Let Her Speak"

We have seen that confessors and other clerical promoters were deeply involved in the production of women's life-narratives in early-modern Europe, ordering their female penitents to write or dictate their memoirs, later publishing or distributing them, and finally appending to the women's texts their own accounts and observations. An even more common occurrence, however, was for priests to turn biographers after the deaths of their penitents and write full-length hagiographies. There were hundreds of such texts produced in Catholic Europe and its colonies in the period between 1450 and 1750.

These, too, could become collaborative works. Often a biographer would intersperse his account with transcriptions of his female penitent's letters, passages from her spiritual diaries, and the like. These excerpts range widely in length and frequency of appearance. The English translator of Vincenzo Puccini's 1609 *Life* of the Florentine Carmelite Maria Maddalena de' Pazzi (1566–1607) explained that he was providing his readers with "divers sufficient touches" of her language, just enough to give them a taste of her passionate, difficult mystical discourse.[57] Other hagiographers included long passages from their subjects' writings that go on for pages and constitute a significant portion of the total book. In any case, the resulting texts alternate between third person and first person voices, move between past and present tenses, and otherwise defy expectations of a univocal and linear narrative.

Why would hagiographers reproduce women's language in this way? Some scholars have stressed the element of control or cooptation here. There is no question that in an inquisitorial age confessors strove to establish the orthodox credentials of their spiritual daughters, both during and after their lifetimes. This protective stance could lead priests to restate or even censor their penitents' words. We have already noted this in relation to Claude Martin, who in his Additions to Marie de l'Incarnation's life-narrative took pains to deflect suspicions that his mother's visions might have been fraudulent or her spiritual writings tinged with Jansenism.[58] Sometimes biographers altered or deleted references that they feared would cause offense or embarrassment to individuals still living.[59] Karen-Edis Barzman claims that Puccini effectively "neutralize[d]" Maria Maddalena de' Pazzi's ecstatic voice, rendering her pronouncements safely bland. This is a common line of argument among scholars examining the male mediation of female-authored texts.[60]

I find this attempt at explanation unsatisfying, however. If clerics were so anxious to "package" their penitents in a certain way, "sanitizing" them for public consumption, why run the risk of citing women's words at all? Why not simply paraphrase or summarize them? This method would seem to offer biographers even greater control over readers' access to their subjects' ideas and provide priests with more opportunities to display their own erudition and stylistic prowess besides.

I suggest that we take seriously the proposition that these *Lives* resulted from a process of genuine collaboration and can tell us something about the spiritual aspirations of pious women as well as their clerical promoters. I examine, therefore, the possible motivations confessors had for including the texts of their female subjects, the various pastoral and authorial choices they made, and the rhetorical strategies they employed. Confessor-biographers frequently struggled with questions of authenticity as well as authority, with establishing credentials as well as control. Feminist literary critics have pointed to an "anxiety of authorship" suffered by numerous women writers,[61] but early-modern priests also manifested certain insecurities as they attempted to convey the spiritual lives of their female penitents. Mystical interactions with the divine, which figure so prominently in these hagiographical accounts, were phenomena that most of these clerics had never personally experienced. Many were intensely aware of their inadequacies in this regard. Pierre François Xavier de Charlevoix, a later biographer of Marie de l'Incarnation, acknowledged to his readers that he transcribed large sections of the nun's own writings but protested that "[s]he soars so high and speaks a language so divine that one would have to be inspired by the same spirit as that which possessed her if one were to find expressions which would equal hers." The learned Jesuit concluded, "[I]t is necessary to let her speak about what transpires in her soul."[62] Two more case studies illuminate some of the methods and purposes with which male hagiographers constructed exemplary lives by interweaving the voices of female subjects with their own.

Miguel González Vaquero and Doña María Vela

María Vela y Cueto was born in the small Castilian town of Cardeñosa in 1561, but was raised in the nearby provincial capital of Avila. Her family, wealthy and well-connected members of the local aristocracy, provided her with a good education and access to the abundant spiritual literature of the day. Despite all her privileges Doña María, as she would continue to be called even inside the convent, resolved to follow a religious vocation. She entered the Cistercian house of Santa Ana at the age of fifteen and remained there for

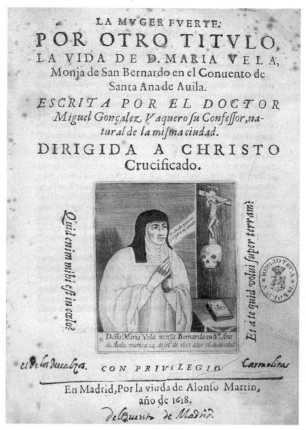

FIGURE NINE

Doña María Vela. From Miguel González Vaquero,
La muger fuerte (Madrid, 1618).
Courtesy of the Biblioteca Nacional, Madrid.

some forty years. But María's decision to adopt the ascetic lifestyle of a humble *beata* was greeted with derision by most of the sisters of this house, the city's oldest, largest, and most elite. When the young nun claimed that she heard celestial voices and received visions and began to exhibit trances, fits, and bodily contortions, displeasure turned to alarm. For over twenty years abbesses and confessors attempted to control María's erratic behavior; some suspected demonic possession.[63]

As in the case of her younger contemporary Isabel de Jesús, María's life and reputation took a significant turn for the better when she at last found a sympathetic confessor. In 1603 a secular priest named Miguel González Vaquero heard about the intense but troubled nun of Santa Ana. Dr. Vaquero, as he was known, was also a native of Avila, born four years after María, in 1565. During his youth Vaquero had come under the influence of the Jesuits and other clerical reformers then active in the city, and had acquired some experience in directing spiritually inclined women. Through mutual acquaintances arrangements were made for Vaquero to hear the Cistercian's confession. Almost immediately the two formed a deep bond of understanding and affection. Convinced of her personal holiness and the authenticity of her divine gifts, Vaquero became María's sole spiritual director, guiding her (and being influenced by her) for the next fourteen years until her death in 1617.[64]

The long and intimate relationship between Miguel González Vaquero and María Vela found textual expression as well. Only five months after his penitent's death Vaquero published *The Strong Woman, or, The Life of Doña María Vela* (*La Muger Fuerte, Por Otro Titulo, La Vida de Doña Maria Vela*). This book enjoyed considerable success, undergoing three more editions in Spanish and two in Italian during the course of the seventeenth century. Included in *The Strong Woman* are numerous selections from María's own writings: a daily record of the graces, or Mercies, bestowed upon her by God (*Libro de las Mercedes*), requested by an earlier confessor named Francisco Salcedo, and a spiritual autobiography (*Vida*) ordered by Vaquero. For many centuries the excerpts in Vaquero's biography offered the only access to María Vela speaking in her voice. Only in the late 1950s were her manuscript writings discovered within the convent of Santa Ana, where they had been carefully preserved by the nuns. They were soon afterwards published and even translated into English.[65] In *The Strong Woman* Vaquero identifies María's words to his readers, setting them in italics or, occasionally, within quotation marks, followed by the expression "the words up to this point are her own," ("Hasta aqui son palabras suyas") or something similar. While the priest includes citations from his exemplary penitent throughout the text, he makes some deliberate editorial decisions regarding their placement and length and also chooses them on the basis of content. For example, the book is divided into three parts; parts 1 and 2 narrate events in María's life up to her first meeting with the biographer. Interestingly, these first two sections contain many more, and longer, transcriptions of the nun's words than does part 3. Here we have, as it were, autobiography in lieu of biography. When relating experiences to which he himself was not a witness and about which he cannot speak from personal authority, Vaquero often allows María to speak for herself. But in part 3 he quite dramatically changes gears, adding himself into the narrative. In fact, the titles of the first two chapters of part 3 do not refer exclusively to María, as in the rest of the book, but to Vaquero himself as well: "On the origins of how I started to direct Doña María Vela," and "How Father Julián de Avila ordered me to hear her confession."[66] In this final section of the biography Vaquero's first-person voice is clearly dominant. Now that he is relating the last fourteen years of María's life, which he observed and in which he played such a prominent role, he does not use her own words nearly as often.

Vaquero also cites passages from the *Mercies* in *The Strong Woman* much more frequently than he does from María's autobiography or other sources. Like Charlevoix, he seems to have believed that mystical encounters were best described by the person who actually experienced contact with the divine. For example, the priest reproduces a Mercy in which María relates how God directly enlightened her about the meaning of suffering during communion, after which she fell to the floor with convulsions (*un pasmo*). Vaquero concludes this passage by noting:

> The words up to this point are her own, and she turned out to know her doctrine so well, that not only did she live forgetting all the things of this world but also all personal concerns . . . Many were the times that I was observing her and considering internally this [topic] of which I am writing . . .[67]

Vaquero's extensive use of María's *Mercies* in *The Strong Woman* reminds his readers of his subject's status as recipient of divine favors but also signals to them his own ability to gain access to her writings. Describing how Salcedo ordered the nun to keep records of her revelations, the biographer cannot help but point out that he keeps "the originals . . . in [his] possession" and is selecting from these papers "in order to write this history."[68] But how did Vaquero gain access to a private spiritual diary compiled for one of his predecessors at least three years before he and María even met?

In anecdotes scattered throughout the text the priest reveals the details. The nun, it seems, had wanted to burn all her writings, but various confessors, monastic superiors—and ultimately God himself—prevailed upon her to preserve them. When he became her confessor, Vaquero took them and kept them for some twelve years until he ordered María to write her autobiography, around 1615. He returned the *Mercies* to her so that she could refer to them while composing her life narrative, but just before her death in September of 1617 "she told me where she had kept her papers, so that I might collect them later."[69]

Vaquero presents this material, of course, in the context of praising his exemplary subject, stressing both María's reception of celestial graces and her humility in desiring to keep her experiences from public view.[70] But in the process he also manages to underscore his own privileged position as trusted confidant to the Servant of God. In part 3 of *The Strong Woman* Vaquero reproduces edifying conversations he held with María, verbal exchanges that he either recalled or recorded at the time. He informs his readers that because of conflicts within Santa Ana he began his acquaintance with María Vela "secretamente"; that is, for several months mutual friends slipped him into the convent to hear her confession. The tone here is of shared confidences by someone whose intimate relationship and exclusive access to information render him the ideal biographer, a note struck by many other early-modern confessor-hagiographers.[71] Miguel González Vaquero may not ever have conversed familiarly with God or received divine messages on his body, as did his charismatic female penitent, but composing a biography that made considerable use of her writings allowed him to establish credentials of a different sort.

Paul Ragueneau and Catherine de Saint Augustin

In the autumn of 1668 the French Jesuit Paul Ragueneau received a letter from far-off Canada. Contained within was a request from Bishop Laval of Québec that he compose a biography of Catherine de Saint Augustin, an exemplary nun who had died in New France five months earlier. Supremely qualified for this task, the priest readily agreed.[72]

Born in Paris in 1608, Paul Ragueneau followed the example of an older brother and entered the Society of Jesus at the age of eighteen. After some years of study and teaching he obtained permission to join the New France mission, arriving in 1637. During a career spanning twenty-five years as a "Black Robe" Ragueneau worked among the Hurons, trained young Jesuits in the field, and rose to the rank of Superior of the Society in Canada. He also wrote a number of the *Relations,* the yearly chronicle of the Canadian mission, in which he reported, among other events, the gruesome deaths suffered by many of his fellow Jesuits at the hands of hostile Iroquois. Ragueneau returned to France in 1662 but continued to raise money and support for the missionary effort. He died in 1680, and like his younger contemporary Claude Martin, soon became the subject of a biography written by an admiring protégé.[73]

The subject of the hagiography Paul Ragueneau agreed to undertake was born Catherine Simon de Longpré in the small town of Saint-Saveur-le-Vicomte in Normandy in 1632. She chose a religious vocation at an exceptionally early age, entering a convent in nearby Bayeux when she was twelve years old.

At sixteen Catherine de Saint Augustin, as she was now called, left France for Canada, where she offered herself as a nursing sister at the recently founded hospital in Québec. Catherine was highly regarded by her fellow religious and settlers for her sweet nature and compassionate care, although she herself suffered from many illnesses. Most people were completely unaware that the nun experienced a turbulent inner spiritual life, receiving divine visions and voices but also devastating bouts of self-doubt, sexual temptation, and demonic attacks. When Catherine died in 1668, at the age of thirty-six, only a handful of her convent sisters, monastic superiors, and confessors knew anything of this sometimes exalted, often tormented existence.[74]

One of those most intimately acquainted with Catherine de Saint Augustin was Paul Ragueneau. He had served as her spiritual director in New France for twelve years, from 1650 to 1662, and continued to correspond with her after his return to France. *The Life of Mother Catherine de Saint Augustin, Hospital Sister of Mercy of Québec in New France* (*La Vie de la Mere Catherine de Saint Augustin, Religieuse Hospitaliere de la Misericorde de Quebec en la Nouvelle-France*), which Ragueneau published in Paris in 1671, is a product of their relationship, as well as of promotional efforts on the part of Canada's new ecclesiastical hierarchy and Catherine's own religious community.[75]

Like Miguel González Vaquero and many other hagiographers of saintly women, Ragueneau includes his subject's own words in his text. However, the Jesuit takes this practice to such an extreme that the *Life* of Catherine de Saint Augustin is really more a collection or compilation of the nun's writings than a conventional biography. Ragueneau makes this editorial decision perfectly clear, opening the book's preface with these words: "This Life is made up almost in its entirety of a Journal, taken from certain papers that her Directors and Confessors commanded her to write . . ."[76]

Why did Paul Ragueneau choose to present Catherine primarily in her own words? One reason may have been the press of time. The bishop and Hospital Sisters of Québec were apparently anxious to make the nun's edifying life and death known to other religious in her order. But what Catherine had left behind was not a systematic, chronologically based autobiography, or even a daily journal in the strict sense, but rather a disjointed set of recollections and meditations, not very accessible to readers. Thus Ragueneau's first task was as editor rather than author. Once he had arranged her writings into a more easily digested form, organizing her descriptions topically rather than chronologically, he may have deemed it faster and easier to simply publish these within a loose biographical framework than to compose an entirely new text.[77]

But though time constraints may have been a factor, Paul Ragueneau also seems to have genuinely relished sharing the words of his extraordinary penitent with his readers. Unlike other hagiographers, the Jesuit keeps his own remarks to a minimum. The chapters into which Ragueneau organizes the *Life* of Catherine typically feature a short title or introductory sentence of one or two lines, then the statement "Here is what she says" ("Voicy ce 'quelle parle") or the like, followed by a citation from Catherine's journal. These passages often go on for many pages. Only rarely does Ragueneau break in with a comment or add an explanatory gloss at the end—a distinct contrast to the method employed by his countryman Claude Martin, as we have seen.[78]

Moreover, in calling the reader's attention to Catherine's voice, the priest highlights not only the content of her words but also the *way* in which she expresses herself. For example, Ragueneau marvels that his penitent received a dazzling vision of the Assumption of the Virgin on that feast day in 1665 and at the compelling way that she described this vision: "Here is how she reports it," ("Voicy comme elle le rapporte").[79] Referring to another encounter, this time with the Holy Spirit in the form of a great cloud, the biographer does not even attempt to paraphrase the mystic, urging instead, "Let us listen to her speak," ("Entendons la parler").[80]

Catherine's extreme youth and the age difference between them undoubtedly accounts for some of the awe that Ragueneau exudes in the *Life*. When they first met in 1650, the Jesuit was forty-two, his penitent, he recalled, "not yet eighteen."[81] And like a proud father (which of course he was, in the spiritual sense), he celebrates her ability to articulate mysteries of the faith obscure to more mature but less gifted individuals. Almost as if anticipating skepticism, he stresses that Catherine is the sole author of these sublime sentiments. "Here is a really remarkable narrative that she herself writes in her Journal," Ragueneau notes in one place. In fact Ragueneau uses the phrase "she herself" ("elle méme") constantly, even to the point of redundancy. Introducing a journal entry on a vision of hell, the Jesuit exclaims, "This is the account that she herself gives of it," his enthusiasm fairly overwhelming his diction.[82]

Catherine de Saint Augustin's original spiritual memoir is no longer extant.

Thus we have no way of knowing how many or which entries (if any) her confessor may have cut or left out of his compilation. But Ragueneau's tone of excited pride suggests showcasing, not suppression. Moreover, he includes long sections on topics one would think a priest in his position might well want to censor, notably Catherine's frequent struggles with sexual temptation and horrific encounters with demons. This latter was a particularly touchy subject in late-seventeenth-century France, where the public had been battered for several decades by reports of possessed nuns.[83]

There is, indeed, at least one occasion in the *Life* in which Ragueneau acknowledges abridging someone's words, but they are his own. He reproduces a letter he had written to Catherine in 1655, consoling her in her many infirmities and assuring her of God's favor. The priest notes that the following year, 1656, "the same Father [that is, Ragueneau himself] writes even more extensively on the same subject." Therefore, he informs his readers, "I will not include here more than a small section [of this second letter]."[84]

The biographer also appears to deliberately downplay the intensity of his relationship with Catherine, muffling his personal response to his prodigious spiritual daughter. Describing their first meeting, toward the end of this 384-page book, Ragueneau opts for the distance of the third-person voice:

> Father Ragueneau, Jesuit, came down from the Huron Mission in the year 1650. Soon after arriving in Québec he found himself engaged in the spiritual direction of this holy Bride of Christ . . . he took charge of her care for twelve consecutive years in that location, and being obliged to return to France in 1662, he was always aware of all that occurred in her interior life through the letters that she wrote to him up until her death.[85]

Even his saintly subject's demise, so often an occasion for effusive narrative on the part of confessor-hagiographers, receives only indirect treatment. "I can do no more than faithfully report here the circumstances of her death that are taken from the circulating letter written by the Reverend Mother Marie de Saint Bonaventure de Jesus, her [Mother] Superior," Ragueneau announces. He adds, "Here is how she speaks"—the "she" in this case referring to Mother Marie—and then proceeds to transcribe the letter, without comment.[86]

The only place in the *Life* where the Jesuit reveals his emotions is at the end of a dedicatory letter to an aristocratic patron of the Québec hospital that precedes the actual text. After receiving the bishop's request, he confesses, he simply could not refuse presenting

for the edification of the public and the consolation of pious souls the example of a life and death so pure and so precious before God, as is this one, of
which I was a witness to my great consolation for the space of eighteen years,
during which time God bestowed upon me the grace of receiving the communications that she gave me herself of all that happened in the most secret
[recesses] of her soul, for which I give thanks to God who truly is wondrous
in his Saints.[87]

This outpouring of passionate gratitude stands in marked contrast to
Ragueneau's apparently "impersonal" way of writing and consistent "self-ef-
facement" in the body of the work, as Guy-Marie Oury has also noticed.[88]
But the priest may have had his reasons for using his penitent's journal entries
so extensively and for minimizing his involvement in Catherine's spiritual life.
In the book's preface Ragueneau first mentions the figure who comes to occupy such a significant place in the narrative that he could be considered its
second subject.

This is Jean de Brébeuf, the celebrated Jesuit missionary and martyr. Paul
Ragueneau had met him upon his arrival in Canada in 1637, come under his
tutelage, and worked closely with him among the Hurons. The capture, torture, and killing of Brébeuf and a companion and attacks on Huron villages
by the Iroquois in the spring of 1649 dealt a serious blow to the French missionary effort and deeply shook Ragueneau. In the *Relations* he composed in
1649 and 1650 and in subsequent writings (including the *Life* of Catherine) he
commemorated Brébeuf's heroism and attempted to persuade others of his
own firm conviction: that his fellow Jesuit merited veneration as a saint.[89]

Catherine de Saint Augustin began corresponding with Brébeuf while she
was still living in Normandy, their common birthplace. His death soon after
her arrival in the colony guaranteed that the two would never meet in the flesh.
But in 1662, some thirteen years after the missionary's demise—and six weeks
after Ragueneau's departure for France—the nun began to experience mystical encounters with Brébeuf. The martyr now became her "Celestial Director," advising her, consoling her, enlightening her about difficult points of
doctrine, and even, on occasion, giving her communion.[90] Interactions with
Brébeuf came to constitute such an important feature of Catherine's inner
spiritual life that she devoted a large proportion of her journal entries to this
theme. At least they are among the ones chosen by Ragueneau for inclusion
in her biography. Of the sixty-nine chapters into which he divides the *Life*,
thirty-two, or a little under half, contain at least passing references to Brébeuf.

In the middle section of the book Ragueneau strings together some twenty consecutive chapters (about 170 pages) consisting almost in their entirety of Catherine's interchanges with her supernatural confessor.[91]

For Paul Ragueneau, then, letting Catherine speak in her own voice was, in large part, to let her speak *about* Jean de Brébeuf. Foregrounding his protaganists' frequent and intense interactions has the effect of reinforcing the privileged status of both: Catherine as the chosen recipient of this remarkable grace and Brébeuf as already a saint in heaven. Wishing to stress this miracle of postmortem spiritual direction, Ragueneau constructs Brébeuf as the nun's "primary" confessor and accordingly deemphasizes his own role in her life and *Life*. His main objective, after all, was the eventual beatification of Brébeuf, the goal for which he had been working for some twenty years.[92]

Predictably, Ragueneau ends the *Life* of Catherine de Saint Augustin not with his own words but with someone else's. He quotes from the letter of a prelate expressing confidence that the visionary nun would become a celestial intercessor "for the good of this new Church" ("pour le bien de cette nouvelle Eglise").[93] Paul Ragueneau had dedicated his entire adult life to this very purpose: the establishment of a new church in a New World. To this end he composed a biographical text that celebrated the lives of two of the people closest to him in this enterprise and gave meaning to their violent and premature deaths.

The life narratives of exemplary women, written either by themselves or, more frequently, by their confessors or other clerical promoters after their deaths, came to occupy an important place in early-modern Catholic culture. The production of these enormously popular and numerous texts was often a fundamentally collaborative enterprise, the voices of authors and subjects interwoven in intricate, sometimes surprising ways. The resulting body of literature reveals as much about male clerics and their agendas as about the women who are their ostensible subjects. Reading the *Lives* of the holy women of one generation, women of the next could aspire to their saintly virtues. They may also have been attracted to the possibility of maintaining intense relationships with priests. In the next chapter I explore the experience and rhetoric of spiritual friendship, a prominent theme in early-modern Catholic life-writing.

CHAPTER FOUR

SOUL MATES

For generations, confessors and other clerical promoters fashioned the life stories of exemplary female penitents, texts that were produced in great number, translated, and disseminated throughout early-modern Europe and its colonies. What messages did readers derive from this literature? Naturally authors continued to construct their subjects as models of virtuous behavior and exhort the faithful to emulate them, as hagiographers had done for hundreds of years. But perhaps more compelling to many readers were the vivid depictions of friendships shared by priests and penitents.

Since the early centuries of the faith Christians had acknowledged that the contemplative, celibate life held the possibility—perhaps the only culturally sanctioned possibility—for a man and woman to have a deep, mutually satisfying relationship outside marriage.[1] Indeed, given that marriages were, for the most part, arranged for economic and procreative purposes, a celibate but otherwise intimate friendship may have struck many as a more attractive option. With the advent of printing in the late fifteenth century and the increased availability of hagiographical texts, this tradition became more widely known to a larger audience than ever before. As people learned of cases of spiritual friendship in earlier generations, did they aspire to participate in such relationships themselves? The potential to achieve a meaningful, even intense, connection with a member of the opposite sex may well have served as a powerful incentive for people to remain within the Catholic fold and even consider a religious vocation. While a pervasive historiography emphasizes the onerous and obligatory aspects of confession, we have seen that many early-modern Catholics, particularly women, embraced the sacrament, frequently and with considerable enthusiasm.[2] In this chapter I examine more closely the themes of spiritual and personal bonding that feature so prominently in the life narratives of early-modern men and women and may offer some clues as to religious choice as well as religious discourse.

Longing and Looking

One of the most common—and most poignant—themes to emerge from the memoirs of religious women generation after generation was their desire for a compatible spiritual director. By this they did not mean simply a priest to hear their confessions and grant them absolution. They longed for a kindred spirit, someone who could offer them advice and consolation and defend them against the slanders and accusations of others, and with whom they could exchange confidences: a true friend. This yearning for a compassionate and companionable spiritual guide permeates the autobiographies written by pious women and the biographical accounts composed by male clerics.

The intense desire for a "good" confessor is understandable given that so many women described having had a "bad" confessor or confessors, sometimes for years at a time. In her autobiography Teresa of Avila painfully recalled how "half-learned" and unsympathetic confessors dismissed her supernatural experiences and methods of prayer, confused her, scolded her, and tried to persuade her that her visions and voices were demonic rather than divine in origin. These confessors, she lamented, "have done my soul great harm."[3] Later, Teresa would insist upon the right of nuns in the Discalced Carmelite order she founded to choose their confessors, advising that a sister with an incompatible director should "tell the prioress that [her] soul doesn't get on well with him and change confessors."[4]

Teresa of Avila may be the most famous example of a woman who complained of ridicule and reproach on the part of confessors, but she is hardly the only one. Indeed, the neglect or mistreatment of penitents by confessors is a virtual commonplace, a theme that female readers of hagiographies would have encountered in the accounts of earlier women with aspirations to the devout life. There is no reason to call into question the pain that each one actually suffered, however. The "bad" confessor may have become such a common topos precisely because it was such a recognizable feature of women's religious experience.

For cloistered nuns a constructive relationship with a confessor was often a question of luck, depending upon which cleric had been appointed the convent's chaplain. Alarmed by her strange, trancelike behavior and poor health,

Margaret Mary Alacoque's Visitandine superiors assigned various confessors to examine the condition of her soul. "But to my grief, " she remembered, "instead of withdrawing me from the state of deception in which I believed myself to be, my confessors and others plunged me still deeper into it."[5] At one point, admitted the Cistercian María Vela, "I was so tired of seeking a confessor that I simply gave up."[6]

María Vela's words illustrate the extent of the despair she felt at this time in her life but also indicate that beyond simply hoping for an understanding confessor she was actively *seeking* one out. Evidence suggests that many women in early-modern Catholic Europe and its colonies set out to find sympathetic spiritual directors and, hopefully, soul mates. Accounts of the lives of *beatas*, tertiaries, and pious laywomen provide the most vivid instances of this sort of searching. Unlike professed nuns, these women without institutional support and formal status as religious were especially vulnerable to accusations of fraud, heresy, demonic possession, and the like, and thus in particular need of the authorization and protection a male clergyman could provide. But also unlike professed nuns, especially those of strictly cloistered orders, laywomen and those who had made simple—that is, nonbinding—vows had the mobility to move about, make inquiries about specific priests and religious orders, and plead their cases to initially skeptical clerics. They would need to draw upon all their resources of persuasion and persistence, as this could be a long and frustrating process.

Mari Díaz, the poor but fervent daughter of landed peasants (*labradores*), left her village in the 1530s for the nearby Castilian city of Avila "because she had heard it said that there were sermons [there]." The *beata* quickly gained the respect of neighbors for her piety and charitable acts but was compelled to search the city for a spiritual director. Later she would wryly recount how she had "exhausted several religious houses with my insistent and tiresome pleas to confess me."[7]

Some two hundred years later María Antonia Pereira would face many vicissitudes in her quest for a religious vocation. Born in 1700 in the village of O Pinedo in Galicia, in the extreme northwest of the Iberian peninsula, she was married at an early age in order to relieve her family's poverty and later moved to the larger town of Baiona. During the 1720s María Antonia began to experience extraordinary graces in prayer. The confessor chosen for her by her mother refused to let her even speak of such matters, and her appeal to the Franciscan friars whose church she frequently attended similarly fell upon deaf ears. In desperation she turned to St. Francis himself, begging him to be her director, and heard him reply, "Do not weary yourself, for I will be your [spiritual] master."[8]

In 1728, María Antonia did find a compatible confessor right in Baiona, José Ventura de Castro, fresh out of seminary. Her happiness was short-lived, however, as Castro's superior, the Bishop of Tui, hearing reports of close contacts between an inexperienced priest and a young married woman, forbade Castro to treat his penitent any longer. The situation deteriorated, with priests and religious in Baiona refusing to even hear María Antonia's confession. Depressed but not deterred, she traveled to Tui to appeal to the bishop personally, cannily first pleading her case before the prelate's own confessor. While standing firm on his decision regarding Castro, the bishop did listen sympathetically to the devout laywoman and arrange for her to return to the guidance of her previous confessor. María Antonia continued to maintain a warm friendship with Castro, however, as their correspondence attests. When, after the death of her husband in 1738, she entered a convent and took the religious name María Antonia de Jesús, it was to José Ventura de Castro that she entrusted the care and education of her son, Sebastián.[9] Examples of women like Mari Díaz and María Antonia, who deliberately sought out spiritual directors, could be multiplied.[10]

Less prominent in the hagiographical literature, but equally suggestive, is the evidence that some priests were searching, too, hoping to find spiritually gifted women to take on as directees. At least they were singularly receptive to the female penitents with whom they came into contact and open to the possibility of a closer relationship than just what their priestly office required.

Take, for example, the case of the Mercedarian friar Juan Bautista del Santísimo Sacramento, profiled in the previous chapter. According to his biographers, as a zealous young priest he harbored a desire to reform his order. For all his piety and hours spent in prayer, however, he never received divine confirmation of this plan. For this he turned to women, his daughters in confession. A chronicler reports that around 1582 Juan Bautista looked to a woman to communicate to him the will of God. At this time he was serving as chaplain to a community of Dominican nuns in Toledo. There was one sister in particular who seemed to him "more advanced than the others" in "exercises of the contemplative life" and favored with "supernatural gifts." The friar "begged her most earnestly" to ask God to resolve his problem for him. At last the nun reported that she had been given to understand that her confessor's dream of founding a new order derived from "divine inspiration and impulse" and that the reform would indeed take place as he planned it.

This interchange greatly consoled Juan Bautista, but as the years went by he seemed to need more assurance. Upon moving to Madrid in 1598 he made the acquaintance of another woman visionary, the *beata* Mariana de Jesús, and became her spiritual director. Mariana, too, provided her confessor with a revelation about the advent of the Mercedarian reform, which "filled [Juan Bautista's] soul with joy, seeming to him that this confirmed that which the divine Majesty had manifested years before to the nun of Toledo . . ."[11]

This anecdote points to a fascinating and not always sufficiently appreciated cultural construct. Juan Bautista del Santísmo Sacramento was, by all accounts, an exemplary friar: austere, prayerful, highly respected as a missionary to Peru, spiritual director, and yes, successful reformer of the Mercedarian order. In the eighteenth century his cause was introduced for canonization. And yet both he and his biographer seem to have accepted the notion that God would not communicate directly with a man, even a saintly one. Being a conduit of divine messages and recipient of divine graces was the prerogative of women, and the best a man could hope for was a vicarious experience through close contact with a charismatic woman. The French Jesuit Paul Ragueneau succinctly conveyed this gendered view of spirituality, which assigned certain characteristics to each sex. Women, he acknowledged, had vivid imaginations and were especially vulnerable to demonic deception. But this priest, who had served as spiritual director to the mystic Catherine de Saint Augustin, also had harsh words for men, whose overly logical minds and pride prevented them from believing any reports of the supernatural. "God bestows his grace on whomever he wishes and whenever he wishes," Ragueneau insisted, "and if at times he rewards more women than men it is often [due] to a lack of humility in us . . ."[12]

In fact, as John Coakley has discussed for an earlier period, the male confidants of holy women frequently expressed both awe and envy of women who received supernatural gifts in a way that did not seem possible for them.[13] Given this expectation, then, it is not surprising to find priests longing and looking for special women to satisfy their various spiritual needs just as women longed and looked for "good" confessors. Many developed sensitive antennae, in any case. One morning in 1696 Angela Mellini entered a confessional in the church of Santo Spirito in Bologna and began to describe her extraordinary visions to the attending priest. Giovanni Battista Ruggieri immediately invited her to become his penitent, a move that angered Mellini's current confessor, who had (predictably) disapproved of her method of prayer and treated her shabbily. Mellini and Ruggieri went on to develop a close and reciprocal relationship, as Ruggieri undoubtedly hoped from the start.[14] Monastic officials requested that Friar Filipe de Santiago examine the Portuguese Franciscan Antónia Margarida de Castelo Branco. She made her first confession to him in December 1675. Antónia Margarida later recorded her excited, somewhat agitated responses to this encounter: "unaccustomed emotions," an "interior commotion," and "shock at his words, and the confident way in which he revealed my [sins and] miseries." When she begged the friar to become "her soul's guide," he admitted that "he had hoped [she] would ask him that." Both understood their coming together as the work of God.[15]

Clerics who were young, newly arrived, or neophytes within a certain religious order were often especially interested in cultivating relationships with women who were older and more established in their communities. Mari Díaz finally found a priest willing to direct her when the Jesuit Baltasar Alvarez arrived in Avila in 1559. At this time the *beata* was approximately sixty years old and had already gained renown at the local level. Her new confessor was twenty-six and had just been ordained a priest. Alvarez's biographer, Luis de la Puente, noted that "this holy woman had good fortune in meeting Father Baltasar, who helped her a great deal in her [spiritual] ascent." He acknowledged, however, that Alvarez likewise had good fortune in meeting and agreeing to guide Mari Díaz, "because she helped him very much by her fine example and, for what she did, he came to be very well known and esteemed by everyone in [Avila]."[16]

Similar considerations may have motivated Juan de Ribera, who became involved with the holy woman Margarita Agullona several years after assuming the episcopal seat of Valencia in 1569. Ribera would eventually become a beloved figure in Valencia and even achieve the status of canonized saint, but his first years as archbishop were rocky ones for the Seville native. Benjamin Ehlers has suggested that Ribera was attracted to the visionary Agullona for both "her sanctity and her popularity." Their long association helped Ribera to integrate himself into the religious life of his adopted city, and he "drew from [Agullona's] popularity both to exhort the Valencian people and to learn about their spiritual needs."[17] For clerics such as Baltasar Alvarez and Juan de Ribera, a watchful readiness to direct spiritually advanced women could yield considerable benefits, personal and professional.

Finding

Given the years of hope, desire, and effort that so many women and priests put into having a meaningful relationship with a like-minded individual, we should not be surprised at the outpouring of emotion when they finally encountered such a person. Nevertheless, it is difficult to avoid being struck by the powerful and eroticized language used by these celibate Catholics, a language strongly reminiscent of the literature of romance. Confessors and penitents frequently portrayed their relationships as divinely ordained and sanctioned and suggested that God had especially chosen them to direct or be directed by this particular person. They used a discourse of destiny to describe instantaneous recognitions, profound personal transformations, and intense feelings of relief, vindication, and gratitude to both their newly found soul mate and God for giving one to the other.

As in the conceit of "love at first sight," many spiritual friends claimed to have known from their first meeting that their years of waiting were over. María Vela went through a whole string of confessors who either died, left town, or treated her with suspicion and disdain. Finally, around 1603, mutual friends arranged for Miguel González Vaquero to hear her confession. In her autobiography María addressed herself to Vaquero, recalling how "the first day I spoke with [you] your spirit suited me so well and I was left with such satisfaction and delight of the heart that I hardly knew myself for having found that which I had so long desired, which was to meet a person who had experience of this sort of spiritual direction [or conversation] and of supernatural prayer . . ."[18] With this María Vela and Vaquero began a relationship that would last some fifteen years until the nun's death in 1617. Soon afterward Vaquero published her hagiography. He, too, remembered that fateful day: "It was the first time that I spoke with our saint, and although I had directed very advanced souls I found something here that caused me notable confusion . . ." He singled out for praise "her way of speaking, so humble and sincere, so full of the love of God, and of such prudent virtue" and expressed his firm conviction that by taking on María as his spiritual daughter "many advantages were to come to my soul . . ."[19]

The future saint Teresa of Avila met Jerónimo Gracián while on a visit to the town of Beas in 1575. The nun was sixty years old and highly respected for having founded the Discalced Carmelite order some thirteen years earlier. Gracián was thirty and had been a friar for only three years. Yet the older woman felt an immediate attraction for the priest, both on a personal level and in terms of what he could do for the reform. Teresa wrote excitedly to a Carmelite sister, "these last few days . . . have been the best days of my life. Father-Master Gracián has been here . . . and although I've gotten to know him . . . I haven't begun to fathom his worth. I think he is perfect; we couldn't have asked God for a better man for our needs." Her correspondence over the next few weeks continued to reveal, in the words of Mary Luti, "a Teresa enthralled."[20]

It was also while on a trip that Diego de Vitoria encountered the *beata* María de Santo Domingo. The two conversed while they traveled with a group from Avila to Toledo around 1507. After Vitoria begged the holy woman to pray for him and ask God to send him contrition for his sins, he soon experienced "a degree of fervor and repentance that he had never felt before." He quickly joined a coterie of Dominican friars who served as spiritual guides and staunch defenders of the controversial peasant prophetess.[21] A number of such relationships were born and nourished during journeys, it would seem. Clergymen had long been considered appropriate chaperones for women, and the road, with its long stretches and leisurely pace, may have offered an opportunity for extended, intimate conversation difficult to find at the confessional or convent grille.[22]

Some women reported having received a premonition of some sort before actually meeting their divinely sent director. María Antonia de Jesús, hearing others speak highly of José Carral, felt an inner conviction that the Jesuit would someday become her confessor, as indeed came to pass.[23] Margaret Mary Alacoque was forced to endure the skepticism of confessors and the taunts of fellow nuns (suspecting demonic possession, some threw holy water on her as she walked by). She prayed to God to stop sending her raptures and visions but heard this reply: "He promised He would, and that He would send me His faithful servant and perfect friend who would teach me to know Him and to abandon myself to Him without further resistance." Soon afterward Claude de la Colombière came to preach at the convent at Paray-le-Monial. As the Jesuit began to address the assembled community, Margaret Mary recalled, "I interiorly heard these words: 'This is he whom I send thee.'"[24]

One of the most famous cases of a deep spiritual friendship in the early-modern period was that shared by Jeanne de Chantal and François de Sales. Their accounts of the early stages of their relationship feature many of the elements noted above: the premonition, the immediate connection between priest and penitent at first encounter, the sense that each was a gift from God to the other.

In the spring of 1604 Jeanne, a young French noblewoman, was still grieving over her husband, killed in a freak hunting accident three years before. In her widowed state her thoughts began to turn toward a life of religious perfection and to finding a spiritual director to aid her in this goal. Jeanne recalled that once, while she was out riding through her country estate, a man dressed in priestly garb had suddenly appeared to her at the foot of a hill. At that moment, she had been given to understand that "this is the man, beloved of God and men, into whose hands you must entrust your conscience."[25]

Jeanne traveled to the nearby city of Dijon to attend a cycle of Lenten sermons delivered by the renowned prelate François de Sales, the Bishop of Geneva (Savoy). The devout widow placed herself in the front row of the church, right beneath the pulpit. As Sales mounted to preach for the first time, Jeanne immediately recognized him as the figure she had seen while riding, her promised spiritual guide. The bishop noticed her, too, asking his local hosts about "the young widow with light brown hair who seats herself across from me during the sermon and who listens so attentively to the words of truth."

Glances led to words. After a few brief interviews Jeanne was finally was able to arrange a full confession with Sales. He penned his response a few days later: "It seems to me that God has given me to you; I am assured of this more keenly as each hour passes."[26] Wendy Wright has shown that as the two began to exchange frequent letters and occasional personal visits, Sales came to recognize that his interactions with Jeanne were enriching his own spiritual life, that perhaps God had given her to him as well. Seven months after their first meeting the bishop acknowledged a new sort of relationship, expressing his thoughts in a new sort of language:

> [F]rom the first time that you consulted me about your interior life, God granted me a great love for your spirit. When you confessed to me in greater detail, a remarkable bond was forged in my soul which caused me to cherish your soul more and more . . . But now, my dear Daughter, a certain new quality has emerged which it seems I cannot describe, only its effect is a great interior sweetness that I have to wish for you a perfect love of God and other spiritual blessings . . . Each affection is different from others. The one I have for you has a certain quality which consoles me infinitely, and, if all were known, is extremely profitable to me. Consider this an absolute truth and have no more doubts about it.[27]

Many religious women highlighted that moment of finding the "right" confessor in their written memoirs. Their sense of relief and gratitude is palpable. Confessors frequently stressed these moments as well. Their narratives describe an experience of personal transformation but also underscore the authors' mastery of the all-important skill of discernment. Unlike those other, "bad" confessors, these priests possessed the intelligence, the sensitivity, and the grace necessary to recognize a genuine "Servant of God." Thus both con-

FIGURE TEN

François de Sales. From Hilarion Coste, *Histoire Catholique* . . . (Paris, 1625). Courtesy of the British Library.

fessors and penitents identified the discovery of a soul mate as turning points in their lives and *Lives*.

Connecting, Body and Soul

These accounts of providential meetings serve as preludes to narratives of relationships that lasted for years, even decades, and describe the crafting of remarkable personal bonds. "[W]henever God worked anything within her,

which [affected] her much in soul or body, she would confer about it all with
her Confessor," recalled the biographer of Catherine of Genoa (d. 1510). Cattaneo Marabotto, "with the grace and light of God, understood well-nigh all,
and would give [Catherine] answers which seemed to show that he himself felt
the very thing that she was feeling herself." The uncanny ability to understand
each other "by just looking each other in the face without speaking" signaled
divine approbation of these two exemplary individuals and of their close
friendship.[28]

The sentiments expressed by François de Sales toward Jeanne de Chantal
and the passionate language he employed were not unique. Others were
equally effusive. The Valencian Jesuit Gerónimo Mur, after guiding the *beata*
Francisca Llopis (López) for seven years, reportedly declared "if I could be
among the most esteemed people in the world, and even with the Queen herself . . . I would leave them all in order to hear the confessions of [Francisca],
such was the purity and grace that I encountered in her blessed soul, and why
I so valued directing her."[29] As we have seen, many priests accepted that they
would not be directly granted raptures, visions, voices, and the like. But they
could be granted the next best thing: intimacy with women who could have
these experiences. Confessors consequently expressed sincere gratitude for
this privileged proximity and its vicarious experience of the divine. In a preface to the *Life* of Catherine de Saint Augustin he published in 1671, Paul
Ragueneau reviewed his eighteen-year relationship with the visionary nun.
During those years, he declared, "God bestowed on me the grace of receiving the communications that she gave herself of all that happened in the most
secret [recesses] of her soul, for which I give thanks to God who is truly wondrous in his Saints."[30]

The bonds of understanding and empathy forged between priests and penitents also found physical expression, manifestations in body as well as soul.
Caring could turn to curing when penitents suffered from illness or other
physical problems. María Quintana, a *beata* from Segovia, spent years inflict-
ing upon herself extreme mortifications in order to repent for an earlier life of
sin. When in 1731 her health broke down completely, her confessor, Francisco
Benito Colodro, actually took her into his home and nursed her. This move
aroused so much gossip that María considered leaving the house to spare the
priest further embarrassment. But God comforted her in the midst of their
troubles, assuring her that "'[t]he love that you have for your Confessor is not
evil, nor does it displease me; rather it gives me much pleasure because it is the
same as loving Me . . .'"[31] The French Jesuit missionary Claude Chauchetière

similarly dedicated himself to caring for the Iroquois convert and holy woman Catherine (Kateri) Tekakwitha until her death in April 1680.[32]

For some religious women, it was as if the vow of obedience they made to their confessors conferred upon these priests an almost thaumaturgic power. The men to whom they submitted their wills could also control their bodies. María Vela, filled with the desire for frequent communion but also with extreme guilt, suffered fits and fainting spells whenever she attempted to receive the eucharist. The solutions offered by a succession of confessors, prioresses, and even an exorcist proved temporary at best. Only after María met and vowed special obedience to Miguel González Vaquero did the situation change. The Cistercian nun later reminisced with her spiritual director: "For a whole year now, it has always been necessary for you to impose obedience upon me in order to enable me to confess . . . [the] same thing has happened with regard to communion . . ." So tight were the bonds of bodily dependency that she observed, "when you were not at hand I have seldom been able to receive [communion]."[33] Catalina de Jesús y San Francisco also experienced difficulty in receiving the sacrament due to a "locking of the tongue" and a "suspension of the senses" that left her "unable to move, afflicted with pains and crippled in the feet and hands." The Franciscan tertiary required "the daily assistance" of her spiritual director in order to confess and receive communion, aid that took the form of "many commands" issued by the priest to his scrupulous penitent.[34]

For their part, priests came to entrust the women they directed with aspects of their physical health as well as their spiritual edification. While still a pious laywoman, Isabel de Jesús traveled to confess to a Franciscan named Francisco de Cogulludo. The friar was so ill at the time that he rode a mule to meet the *beata*. Before Isabel could even speak, Cogulludo dismounted and threw himself on his knees, asking for her blessing.[35] In 1725, while serving as prebendary of the Cathedral of Santa Fe in New Granada (Colombia), Juan de Olmos y Zapiaín received news of his promotion to the rank of canon. Although this was a much more prestigious position, the priest had many qualms about accepting because, he explained, "my health had deteriorated, I was about sixty-two years old, and I feared a serious decline in my heath." Olmos's response was to talk this over with his penitent, the Poor Clare Jerónima Nava y Saavedra, and entreat the nun to pray for him and determine God's will.[36]

Miguel González Vaquero and María Vela described their lives as so intertwined that they shared experiences of sickness, sacrifice, and recovery. María recalled to him one of her many bouts of serious illness:

You decided to say a mass for me and offer your health for mine. Your prayers were heard and you were given a very great fever. My health improved over a period of three or four days, but then my troubles returned . . . I turned to His Majesty, entreating him not to pass on this illness to [you], for then I would have no peace, and thus His Majesty improved your health, although you spent fifteen days without being able to see me, and I spent them . . . without being able to receive communion, which I can never do when [you] are away . . .[37]

Certain themes thus emerge in the accounts of early modern religious women and their male confidants as they described intense, often long-lasting relationships. They remembered exchanging confidences, even secrets, soliciting the other's advice or opinions before making a decision, and learning how to tell, just with a glance, what the other person was thinking. They expressed pleasure when their chosen partner was present and distress at separation. They cared for each other in sickness and in health, sometimes experiencing sympathetically the other's bodily afflictions. In short, they interacted like many married couples. The only significant difference was the lack of sexual congress.[38]

But this does not mean that their partnerships were devoid of desire, passion, and love. Indeed, a vivid imagery of marital or erotic union animates many of the writings and reminiscences of these men and women. After knowing Jeanne de Chantal and working closely with her for years, François de Sales found it difficult to disguise his feelings. "O, God, my dearest Daughter," he exclaimed in a letter of 1610, "how tenderly and ardently I feel the sacred bond and the good of our holy unity!" In another letter he insisted that "it will be impossible for anything to ever separate me from your soul. The bond is too strong. Death itself would not have the power to dissolve it because it is of a quality that lasts forever."[39]

Isabel de Jesús recalled how once a confessor of hers, whom she declined to name (almost certainly Francisco Ignacio, her future biographer), begged her to petition God on his behalf. While complying with this request she was granted a breathtaking vision. The Lord "showed me the heart of this man as one most greatly to be envied," she remembered. "I saw him wrapped up in a very hot fire and surrounded by the angels who accompanied him. I saw that . . . his heart rose and fell most lightly; I knew full well that it burned with divine love . . ." Isabel offered a prayer of thanks: "Blessed be He who gave [my confessor] such a great gift of love in this life . . ."[40]

The classic theme of mystical marriage between a woman and Jesus Christ

was well known by the fifteenth century, and women continued to describe ecstatic, erotic encounters with a divine spouse throughout the early-modern
period.[41] However, in a fascinating variation, some women perceived Christ
arranging and officiating over a union between themselves and their confessors. Then again, as many women understood their confessors to take the
place of God or Christ on earth, perhaps these two cultural constructs are essentially the same.

Recall that in 1575 Teresa of Avila resolved to give her total obedience to
Jerónimo Gracián, the man who was, she was certain, "a great servant of
God" and "the one who stood in God's place." Soon afterward she experi-
enced a powerful vision, "like a flash of lightning":

> It seemed to me that our Lord Jesus Christ was next to me in the form that he
> usually appears, at His right side stood Master Gratian himself, and I at His
> left. The Lord took our right hands and joined them and told me he desired
> that I take this master to represent Him as long as I live, and that we both
> agree in everything because it was thus fitting.

Teresa concluded her recollection of this experience, so reminiscent of a betrothal or wedding ceremony, with a fervent prayer: "Blessed be He who created a person who so pleased me that I could dare to do this."[42]

A most striking example of imagery of this type comes from the relationship between Margaret Mary Alacoque and her director, Claude de la Colombière. As we have seen, Margaret Mary understood this priest to be the one
chosen by God to be his (and her?) "perfect friend." Many criticized the Jesuit when he decided to take on the troubled nun as a penitent in 1678; she herself marveled that "he did not abandon me as others have done." But soon
afterwards, God vindicated them both:

> One time when [de la Colombière] came to say mass in our church, Our Lord
> granted very great [spiritual] graces to both him and me. As I went up to re-
> ceive [Jesus Christ] in the holy communion, He showed me His sacred Heart
> as a burning furnace, and two other hearts were on the point of being united
> and absorbed into it, and He said to me: "It is thus my pure love unites these
> three hearts forever." And afterward, he gave me to understand that this
> union was all for the glory of his sacred Heart, and that he desired that I re-
> veal to [de la Colombière] its treasures, so that he might make known and
> publicize its worth and utility, and to that end he wished that we be like
> brother and sister, sharing equally in these spiritual riches.[43]

Contained within this one revelation we find many of the themes examined thus far: reference to earlier "bad" confessors and relief at finding a "good" one; God choosing a particular priest to serve as director (and in this case, messenger) of a particular woman; the bonds between confessor and penitent consecrated in a "marriage ceremony" with Christ as officiating priest; the erotically charged images of heat, fire, union, absorption, the heart. Margaret Mary's vision also points to the critical importance of the eucharist for religious women and their male promoters, a topic to which we will return.

Parting

One of the most powerful gestures of solidarity between priests and exemplary women was also the final one. Many confessors attended and recorded the deaths of their penitents. This was a moment fraught with multiple, even conflicting, meanings for these devout Catholics. As theologians and authors of edifying texts clerics hastened to express joy and the conviction that the Servant of God was assured a blessed afterlife and saintly status. As human beings, they mourned the loss of a beloved partner.

This potent mix of emotions can be found in the deathbed scene that generally concluded a hagiographical account, or at least its first part, with subsequent sections detailing the subject's many virtues and/or her postmortem miracles and cures.[44] Here the confessor-hagiographer functions as both narrator and participant.

André Duval, for example, vividly recounted the death of Barbe Acarie (in religion, Marie de l'Incarnation) in 1618. In the last chapter of the biography he published in 1621, conventionally titled "On her happy death" ("De son heureuse mort"), the priest recalled that he was in Paris when his penitent fell ill at her convent in Pontoise. For several days Marie's great humility prevented her from notifying her preferred confessor, but finally, about to succumb to anguishing attacks of fever, she asked the other nuns to summon him. Duval hurriedly made the journey, arriving at the convent at half past five in the morning. He was indeed able to spend the last hours with her, anoint her, and prepare her for death. It is important to note that another priest had been present this whole time, the house's chaplain, a certain M. Fontaine, who was presumably as capable of giving the last rites as was Duval. From a canonical point of view, of course, any priest could have attended the dying woman. Clearly, Marie desired the presence of this particular priest, whom she had known for years, who had guided her as both a laywoman and a religious and had aided her in bringing the Discalced Carmelite order to France. When Marie at last expired, her convent sisters were devastated, and Duval "tried to console them as best [he] could." But, the priest allowed, "I was in as great need of consolation as they were."[45]

Using typical hagiographical tropes, Miguel González Vaquero insisted that María Vela greatly "desired" the "happy death" God granted her as a reward for "the trials and tribulations of [her] saintly life." But there was apparently one person whom the nun found difficult to leave. At the end she, too, called for a particular priest, Vaquero, who had been her spiritual guide, confidant, and defender for fifteen years. María even obtained permission from her abbess to speak to the priest alone for a time in her cell. Vaquero stayed by her side as she struggled to keep up with her monastic devotions. Later he poignantly recalled that even after María had lost the power of speech, "she helped herself as best she could to keep saying [her prayers] with me until the blessed moment arrived . . ."[46]

Juan de Olmos assured his readers that Jerónima Nava y Saavedra enjoyed a quiet, gentle passing, like "a sweet dream." Yet the priest who had confessed and directed this woman "with special attention and care" for some twenty years admitted that "the pain of her loss pierced [his] heart." The sixty-five-year-old Olmos had to be helped to the door of the convent. He excused himself to the nuns for missing Jerónima's burial, citing the extreme "grief of her death."[47]

Confessors represented themselves as solicitously caring for fatally ill penitents up to the end, hearing their last confessions, administering the final sacraments. For their part, holy women had something to offer the priests. Two or three days before she died in 1607 the Florentine Carmelite Maria Maddalena de' Pazzi made a promise to her confessor, Vincenzo Puccini. The nun vowed that "if she went to heaven, she would pray earnestly to God both for [Puccini] and all the religious [of her convent], that after this short life they might meet in that celestial kingdom." The Jesuit remembered these words. After he completed his account of her "happy death" Puccini switched into the first person voice to address the Servant of God:

> I will not now express myself to thee in many words to entreat thy prayers to the eternal God for me, who yet find myself in this valley of tears; for I confide in that which thou didst so often promise me with careful charity while I ministered to thee the most holy sacraments in thy last sickness.[48]

Serafino Razzi attended Caterina de' Ricci at her death in 1590. The Dominican friar likewise ended the hagiography he published two years later with a moving plea for personal intercession. "[B]lessed mother and beloved bride of Christ," he appealed, "now that you find yourself . . . enjoying the glory of the blessed in heaven and the reward of your honorable deeds and holy merits . . . pray, in charity, for my salvation and good death. Amen."[49]

Moreover, many holy women reported experiencing visions and even the ability to converse with their spiritual directors after the priests had died. Catherine de Saint Augustin, for example, had corresponded with the renowned Jesuit missionary Jean de Brébeuf for several years before deciding to emigrate to Canada herself. Only a few months after her arrival in 1649 Brébeuf was brutally killed in an Iroquois attack. Nevertheless, thirteen years later, in 1662, Catherine reported mystical encounters with the martyred priest. Brébeuf now became her "celestial director," advising and teaching her, even on occasion giving her communion. This sort of supernatural, post-mortem endorsement by a female visionary could do wonders for a priest's reputation, proving especially helpful in cases such as that of Brébeuf, whose cause was soon introduced for canonization.[50]

The numerous deathbed testimonies composed by confessors could serve a variety of doctrinal and rhetorical purposes. Priests once again underscored the exemplary virtues and privileged status of their female penitents, as well as their own faithful proximity. They reaffirmed key Catholic teachings concerning the immortality of the soul, the cult of the saints, and the efficacy of intercessory prayer. They depicted "model priests" devoutly and conscientiously completing their pastoral and sacramental duties. And they imbued with a sense of eternity narratives of desire, searching, providence, and fulfillment. Not even the popular romances of the day could rival these riveting accounts of men and women forging bonds that united them in body as well as soul, lasted for years, and persisted beyond the grave.

Communion

Central to these dramas of spiritual and emotional connection was the sacrament of the eucharist. Women and priests frequently described significant moments of encounter and union as taking place just before, during, or after they had given or received the body of Christ. Communion, of course, was just as heavily criticized and contested during the Reformation as was confession. It is therefore necessary to turn now from the personal to the polemical and to place this sacramental relationship within contemporary debates over religious practice, theology, and sexuality.

As we have seen, around 1400, a number of clergyman began to urge laypeople to receive communion more frequently than just once a year with the annual confession that had been established at the Fourth Lateran Council in 1215. The trend of receiving the eucharist more frequently, anywhere from once a month to once a week, began in religious houses and spread to the numerous penitential confraternities established for devout members of the laity by the end of the Middle Ages. Many clerics, such as the influential Jean Gerson, hoped that this habit would eventually take hold among all the faithful, and they vigorously promoted it in sermons and written tracts. In the sixteenth century the campaign for more frequent communion was enthusiastically taken up by some of the new reforming groups, such as the Oratory of Divine Love and, most notably, the Society of Jesus.[51] More frequent confession was encouraged as well. The Council of Trent (1545–63) reinforced the need for prior confession in order that "one may receive the Sacred Eucharist worthily."[52]

Promoters argued that more frequent contact with the body of Christ had numerous salutary effects. It made people more devout and more likely to attend the mass and the many processions and rituals in which the consecrated host was displayed. Catholics would become more self-reflective, more conscious of sin, and thus more desirous of its purgation. Pious and purified individuals in turn made for godly communities, ones that could serve as potent bulwarks against heresy. As Frederick McGinness summarizes this viewpoint: "[T]he collective reform of a city or country could occur only through the reform of individuals sanctified through the Sacraments."[53]

Frequent communion also had its detractors, however. Many critics objected, fearing that overuse would diminish a desired sense of mystery toward the sacrament and respect for priests. Receiving communion would become, they fretted, a matter of routine rather than a moment of union with the divine. These clerics insisted upon prior fasting and sexual abstinence, and generally advocated "infrequent and awesome communion."[54]

There may have been another reason why some clerics worried about the frequency of confession and communion. They noticed, as have some historians, that a great many, perhaps the majority, of the persons who responded to this call, clamoring to receive the consecrated host several times a week or even every day, were women.[55] Why should this have been the case? Caroline Bynum and others have called our attention to the ways that medieval women and men associated women with the body and bodily functions and therefore with the suffering and humanity of Christ. Consequently, union with and ingestion of the body of Christ through the eucharist came to hold particular significance for women.[56] Some scholars also point to a certain "feminization" of values and practices in late-medieval and early-modern

Catholic cultures. Stephen Haliczer, for example, observes that the development of many new devotions "allowed women greater participation since these did not require educational qualifications that were denied them, but depended only on spiritual and emotional commitment."[57] Moreover, as we have seen, many spiritually inclined women longed for meaningful relationships with priests. For them, more frequent communion meant an opportunity for more frequent confession and interaction with priests, often the one particular priest they felt God had chosen for them.

Bishops, monastic superiors, and other clerical authorities thus found themselves in something of a quandary. One the one hand, greater frequency and intensity of confession and communion contributed to personal holiness and helped to foster the reverence due to ordained priests as the purveyors of both absolution and eucharist. On the other hand, many believed that all women, no matter how virtuous, represented sexual temptation and that priests did well to limit their interactions with them to the minimum. A priest's willingness to attend to the spiritual and sacramental needs of a female penitent on a frequent, even daily, basis not only constantly exposed him to temptations of the flesh, but also distracted him from other tasks. The Jesuit Baltasar Alvarez, for example, was admonished by his superiors "not to waste time with women . . . in person or by letter" but rather to "apply himself to the treatment of [or conversation with] men, where there is less danger and greater advantage."[58] Critics may have recognized a potential theological problem as well. Many devout women insisted upon receiving communion only from their own confessors, a stance that threatened to "overpersonalize" the sacrament, shifting the emphasis from the salvific power of the body of Christ to that of the officiating priest. One Spanish cleric complained that female penitents were "in such a state of vassalage to their confessors that it is deemed a great infidelity or sacrilege to confess to or hear the sermons of anyone else."[59]

It is important to recognize, then, that early-modern promoters of pious women were participating in a polemic, endorsing the pro-frequent communion position, at least implicitly. At many points in their hagiographies they detailed, praised, and held up as exemplary the intense eucharistic piety of their subjects. In this, as in other aspects of religious practice and behavior, they may have been quite effective at constructing models for emulation, as generations of women continued to express what Miguel González Vaquero called "a thirst for communion."[60] As this was a desire that only a priest, invested with the power to consecrate the host, could satisfy, narratives of frequent and fervent communion, and of bonding between priests and female penitents, often overlapped and intertwined.

Indeed, for many hagiographers the issue of frequent communion provided a way of organizing accounts of saintly lives and friendships of the sort we have been examining. In this formulation, the story begins with the Servant of God pining to receive the host ever more frequently, even on a daily basis. She undergoes a period of testing, suffering the ridicule and rejection of disapproving confessors.[61] Finally she meets (or is granted) a priestly soul mate who gives her permission to receive communion more frequently.[62] Her abundant access to the body of Christ is understood as a reward for years of patience and penitence, as a sign of signal grace, and as virtuous religious behavior to be imitated by others. This powerful experience of spiritual and bodily incorporation is rendered even more meaningful for being mediated by the man chosen by God to console her spirit and direct her soul. For her Christ is doubly present: in the consecrated host and in the person of her confessor. It is hard to imagine a more effective endorsement for either holy woman or officiating priest or a more visceral way of affirming the doctrine of transubstantiation.[63]

Life narratives that described the forging of strong and lasting bonds of friendship between women and their spiritual directors may have served another polemical purpose as well. Both Protestants and many Catholic laypeople charged that clerics preyed upon women sexually, using confession merely as a tool of seduction.[64] Given this pervasive cultural stereotype, one might think that these descriptions of intense male-female relationships and the use of highly affective language would only fan the flames. Nevertheless, the authors of hagiographical texts challenged conventional wisdom by insisting upon the possibility of chaste but passionate friendships between priests and their female penitents. Defiantly they deployed intensely personal experiences as public weapons in support of the Catholic faith and of the Catholic priesthood. In their accounts the much-maligned sacraments of confession and communion profoundly change the lives of individuals and communities. And God bestows upon a virtuous clergy something longed for by all men and women: the ability to understand and be understood by a special friend. This most rare and wonderful gift invited only envy and emulation. Surely the risk of arousing gossip was outweighed by the rewards of spiritual and personal fulfillment and the promise of continued recruitment to the religious life in generations to come.

CHAPTER FIVE

READING HABITS

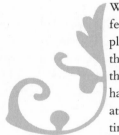We have explored the motivations and activities of confessors as authors and some of the strategies they employed and themes they developed in writing the *Lives* of their exemplary female penitents. But how do we know that anyone actually read the books they produced? I have referred to hagiography as a popular form of literature in early-modern Europe and its colonies; now it is time to investigate this claim. After looking at some numbers I turn to women's autobiographies for what they reveal about reading choices and the impact of books on women's lives and *Lives*.

Numbers and Networks

Thanks to the painstaking efforts of scholars, we now have a quite sophisticated understanding of book production in Italy, Spain, France, Portugal, and the Spanish and French colonies during the early-modern period. Bibliographies of works printed between 1450 and 1800 leave no doubt that presses in these Catholic lands were kept busy publishing the *Lives* of saintly persons. Not that printed books were the only means by which the faithful encountered models. Unpublished manuscripts, letters, convent chronicles, and the like continued to circulate widely, and forms of oral discourse, notably sermons, remained important, as they had for hundreds of years.[1] However, the advent of printing in the later fifteenth century greatly accelerated the transmission of information and expanded access to books in the vernacular, including hagiographies.[2] I thus use printed books as a means of gauging the production and distribution of *Lives* to a Catholic reading public.

The evidence for Italy alone is impressive. In 1996 Gabriella Zarri and her colleagues published a bibliography of texts by and about women and religion printed between 1450 and 1700, a reference of over 2,600 entries. Of these some 242 texts detail the lives of individual women from this period, the "modern" saints discussed below. These include full-length biographies, as well as sermons, funeral orations, panegyrics on the occasion of beatifications and canonizations, and other short works. If one were to add the collected lives of "illustrious women" and the biographies of female figures from earlier epochs of Christian history, the figure would certainly double.[3]

The publication histories of these texts attest to their popularity among readers and publishers, especially during the seventeenth century. About a third (88) were reprinted at least once, and many enjoyed two or more editions spanning years or even decades. Examples of hagiographical "best-sellers" include Ottavio Gondi's *Life* of Angela Merici (six editions, 1600–38), Giacomo Grasetti's *Life* of Catherine of Bologna (six editions, 1610–54), the *Life* of Catherine of Genoa by Cattaneo Marabotto and Ettore Vernazza (nine editions, 1551–1681), and Vincenzo Puccini's *Life* of Maria Maddalena de' Pazzi (eleven editions, 1609–75).[4] Raymond of Capua's *Life* of Catherine of Siena held something of a record. This extraordinarily influential work, composed in Latin between 1385 and 1395, was first published in Italian in 1477 and thereafter reprinted every few years until 1617, undergoing twenty-six editions in three different cities over a 140-year period.[5]

Bibliographical data on spiritual autobiographies and hagiographies of women written in Spain during the sixteenth, seventeenth, and eighteenth centuries reveals similar trends. Isabelle Poutrin has documented approximately two hundred *Lives* of saintly women produced in Spain in this period, confirming some of the earlier estimates made by José Luis Sánchez Lora.[6] Here, too, many texts enjoyed lengthy publication runs, such as Antonio Daza's *Life* of Juana de la Cruz (five editions, 1610–17) and Miguel González Vaquero's *Life* of Doña María Vela (five editions, 1618–74).[7]

For Henri-Jean Martin, the "incredible" expansion of hagiographical literature was a key feature of a "religious Renaissance" that transformed French culture in the seventeenth century.[8] Of the nearly three hundred *Lives* published during this time at least several dozen treated saintly women of the recent past. Some books enjoyed immense popularity, such as André Duval's biography of the Parisian *dévote* Barbe Acarie, which underwent nine editions between 1621 and 1638.[9] In Portugal, too, readers avidly consumed hagiographies, some composed in their native language and some available in translation.[10]

This last point underscores an important observation, that books frequently crossed national and linguistic borders. A great many of the *Lives* published in early-modern Catholic Europe were translations. Just to cite one prominent example: the autobiography of Teresa of Avila, first published in Spain in 1588, enjoyed at least eight editions in Italian and fourteen in French during the course of the seventeenth century.[11] The active involvement of translators as well as hagiographers ensured that readers across Europe would have access to numerous accounts of exemplary women from many different regions.

During the seventeenth and eighteenth centuries this network of books and readers extended across the Atlantic as well. As nuns, *beatas*, and tertiaries in the Spanish colonies achieved recognition for their holiness, devotees compiled and published hagiographical accounts. At least fifty *Lives* of exemplary women were produced in Spanish America between 1636 and 1782. Some books were published in Spain, but most were printed in the burgeoning cities of the New World, notably Mexico City but also Puebla, Lima, and some smaller centers. Adding testimonies, letters, and institutional histories that remained unpublished but circulated within convents and other pious circles would push the total to around seventy.[12] Even in New France, where the European population remained fairly small and the number of presses was extremely limited, at least thirteen narratives of holy women appeared in print.[13]

Thanks to a vigorous program of publication, translation, and distribution, then, hundreds of *Lives* of exemplary women circulated throughout Europe and its colonies. By the mid-seventeenth century an English nun living in Brussels and a Poor Clare in New Granada (Colombia) could possess the biography of the Florentine Maria Maddalena de' Pazzi, in English and Spanish translations, respectively.[14] Devout persons in Padua and in Quito could read the *Life* of the Peruvian *beata*—and the New World's first canonized saint—Rose of Lima.[15] In Paris and in Mexico City the faithful could learn the virtues of the Mohawk woman Catherine (Kateri) Tekawitha, converted by French missionaries in the North American woodlands.[16] Printed texts such as these helped to connect individual Catholics to a pan-European, trans-Atlantic, inter-American community of believers.

Encountering Books, Choosing Models

Though the sheer numbers are compelling, they do not, of course, tell the whole story. Who was actually reading these books? We can document at least one sort of readership for the *Lives* of saintly women. They were read by other devout women, who may have been, after all, the primary target audience of clerical authors. Many of these female readers later became writers, recording their own life narratives. Their autobiographical accounts provide fascinating, if sometimes frustratingly brief, clues about the ways women in one generation encountered and made use of the *Lives* of women from previous generations.

How were female readers first introduced to hagiographical texts? Many described growing up in households in which the reading of devotional literature was strongly encouraged. Teresa of Avila remembered a father who was "fond of reading good books" and thus "had books [in the vernacular] for his children to read," and other women evoked similarly book-filled childhoods.[17] Some identified the "good books" shared within the family circle as saints' lives. Growing up in mid-seventeenth-century France, Margaret Mary Alacoque recalled: "I scarcely read any other books than Lives of the Saints, and on opening a book, I used to say to myself: I must find one that is easy to imitate, so that I can do as she did in order to become a saint, such as she was." A generation later, the Colombian Francisca Josepha de Castillo recorded: "My mother used to read to me the books of St. Teresa of Avila . . . and this gave me a great desire to be like one of those nuns . . ."[18] This sort of response was, of course, precisely what hagiographers intended. These two pious young girls, avid consumers of hagiographies, did in fact become nuns and eventually wrote autobiographies and other works that were in turn read by others.

Women who entered the religious life often became acquainted with exemplary lives in convents, where they had many opportunities to both read books and hear them read aloud. Soon after María de Jesús (Gallart) professed as an Augustinian Recollect in 1633, some sisters "brought [her] the book of Doña María Vela," that is, *La muger fuerte*, the biography by María Vela's confessor Miguel González Vaquero. After reading the *Life* of this ascetic Cistercian who had died twenty-six years earlier, the younger Spanish nun resolved to undergo the same trials and tribulations.[19] French Discalced Carmelites and Mexican Augustinian Recollects participated in reading together the *Lives* of their orders' founders, Teresa of Avila and Mariana de San José, respectively, an experience undoubtedly shared by members of other religious communities as well.[20]

One of the most common ways for spiritual women to discover the lives of saintly predecessors was through their confessors, a development that should not be surprising given the close relationships they frequently maintained, as we have seen. Confessors recommended or even ordered their penitents to read certain books.[21] They shared their own copies or bestowed them as gifts.[22] They read aloud to women who were illiterate.[23]

The case of María Antonia de Jesús illustrates several of these themes and demonstrates how hagiographical texts could affect women's lives and serve as tools of spiritual direction for confessors. Born in poverty in rural Galicia in 1700, María Antonia was, like most people of her estate, illiterate. However, around the age of twenty-nine she conceived a great desire to read and begged God to instruct her. One day she opened a book (alas, not specified), recognized the words "Love of God," and then read it all in a rush, realizing that "the Lord had conceded to her the favor of learning to read, with no other teacher than Himself."[24]

María Antonia reported this and other supernatural graces to her confessor, José Ventura y Castro, an enthusiastic young man who had just received ordination. Castro struggled with how best to guide this wife and mother who claimed extraordinary spiritual gifts. Just then someone gave him the *Life* of Teresa of Avila. Castro saw this as providential, as he found so many helpful parallels between Teresa's experiences and those of his penitent. After he had read the book, he gave it to María Antonia, who was also much consoled by it. She came to enjoy reading Teresa together with a small group of female followers (*discípulas*), anticipating, as it were, her later life as widow, nun, founder of the first Discalced Carmelite convent in Galicia, and author of her own autobiography and devotional writings.[25]

Like María Antonia de Jesús, many women in early-modern Catholic Europe and its colonies presented the practice of reading and encountering the *Lives* of saintly exemplars as integral to their personal and spiritual formation. Which books did they decide to read and on which exemplars did they attempt to model their lives? By the seventeenth century, as we have seen, Catholics had hundreds of hagiographical texts from which to choose: lives of men and women, saintly figures who lived (or were reported to have lived) many centuries before, and virtual contemporaries, saints from distant lands and from the readers' own hometowns. The process of selection was not simply random or obligatory. An examination of autobiographies composed by spiritual women in the period between 1450 and 1750 suggests certain patterns and preferences.

Some women, to be sure, read, and were deeply influenced by, the lives of male saints. These included "saints of old," figures from the scriptural, patristic, and medieval past. A famous case is that of Teresa of Avila, upon whom Augustine's *Confessions* made a deep and lasting impression. She was, she explained, "very fond of St. Augustine," because she had been educated in an Augustinian convent as a girl and closely identified with the life narrative of a "sinner" whom "the Lord brought back to Himself." One might add that Augustine was also the originator of the autobiographical tradition in which Teresa was at that moment participating.[26]

Spiritual women also read and took inspiration from the *Lives* of "modern" male exemplars such as Ignatius Loyola, John of the Cross, and Gregorio López, famed as the New World's first hermit. Jerónima Nava y Saavedra (1669–1727) was already "greatly devoted to those saints who have shown [others] the path of the love of God" when her confessor introduced her to the life and works of François de Sales (1567–1622; canonized 1665). Ever since then, she explained, she had maintained "a great affection for that saint and his most sweet and clear doctrines."[27]

Despite the warmth of feeling for many male figures, however, early-modern women demonstrated a clear preference for saints of their own sex. But here, too, the pool was large. Many found meaningful models among female saints of biblical, early Christian, and medieval times, reading about, hearing about, and even having visions of figures such as Mary Magdalene, Clare of Assisi, and Angela of Foligno.[28] Margaret Mary Alacoque declared that Clare of Montefalco was "very dear to me." The devotion of a seventeenth-century French nun to a Tuscan mystic of the thirteenth century may seem puzzling at first, until one examines the experiences of both women. During one of her many ecstasies Margaret Mary heard God tell her that he would bestow upon her "the same reward as He had given St. Clare of Montefalco." Clare's "reward" was to have the instruments of Christ's passion impressed upon her heart, a miracle made famous when, at her death in 1308, her fellow nuns ordered an autopsy and reportedly discovered the implements still embedded there. Margaret Mary evoked this earlier instance of divine grace just after reporting how Christ had appeared to her during communion and exchanged his heart with hers, the event considered to have inaugurated the modern devotion to the Sacred Heart. Margaret Mary Alacoque, it would seem, regarded Clare of Montefalco not as an abstract saintly figure from the distant past but as someone whose mystical experience anticipated and authorized her own, a kindred spirit.[29]

This engagement with the Christian past could point to differences between pious women and their male promoters, revealing varying techniques and agendas. Clerical authors frequently situated their female penitents within a genealogy of saintly women. Some historically conscious biographers constructed lists that stretched back to the heroines of the Old Testament; others ranked their spiritual daughters among notable women of the early church and medieval centuries.[30] Serafino Razzi, for example, composed an epilogue to the *Life* of Caterina de' Ricci he published in 1594 called "On the Comparison of this Servant of God with Some Other, Earlier Virgins." Attempting to establish the orthodox credentials of his charismatic penitent, the Dominican cited such authorizing precedents as Catherine of Siena and Brigit of Sweden. Perhaps anticipating skepticism from those who claimed God would never reveal himself to a mere woman, Razzi pointed out, somewhat defensively, that the deity "bestows his gifts however, whenever, and on whomever he pleases." Nearly a century later this sentiment would be expressed in virtually the same terms by Paul Ragueneau, who also included his spiritual daughter, Catherine de Saint Augustin, within a genealogy of holy predecessors.[31]

This approach could have served another rhetorical purpose as well, which perhaps accounts for its popularity among early-modern hagiographers. The strategy had the effect of locating not only female subjects but also male confessors within the annals of sacred history. This may explain why clerics frequently evoked well-known cases of male-female spiritual partnerships, such as Jerome and Paula, Augustine and Monica, and Catherine of Siena and Raymond of Capua. If their penitents were to be "new" Paulas or Catherines, they were, at least by implication, the "new" Jeromes or Raymonds.[32] Women, however, rarely if ever claimed to belong to an illustrious spiritual lineage, as did their male supporters. Such an assertion surely would have aroused accusations of excessive pride. They tended, rather, to choose one figure at a time, or perhaps two or three, taking care to characterize them as models to whose virtues they aspired.

Men and women could diverge even in their choice of a single exemplar. To José Esteban Noriega, the life of his penitent María Quintana, an impoverished concubine and possible prostitute turned chaste and ultra-ascetic *beata*, had obvious parallels with that of Mary Magdalene. In his 1737 biography the priest made frequent references to the biblical figure, even choosing as the book's title *La pecadora arrepentida* (*The Repentant Sinner*).[33] María, however, did not take the abject Magdalene as her personal patron but instead chose a saint whose status and life experiences were quite different from her own. This was Gertrude the Great, the thirteenth-century mystic and theologian of aristocratic origins from the German convent of Helfta. María de-

La V. Maria del S.^{mo} Sacramento (llamada La Quintana) natural de Segovia murio de 49 años en el de *1734* à 16. de Agosto.

FIGURE ELEVEN

María Quintana. From José Esteban Noriega,
La Pecadora arrepentida . . . (Madrid, 1737).
Courtesy of the Biblioteca Nacional, Madrid.

scribed a turning point in her life. Homeless, forced to sleep in a filthy, freezing stable, she remembered that one night, "St. Gertrude (whom I have loved very much since I was a child) appeared to me in the habit of a Benedictine nun, very beautiful, as she was in the world . . ." This powerful vision signaled the beginning of a profound conversion experience. After this, María explained, she strove to adopt for herself certain qualities of the saint who had just visited her: "on the outside: moderation [*compostura*], in the inside: devotion, inclination for all that is good and a total hatred of all that is evil, which is sin." María Quintana did not look toward a saint whose circumstances resembled her own but rather toward a strong and dignified female figure, a model for the life to which she now aspired, not a reminder of her wretched past and present.[34]

Most spiritual women in early-modern Europe and its colonies, however, looked to much closer "contemporaries" for inspiration, that is, women who lived between roughly 1450 and 1700. In his 1671 *Life* of Catherine de Saint Augustin, Paul Ragueneau compared his penitent to various saintly exemplars from the Middle Ages but also to a figure from "our most recent era" ("en nos derniers siècles"), namely, Teresa of Avila. Although the Spanish nun had died nearly a hundred years earlier, in 1582, the French Jesuit still thought of her as someone from his own time.[35] This sensibility was apparently shared by many religious women, whose reading preferences reflect a strong interest in the experiences of other women who lived within this broad chronological community. Perhaps they found that they could identify more readily with figures from a more recognizable past than with those in distant historical periods. And, of course, the advent of printing in precisely this period had greatly facilitated the production and distribution of books.

Many early-modern readers were attracted to the *Lives* of predecessors who were close to them not only chronologically but also geographically. Understanding this sense of local identity and connectedness can help to explain why women sometimes evoked earlier female figures who are virtually unknown today. For example, Maria Maddalena de' Pazzi maintained an intense devotion to a Maria Bagnesi. In one of her mystical treatises, the *Dialogues*, the nun described how she was granted a vision of the now-departed soul seated on a throne in heaven, "all resplendent and full of wonderful majesty."[36] Maria Bagnesi was, like Pazzi herself, a Florentine of noble birth. During the middle decades of the sixteenth century this Dominican tertiary had attracted numerous followers for her many reported miracles and patient endurance of illness. Maria Bagnesi, like many such local charismatic figures in late-medieval and early-modern Europe, helped to form the core of an urban spiritual community in Florence. At her death in 1577 she was given solemn burial at the Carmelite convent of Santa Maria degli Angeli.[37] When, four years later, in 1581, Maria Maddalena de' Pazzi entered this house, recollections of the holy woman were still strong.

In addition to hearing tales about the tertiary, the nun would have had ample opportunity to read about her exemplary life. The convent kept many of the writings of Alessandro Capocchi, a respected Dominican friar who had served as both chaplain to the community and spiritual advisor to Maria Bagnesi. These included his sermons and a manuscript biography of his penitent. And within Maria Maddalena's lifetime Florentine presses brought out several collections of saintly lives that included profiles of Maria Bagnesi.[38] Put simply, Maria Maddalena de' Pazzi lived in an atmosphere saturated with the oral and textual memory of a beloved local holy woman.

As she mulled over whether or not to accept election to an administrative office among the Hospital Sisters of Québec in 1663, Catherine de Saint Augustin directed her prayers to a Marie des Vallées. Although Marie had died seven years earlier, in 1656, Catherine felt confident of her presence and guidance.[39] Who was Marie des Vallées and why did the Hospital Sister call upon her aid? Like Maria Bagnesi, Marie exerted significant spiritual influence on the local level, in this case in Normandy in the first half of the seventeenth century. According to her biographer, Catherine had a providential encounter at the age of twelve with the woman known as the "Saint of Coutances." Passing through Catherine's village, in the same bishopric, Marie predicted with all certainty that the girl would become a nun. "And this," the Jesuit commented, "is what happened, no doubt due to the intervention of that good Soul, to whom [Catherine] had commended herself."[40]

In addition to this intimate local and personal connection, there may have been other reasons why Catherine de Saint Augustin identified with her countrywoman. In 1641 the charismatic Marie fell under suspicion of demonic possession. The bishop of Coutances called in the renowned theologian—and native of Normandy—Jean Eudes (1601–80) to pass judgment on this troubling case. Eudes not only exonerated Marie; he enthusiastically declared her holiness. During the 1650s and '60s Catherine too would be tormented by devils, and her confessor, Paul Ragueneau, also obligated to defend his penitent as saintly victim rather than dangerous demoniac. As Guy-Marie Oury has suggested, Catherine probably learned of Marie's travails, either through correspondence with fellow Normans or by reading about them in the hagiographical account prepared by Eudes and circulated in France and New France by 1663. This sense of shared experience, as well as shared homeland, may well have inspired Catherine to choose the "Saint of Coutances" as a "model and celestial protector."[41]

Of course, religious women frequently cited the *Lives* of exemplars who were famous in their own times and also well known to us today. Chief among these were Catherine of Siena (died 1380, canonized 1461) and Teresa of Avila (died 1582, canonized 1622).[42] Dozens of women in early-modern Europe and its colonies described reading and/or hearing the *Lives* of these two luminaries of female spirituality. But while Catherine and Teresa in some ways transcended space and time in their appeal to later generations, quite specific considerations could still come into play as women made choices regarding reading matter and role models.

Let us consider some of the circumstances under which seventeenth- and eighteenth-century women cited Teresa of Avila and the ways in which they connected their own lives with hers. The future nun Teresa de Jesús María was born in the Castilian city of Toledo in 1592 and given the name María. As early as three years old, she would later claim, she heard the Lord call her to the religious life, specifically to be a nun in an ascetic order. Several influences would point her toward the recently founded Discalced Carmelites. María often attended the church attached to their monastery. Her parents were apparently acquainted with certain Discalced Carmelite friars. Moreover, her mother made an astonishing admission to her sensitive and impressionable young daughter: that she, too, had once dreamed of the convent and often felt distressed by her inability to fulfill this vocation. Her own convictions, her family's connections, and, one can imagine, the promptings of her pious mother led to María's entrance into Toledo's Discalced Carmelite convent at the unusually young age of nine. When she professed eight years later, she recalled that "out of devotion for our Mother Saint Teresa [the sisters] gave me that name."[43]

This case points to a number of interlocking issues of identity: regional, institutional, personal, familial. Teresa de Jesús María was from Toledo, a city not only close to Avila but also one in which Teresa had personally founded a Discalced Carmelite convent. Visible reminders of the saint filled her everyday landscape. The same was true for Isabel de Jesús (Sosa), also of Toledo, Marina de Escobar, of Valladolid, María Quintana, of Segovia, Juana Rodríguez, of Burgos, and María Vela, of Avila itself, just to name a few examples. For these Castilian women Teresa was not only a great Saint of the Church, but also a local figure, a *compatriota*.[44]

In his preface to the first printed edition of Teresa's works (1588), Fray Luis de León proclaimed that the saint had left behind "two living images of herself," namely, "her daughters and her books." One might add, daughters who read her books. Indeed, many of the women who evoked Teresa were members of the religious order she founded. These included Discalced Carmelites from the saint's native Spain but also as far away as Mexico and Flanders.[45] This sense of institutional identity inspired women religious in other orders as well and frequently crossed regional borders. The Mexican Augustinian Recollect María de San José avidly read the *Life* of that order's founder, the Spaniard Mariana de San José.[46] Catherine of Siena continued to serve as the preeminent exemplar of Dominican spirituality for nuns and tertiaries from Tuscany to Peru.[47]

Women also read and identified with Teresa for very personal reasons, often involving relationships within the family. We have already seen the young Teresa de Jesús María's response to her mother's vicarious desire for the cloister. Recall also that it was her mother's act of reading that introduced Francisca Josepha de Castillo to Teresa's works and awakened in her an interest in the religious life. After she lost her mother at the tender age of eight, the Catalan Teresa Mir began to frequent the Discalced Carmelite convent near her home in the town of Olot; her only sister would later take vows there. By 1709 Mir had adopted the saint of Avila as her special "patrona." For Juana Rodríguez, recollections of Teresa, her family, and her earliest desires for a religious vocation were inextricably linked. When Teresa came to Burgos to establish a convent in the winter of 1582, she apparently met Juana's parents, well-to-do merchants of that city. According to the lovingly repeated story, on that occasion the saint embraced the eight-year-old Juana, offered her blessing, and admonished her parents, "take good care of that little girl, because God is going to work many miracles though her."[48]

Naturally, these sorts of connections were made with other saintly figures, too. An intriguing case is that of Ursula Suárez (1666–1749), a nun who often struggled with issues of authority in colonial Chile. In her autobiography Ursula mentioned two books that had made especially strong impressions upon her, those of Doña Marina de Escobar (1554–1633) and María de la Antigua (1566–1617). "I enjoyed reading the *Lives* of these two servants of God, and I had great desires to be like them," she recalled.[49]

Ursula's assertion has puzzled some scholars, as she does not appear to have used these predecessors as literary models. Nevertheless, I suggest that the Chilean could find details in these particular texts that resonated with her own life. For example, Ursula's mother's family name was Escobar; thus her full name was Ursula Suárez y Escobar. This linguistic coincidence alone may account for a certain affinity with Doña Marina de Escobar, a pious laywoman and visionary from the Castilian city of Valladolid.[50]

FIGURE TWELVE

Frontispiece to *Vida maravillosa de la Venerable Virgen Doña
Marina de Escobar* . . . (Madrid, 1665). At bottom,
portrait of the author, Luis de la Puente.
Courtesy of the Biblioteca Nacional, Madrid.

María de la Antigua experienced a rather unsettled family life before entering a convent of Poor Clares near Seville and was involved in many
conflicts with fellow nuns and superiors thereafter. In broad outline this describes the trajectory of Ursula Suárez's life in Santiago, Chile, as well. The
Spanish nun compiled a didactic autobiography in successive notebooks

(*cuadernos*), the method that the Chilean would later employ in constructing her own narrative. Ursula apparently took María's advice to heart. She resolved to end a long-standing friendship with a certain "gentleman" who visited her in the convent "once [she] knew what la Antigua had said" on such matters. "Only God could give me the courage" to make this break, she later concluded, but reading the travails and teachings of a fellow Franciscan had first alerted her to the dangers and motivated her to change her life.[51]

For many women, then, reading hagiographies was an intensely personal and meaningful experience. Some, moreover, understood this process of textual encounter, identification, and authorization as divinely sanctioned. They reported receiving visions or other supernatural favors during or following the act of reading *Lives*. Again, interactions with Teresa of Avila prove instructive. As Isabel de Jesús (Sosa), a Discalced Carmelite in seventeenth-century Toledo, read Teresa's works, she perceived the words illuminated by a ray of light emanating from a figure of Christ.[52] The Portuguese Poor Clare Antónia Margarida de Castelo Branco (1652–1717) suffered from excessive doubts and scruples, a condition much alleviated by reading Teresa's *Life*. Thereafter taking the saint as her spiritual guide, the nun insisted, "A number of times I have experienced her favor in many matters that could not be helped by natural means."[53] André Duval, the confessor of Barbe Acarie (1566–1618), recalled that the pious noblewoman devoured Teresa's works and also Francisco de Ribera's biography of the Spanish nun, as soon as these texts became available in French translation early in 1601. A few days later Teresa appeared to the *dévote* and announced that God wanted her to establish Discalced Carmelite houses in France. Acarie threw herself into this work and eventually entered the order as a tertiary after the death of her husband.[54]

Women reported supernatural interactions with other *Lives*, too. Francisca Josepha de Castillo read the biography of Maria Maddalena de' Pazzi and became a fervent devotee. Several years later, during a difficult period in her life, she was granted a rapturous union with the Florentine mystic: "It seemed to me that Saint Maria Maddalena de' Pazzi, my mother and lady, came lovingly to my soul and united her spirit with mine with a very tight and intimate embrace, encouraging and consoling me."[55] It is difficult to imagine a more powerful testimony to the impact of *Lives* on spiritually minded women in early-modern Europe and its colonies.

Thus we see that the extraordinary efforts of hagiographers, translators, and publishers were not in vain. Women actually read the books they produced and distributed by the hundreds. For many of these fervent readers, encountering the *Lives* of exemplary, writing women of the recent past influenced their own lives in profound ways. They, in turn, composed autobiographies that were read by subsequent generations of pious women. This cycle of creativity and imitation, I suggest, played a pivotal role in the preservation and perpetuation of Catholic culture.

CONCLUSION

Close associations and strategic alliances between male clergy and pious women were not new to the early-modern period. Indeed, some have suggested that this particular male-female dynamic was a salient feature of western Christianity right from its beginnings, a factor that helps to account for both the religion's appeal among certain constituencies and the latent tensions with husbands, family members, and political authorities it often produced.[1] By the last two centuries of the Middle Ages, during the flourishing of an intensely penitential culture, clerics increasingly dedicated themselves to the spiritual direction of devout individuals, especially women. As they encountered women they deemed especially virtuous, they recorded their lives, promoting them as models for all Christians. Their efforts have been the topic of this book.

By the sixteenth century, the practices of confession and spiritual direction and the writing of hagiographical texts began to take on new meanings. The advent of printing and the subsequent rise in literacy meant that exemplary lives could be produced, translated, and distributed to a much greater reading public than ever before. The rise of Protestantism and the conquest and colonization of the New World posed unprecedented challenges. Early-modern Catholics responded in a number of ways to defend, reaffirm, and expand the faith. The forging of close sacramental and personal relationships between clerics and women, and their expression in written texts, now became more important than ever. The *Lives* of saintly women written by their confessors, in particular, could serve a number of rhetorical purposes.

For example, Protestants rejected the sacraments of confession and ordination, as well as transubstantiation, monasticism, celibacy, and the cult of the

saints. In these hagiographical accounts, however, these basic Catholic doctrines are not only still valid but profoundly transform individuals and communities. Stories of heroic lives and holy deaths—much more compelling and
accessible to readers, including women readers, than, say, technical doctrinal
treatises—nevertheless succeeded in conveying the same messages regarding
orthodox Catholic belief and practice.

As we have seen, early-modern confessor-hagiographers used many different techniques and styles to narrate the lives of exemplary women penitents. As a group, however, they tended to stress certain virtues as particularly
worthy of imitation, especially (although not exclusively) for women. These
included a deeply contemplative, sometimes mystical, prayer life, asceticism
and the denial of material possessions and pleasures, patient suffering in the
face of illness, demonic attacks and other afflictions, humility, and obedience,
at least to the will of God. At the core of these discussions was a fundamental Catholic tenet: the efficacy of intercessory prayer in the process of salvation. At a time in which Protestants challenged this entire system, clerical
promoters insisted upon the holiness of women who voluntarily separated
themselves from the world (sometimes in convents, sometimes in more informal arrangements as tertiaries and pious laywomen) so as to better pray for
the souls of living and departed Christians.

By living saintly lives and writing the *Lives* of the saintly, then, pious
women and male clerics contributed to the vast enterprise variously known as
Catholic Reform, Catholic Revival, or the Counter-Reformation.[2] The hundreds of hagiographical texts composed and translated into all European languages and consumed on both sides of the Atlantic between 1450 and 1750
established models of behavior, reinforced key points of doctrine, and insisted upon the truth of Catholic teachings. What may have held the greatest appeal for many readers, however, were vivid accounts of spiritual friendships
shared between clerics and religious women. In any case, in an age of confessional competition, when the continued participation of men and women in
the priesthood and the monastic life could no longer be taken for granted, the
role of hagiographical texts as recruitment tools could prove critical. Their
authors undoubtedly hoped that they would yield results, as in the case of the
Colombian Francisca Josepha de Castillo. Raised on the *Life* of Teresa of
Avila and other holy women as a child, she later recalled that this reading matter "gave me a great desire to be like one of those nuns . . ."[3] Francisca indeed
went on to enter a convent and eventually wrote her own spiritual autobiography and devotional works for the edification of the next generation of be-

lievers. Her life choices serve as eloquent testimony to the influence of exemplary models and the written word in the formation of religious identities during the early-modern period.

And yet, by Francisca's death in 1742 the Catholic culture in which she had been raised was already experiencing significant changes. Among these was a general reduction in the number of hagiographies of pious women written by confessors and other clerical promoters. During the second half of the eighteenth century the genre certainly did not disappear, but neither did it enjoy the popularity of earlier decades. Evidence from Spain illustrates this pattern. In her meticulous study of religious life-writing Isabelle Poutrin shows that of seventy-three hagiographical texts of this sort composed between 1500 and 1800, only eight were written after 1740 and only four after 1750, the last appearing in print in 1779. Poutrin's observations are borne out by research on the Spanish American colonies, which shows that after a few texts were produced in the 1750s and 1760s, the numbers dwindled. This trend may have begun even earlier in the eighteenth century in France and Italy.[4]

How do we explain the decline in an interpersonal dynamic and its literary expression that had previously played such a compelling role in Catholic culture? A thorough answer to this question would require an extensive study of social and religious change during the eighteenth and early-nineteenth centuries, a task that falls beyond the purview of this book. Nevertheless, I offer some observations in the hope that others will take up the story where I leave off.

After nearly 150 years of extraordinary vitality in renewing their church and opposing Protestantism, by the second half of the seventeenth century Catholics no longer seemed capable of maintaining a united front. Troubling internal conflicts erupted, the most serious of which was the theological dispute sparked by the posthumous publication of a treatise by the Flemish bishop Cornelius Jansen in 1640. Having immersed himself for years in the works of St. Augustine, Jansen came to some rather pessimistic conclusions regarding human nature and the role of human beings in effecting their own salvation. In what has sometimes been described as a "Puritanical" interpretation of Catholic doctrine, Jansen suggested that only a small elite of exceptionally ascetic and disciplined individuals had been elected for salvation through divine grace.[5]

Catholic thinkers, first in France and Flanders, and then in other parts of Europe consequently became embroiled in seemingly endless debates over predestination, free will, original sin, and the efficacy of good works, including acts of penance. What started out as a rather arcane and technical quarrel among specialists over time became more acrimonious and deeply polarizing, dividing members of religious orders, lay elites, secular rulers, and the papacy into camps of supporters and opponents. The Jesuits quickly emerged as the most vocal critics of the Jansenist position, and they continued to champion free will, individual conscience, and participation in the traditional penitential system as crucial components of the path to salvation.[6]

By the eighteenth century, high-minded discussion had degenerated into an "ecclesiastical civil war" that pitted Jesuits against an assortment of enemies. At one point a French cardinal identified "Jansenists" as "simply fervent Catholics who don't like the Jesuits."[7] The conflict, many believe, had also become much more political than theological in nature, with Jansenists and their supporters accusing the Jesuits of promoting the unchecked power of the papacy and undermining monarchical authority. By midcentury the anti-Jesuit forces had the upper hand, and one by one the kings of Catholic Europe—Portugal in 1759, France between 1761 and 1764, Spain in 1767—expelled all Jesuits from their realms and colonies. In 1773, under intense pressure from these absolutist rulers, Pope Clement XIV agreed to dissolve the Society of Jesus.

Naturally these momentous events had many consequences. Some scholars suggest that over the long run the Jansenist-Jesuit conflict dealt blows to clerical morale, religious unity, and the esteem of the laity for ecclesiastical authority from which Catholic culture never entirely recovered.[8] It may also have contributed to the eventual waning of sacramental relationships and hagiographical texts. Interestingly, one category of exemplary life-writing actually experienced an increase in the eighteenth century. In France, dozens of memoirs and admiring biographies of female supporters of the Jansenist cause had been composed during the seventeenth century. The ascendancy of Jansenism in the eighteenth century now meant that these texts celebrating the lives of Jansenist women could be published and distributed.[9] Nevertheless, the overall trend toward decline continued. Clerics on both sides of the debate devoted enormous amounts of time and energy to writing polemical tracts, time that could have been spent on composing hagiographies. And intriguingly, the decline in the relating of lives and *Lives* essentially coincided with the final struggles and then expulsion of the Jesuits. The departure of a group that had played such a pivotal role as spiritual directors and hagiographers for the previous two hundred years certainly must have left a void in Catholic devotional and literary life, especially for the devout women who had been their penitents, patrons, readers, and subjects.[10]

Perhaps even more profound, if less dramatic, than these political and ecclesial upheavals were gradual but perceptible changes in the values held by Catholics. New perspectives on saintliness and service would evolve over the course of the seventeenth and eighteenth centuries, resulting in altered expectations for women and men pursuing the religious life.

The close relationships between confessors and female penitents explored in this book were, I suggest, the products of a culture that placed a high value on intercessory prayer. Women had long been regarded as particularly well suited for this task but only when they withdrew from the world and adopted lives of contemplation and sacrifice. Whether they took formal vows as nuns or followed more informal vocations in pious associations or as individuals in their families' homes, religious women were expected to spend long hours examining their own lives and sins and then purifying themselves through various penitential practices in order to carry out their most essential work: praying for the salvation of souls, their own and those of others. This is where confessors and spiritual directors came in. Many dedicated themselves to guiding individual women to lives of greater perfection and, in cases of exceptional saintliness, publicizing their orational and penitential contributions to a wider Christian community. Teresa of Avila succinctly articulated this worldview. She wistfully acknowledged that only male clerics were permitted to serve God in the world as preachers and missionaries, but, she assured her Discalced Carmelite daughters, by strictly adhering to their monastic rule and engaging in constant prayer "we shall be fighting for Him even though we are very cloistered."[11]

Within a few decades of Teresa's death in 1582, however, the active apostolate for which she had yearned became a reality for many women throughout Catholic Europe and its colonies. The Daughters of Charity, Sisters of Mercy, and various groups of Hospital Sisters had their beginnings in France in the late 1620s and 1630s. Founded to address pressing social needs, as well as the spiritual aspirations of their members, these new orders devoted themselves to active work in the world, distributing relief to the needy, teaching girls, and caring for the sick and the indigent. They expressed their vocation not primarily through continuous prayer but by service to the poor. It is important to note that many of these new active communities for women had to undergo numerous vicissitudes before finally becoming firmly established, usually at the local level, and they did not immediately replace the more traditional contemplative orders. Nevertheless, they continued to grow in number and popularity, so that by the end of the seventeenth century there were

dozens of teaching, nursing, and charitable orders throughout France and
French Canada and eventually other parts of Europe as well.[12] Even during
the eighteenth century, when educated elites influenced by Enlightenment
ideas began to criticize monastic houses generally as parasitic bastions of medieval superstition, no one could question the "usefulness" of these hard-
working women. As Olwen Hufton observes, the only complaint about these
charitable orders and the women who ran them was that "there were not
enough of them to assuage the problems of needy old age or suffering pauper
children."[13]

The success of active orders for women suggests an important shift in pri-
orities, one that challenged the age-old primacy of prayer as the most sublime
expression of Christian service. Many Catholics, it seems, now placed a higher
value on pragmatic intervention in the needs of this world. The work of religious women was slowly being redefined as service to minds and bodies, not
only to souls. The transfer of women (and donations) to the active orders had
many implications, among them the decline in confessor-penitent relationships and the writing of exemplary lives. This new religious style did not favor the same type of contemplative environment in which intense spiritual
direction had taken place. Members of active orders simply did not have the
time or social space for long periods of meditative prayer, rigorous self-
inspection, and the careful reconstruction of past sins and current aspirations
necessary for the composition of spiritual life-narratives. Thus it does not
seem merely accidental that the consolidation of active orders for women during the eighteenth century coincided with the waning of hagiographical accounts of female penitents written by their confessors or spiritual directors.
Interestingly, in Spain and Spanish America, where the transition from contemplative to active orders occurred more slowly, the tradition of religious
life-writing persisted the longest.[14]

Priests, too, began to reassess their vocations in light of changing times and
the changing roles of women in the religious life. Clerics continued to inter-
act with pious women, of course, but more often perhaps as partners in re-
lieving human misery than as spiritual guides or biographers. By the second
half of the eighteenth century the imperative to promote exemplars for the
edification of the faithful that had motivated churchmen for hundreds of years
seemed to wane in importance. Less likely now to forge close relationships
with women they directed as spiritual daughters and admired as Servants of
God, priests would find new ways to fulfill their missions and form their
identities.

In the mid-nineteenth century Jacob Burckhardt proclaimed the Renaissance as the age that first saw "the development of the individual." While scholars have challenged many of Burckhardt's assumptions—the role of the state in identity formation, for example—they have continued to explore an emerging "individualism" or "sense of the self" as a salient feature of western European society in its transition from medieval to modern times.[15] Certainly the period between 1450 and 1750 witnessed an explosion in biographical and autobiographical writing of all kinds. The experience of narrating and recording lives within a Catholic culture of confession, I suggest, contributed to this fundamental cultural shift.

Women's spiritual autobiographies have received much scholarly treatment of late, but this study has focused attention on the much more numerous hagiographies of women composed by male clerics. Discussing the autobiographical impulse in sixteenth-century France, Natalie Zemon Davis notes that "[v]irtually all the occasions for talking or writing about the self involved a relationship: with God or God and one's confessor, with a patron, with a friend or lover, or . . . one's family . . ."[16] In composing the *Lives* of exemplary female penitents priests located themselves within these webs of relationships as well. In richly layered and complex texts clerical authors described their sense of connectedness to their female subjects as mentors, disciples, spiritual friends, patrons, symbolic (and sometimes biological) kin, and coworkers in the vineyard of the Lord. In the process of promoting saintly women as models for all Christians and for posterity, they revealed a great deal about themselves. Suddenly, as it were, men so often lumped together as "the clergy" or, even less accurately, "the Church" emerge as fully drawn individuals. A genre supposedly so sterile and formulaic in fact yields manifold insights about men, women, and the role of religion in the construction of cultural and personal identities. This realization would have come as no surprise to early-modern hagiographers, convinced as they were of the power of exemplary lives to move the human heart.

Introduction

1. Thomas N. Tentler, *Sin and Confession on the Eve of the Reformation* (Princeton: Princeton University Press, 1977), chap. 1.

2. See, for example, *Penitence in the Age of Reformations*, ed. Katharine Jackson Lualdi and Anne T. Thayer (Aldershot, U.K.: Ashgate, 2000); Wietse de Boer, *The Conquest of the Soul: Confession, Discipline, and Public Order in Counter-Reformation Milan* (Leiden: Brill, 2001), esp. chaps. 2, 3; Abigail Firey, ed., *A New History of Penance* (Leiden: Brill, forthcoming).

3. Tentler, *Sin and Confession*, chap. 2; W. David Myers, *"Poor Sinning Folk": Confession and Conscience in Counter-Reformation Germany* (Ithaca: Cornell University Press, 1996); *Handling Sin: Confession in the Middle Ages*, ed. Peter Biller and A. J. Minnis (Woodbridge, U.K.: York Medieval Press, 1998); Lu Ann Homza, *Religious Authority in the Spanish Renaissance* (Baltimore: Johns Hopkins University Press, 2000), chap. 5.

4. Cited in Jaroslav Pelikan, *The Christian Tradition: A History of the Development of Doctrine* (Chicago: University of Chicago Press, 1971–84), 4:129.

5. Cited and discussed in Thomas N. Tentler, "Sacramental Privacy: The Myth, Law, and History of the Seal of Confession, 1215 to 1965." My sincere thanks to Professor Tentler for making available to me this unpublished paper.

6. See, for example, Alexander Murray, "Confession as a Historical Source in the Thirteenth Century," in *The Writing of History in the Middle Ages: Essays Presented to Richard William Southern*, ed. R. H. C. Davis and J. M. Wallace-Hadrill (Oxford: Oxford University Press, 1981), 275–322.

7. "Je ne pouvois refuser à l'édification du public & à la consolation des bonnes ames, l'exemple d'une vie & d'une morte ausi pure & ausi precieuse devant Dieu . . . les communications qu'elle me donnoit par elle-même de tout ce qui se passoit dans le plus secret de son ame. . . ." Paul Ragueneau, *La Vie de la Mere Catherine de Saint Augustin, Religieuse Hospitaliere de la Misericorde de Quebec en la Nouvelle-France* (Paris, 1671), dedicatory letter.

8. For the use of the term "confessor" to denote a category of saint in the early Church see Kenneth L. Woodward, *Making Saints: How the Catholic Church Determines Who Becomes a Saint, Who Doesn't, and Why* (New York: Simon and Schuster, 1990), 54–55, 61–62.

9. On penitential movements and third orders see, for example, André Vauchez, *The Laity in the Middle Ages: Religious Beliefs and Devotional Practices*, trans. Margery J. Schneider (Notre Dame: University of Notre Dame Press, 1993; orig. publ. 1987), esp. chap. 10; Anna Benvenuti Papi, *"In Castro Poenitentiae:" Santità e Società Femminile nell'Italia Medievale* (Rome: Herder, 1990).

10. André Vauchez, *Sainthood in the Later Middle Ages*, trans. Jean Birrell (Cambridge: Cambridge University Press, 1997; orig. publ. 1988), esp. chaps. 9, 10. See also Donald Weinstein and Rudolph M. Bell, *Saints and Society: The Two Worlds of Western Christendom, 1000–1700* (Chicago: University of Chicago Press, 1982).

11. Regrettably, speakers of German, Dutch or Flemish, and Czech, as well as Catholics in Eastern Europe, fall outside the purview of this study simply because of linguistic limitations. I had also originally intended to include cases from Brazil but soon learned that the historical trajectory of Portuguese immigration (especially of women) and the establishment of Catholic institutions differed significantly from that of the Spanish and French colonies, effectively placing it outside the chronological limits of this study. See, for example, Leila Mezan Algranti, *Honradas e devotas: mulheres da colônia: condição feminina nos conventos e recolhimentos do Sudeste do Brasil, 1750–1822* (Rio de Janeiro: José Olimpyo, 1993).

12. Thomas J. Heffernan, *Sacred Biography: Saints and Their Biographers in the Middle Ages* (New York: Oxford University Press, 1988) 15–18. Other important studies that end by 1400 include Vauchez, *Sainthood in the Later Middle Ages;* Caroline Walker Bynum, *Holy Feast and Holy Fast: The Religious Significance of Food to Medieval Women* (Berkeley: University of California Press, 1987); Aviad Kleinberg, *Prophets in Their Own Country: Living Saints and the Making of Sainthood in the Later Middle Ages* (Chicago: University of Chicago Press, 1992); Catherine M. Mooney, ed., *Gendered Voices: Medieval Saints and Their Interpreters* (Philadelphia: University of Pennsylvania Press, 1999).

13. Anne Jacobson Schutte, *Aspiring Saints: Pretense of Holiness, Inquisition, and Gender in the Republic of Venice, 1618–1750* (Baltimore: Johns Hopkins University Press, 2001), chap. 3; Moshe Sluhovsky, "The Devil in the Convent," *American Historical Review* 107:5 (2002): 1379–1411; Nancy Caciola, *Discerning Spirits: Divine and Demonic Possession in the Middle Ages* (Ithaca: Cornell University Press, 2003).

14. For Battista da Varano (1458–1524) see Joseph Berrigan's introduction to Battista da Varano, *My Spiritual Life*, trans. Joseph Berrigan (Toronto: Peregrina Publishing, 1986), 7–13. For María de Ajofrín (d. 1489) see Ronald E. Surtz, *Writing Women in Late Medieval and Early Modern Spain: The Mothers of Saint Teresa of Avila* (Philadelphia: University of Pennsylvania Press, 1995), chap.3.

15. A number of scholars have investigated the role of confessors and other clerical authorities in the composition of Teresa of Avila's autobiography. See, for example, Carole Slade, *St. Teresa of Avila: Author of a Heroic Life* (Berkeley: University of California Press, 1995), chap. 1; Elizabeth Rhodes, "What's in a Name: On Teresa of Avila's *Book*," in *The Mystical Gesture: Essays on Medieval and Early Modern Spiritual Culture in Honor of Mary E. Giles*, ed. Robert Boenig (Aldershot, U.K.: Ashgate, 2000), 79–106; Alison Weber, "The Three Lives of the *Vida:* The Uses of Convent Autobiography," in *Women, Texts and Authority in the Early Modern Spanish World*, ed. Marta V. Vicente and Luis R. Corteguera (Aldershot, U.K.: Ashgate, 2003), 107–25.

16. "Pource qu'estant en plusieurs lieux pleine d'un grand nombre d'heretiques. . . ." André Duval, *La Vie admirable de la Bienhereuse Soeur Marie de l'Incarnation . . . appelée dans le monde Mademoiselle Acarie* (Paris: Librairie Victor Lecoffre, 1893; orig. publ. 1621), xxii.

17. For more on Catholic devotions in the context of anti-Protestant polemics see, for example, Frederick J. McGinness, "'Roma Sancta' and the Saint: Eucharist, Chastity, and the Logic of Catholic Reform," *Historical Reflections/Reflexions Historiques* 15 (1988): 96–116; Philip M. Soergel, *Wondrous in His Saints: Counter-Reformation Propaganda in Bavaria* (Berkeley: University of California Press, 1993).

18. Woodward, *Making Saints*, chap. 2.

19. Allan Greer and Jodi Bilinkoff, eds., *Colonial Saints: Discovering the Holy in the Americas, 1500–1800* (New York: Routledge, 2003), especially essays by Dominique Deslandres, Allan Greer, and Kathleen Ann Myers.

20. See, for example, Craig Harline, "Actives and Contemplatives: The Female Religious of the Low Countries before and after Trent," *Catholic Historical Review* 81, no. 4 (1995): 541–67; Elizabeth A. Lehfeldt, "Discipline, Vocation, and Patronage: Spanish Religious Women in a Tridentine Microclimate," *Sixteenth Century Journal* 30, no. 4 (1999): 1009–30; Susan E. Dinan, "Spheres of Female Religious Expression in Early Modern France," in *Women and Religion in Old and New Worlds*, ed. Susan E. Dinan and Debra Meyers (New York: Routledge, 2001), 71–92.

21. Isabel Poutrin, "Juana Rodríguez, una autora mística olvidada (Burgos, siglo XVII)," in *Estudios sobre escritoras hispánicas en honor de Georgina Sabat-Rivers*, ed. Lou Charnon-Deutsch (Madrid: Castalia, 1992), 268–84.

22. Doña María Vela y Cueto, *Autobiografía y Libro de las Mercedes*, ed. Olegario González Hernández (Barcelona: Juan Flors, 1961). For an analysis of María Vela's relationships with her confessors see Susan D. Laningham, "Gender, Body, and Authority in a Spanish Convent: The Life and Trials of María Vela y Cueto, 1561–1621" (Ph.D, diss., University of Arkansas, 2001).

23. I offer some reflections on the changing chronology and geography of female charismatic spirituality in Jodi Bilinkoff, "Navigating the Waves (of Devotion): Toward a Gendered Analysis of Early Modern Catholicism," in *Crossing Boundaries: Attending to Early Modern Women*, ed. Jane Donawerth and Adele Seeff (Newark, Del.: University of Delaware Press, 2000), 161–72.

24. Catherine Mooney, "Voice, Gender, and the Portrayal of Sanctity," and Karen Scott, "Mystical Death, Bodily Death: Catherine of Siena and Raymond of Capua on the Mystic's Encounter with God," offer cogent discussions of these objections and of the methodological and interpretive challenges involved in using hagiographical texts as sources. In *Gendered Voices* 1–15; 140–44.

Chapter 1. Spiritual Directions

1. Roland H. Bainton, *Here I Stand: A Life of Martin Luther* (New York: New American Library, 1950), 40–42. This section is called "The Failure of Confession."

2. André Vauchez, *The Laity in the Middle Ages: Religious Beliefs and Devotional Practices*, trans. Margery J. Schneider (Notre Dame: University of Notre Dame Press, 1993; orig. publ. 1987), 119–27; quote at 122. See also Richard Kieckhefer, *Unquiet Souls: Fourteenth-Century Saints and Their Religious Milieu* (Chicago: University of Chicago Press, 1984), esp. chap. 5; Caroline Walker Bynum, *Holy Feast and Holy Fast: The Religious Significance of Food to Medieval Women* (Berkeley: University of California Press, 1987,) esp. chaps. 1–2.

3. There is an extensive bibliography on late medieval preaching. See, for example, Larissa Taylor, *Soldiers of Christ: Preaching in Late Medieval and Reformation France* (Toronto: University of Toronto Press, 2002; orig. publ. 1992); Cynthia L. Polecritti, *Preaching Peace in Renaissance Italy: Bernardino of Siena and His Audience* (Washington, D.C.: Catholic University of America Press, 2000); Anne T. Thayer, *Penitence, Preaching and the Coming of the Reformation* (Aldershot, U.K.: Ashgate, 2002).

4. Corrie Norman, "The Social History of Preaching: Italy," in *Preachers and People in the Reformation and Early Modern Period*, ed. Larissa Taylor (Leiden: Brill, 2001), 147–48. Norman characterizes late-medieval and early-modern Italy as "a preaching culture" (126). See also Francesco C. Cesareo, "Penitential Sermons in Renaissance Italy: Girolamo Seripando and the Pater Noster," *Catholic Historical Review* 83 (1997): 1–19.

5. Taylor, *Soldiers* 126–33; quotes at 127.

6. Norman, "Social History," 177; Thayer, *Penitence, Preaching,* esp. chap. 3. For another study that examines the links between preaching and confession see Donald Weinstein, "The Prophet as Physician of Souls: Savonarola's Manual for Confessors," in *Society and Individual in Renaissance Florence,* ed. William J. Connell (Berkeley: University of California Press, 2002), 241–60.

7. The literature on confraternities is vast as well. See, for example, Vauchez, *Laity,* chap. 9; Herbert Grundmann, *Religious Movements in the Middle Ages,* trans. Steven Rowan (Notre Dame: University of Notre Dame Press, 1995; orig. publ. 1935), esp. 75–152; *Confraternities and Catholic Reform in Italy, France, and Spain,* ed. John Patrick Donnelly and Michael W. Maher (Kirksville, Mo.: Thomas Jefferson University Press, 1999).

8. Vauchez, *Laity,* chap. 10; Giles-Gérard Meersseman, *Dossier de l'ordre de la Pénitence au XIIIe siècle* (Fribourg: Editions Universitaires, 1961), 1–38; Anna Benvenuti Papi, *"In Castro Poenitentiae:" Santità e Società Femminile nell'Italia Medievale* (Rome: Herder, 1990); John Henderson, "Penitence and the Laity in Fifteenth-Century Florence," in *Christianity and the Renaissance: Image and Religious Imagination in the Quattrocento,* ed. Timothy Verdon and John Henderson (Syracuse: Syracuse University Press, 1990), 229–49.

9. Thomas N. Tentler, *Sin and Confession on the Eve of the Reformation* (Princeton: Princeton University Press, 1977), chap. 1.

10. D. Catherine Brown, *Pastor and Laity in the Theology of Jean Gerson* (Cambridge: Cambridge University Press, 1987), 56–72; quote at 57.

11. Taylor, *Soldiers,* 171–78; quote at 172. This trend has been documented for other parts of Europe as well. See, for example, Norman "Social History," 180–84; Stephen Haliczer, *Sexuality in the Confessional: A Sacrament Profaned* (New York: Oxford University Press, 1996), chap. 2; W. David Myers, *"Poor, Sinning Folk:" Confession and Conscience in Counter-Reformation Germany* (Ithaca: Cornell University Press, 1996), chap. 1.

12. Cited in R. N. Swanson, "Angels Incarnate: Clergy and Masculinity from Gregorian Reform to the Reformation," in *Masculinity in Medieval Europe,* ed. D. M. Hadley (London: Longman, 1999), 160–77; quote at 170. For more on the underlying sexual tensions and jealousy of husbands with respect to their wives' confessors see Colleen Seguin, "Ambiguous Liaisons: Women's Relationships with Their Confessors in Early Modern England," *Archive for Reformation History* 95 (2004): 156–85.

13. Norman "Social History," 180–81; Adrian Randolph, "Regarding Women in Sacred Space," in *Picturing Women in Renaissance and Baroque Italy,* ed. Geraldine A. Johnson and Sara F. Matthews Grieco (Cambridge: Cambridge University Press, 1997), 38–40; quote at 38.

14. Katherine L. Jansen, *The Making of the Magdalen: Preaching and Popular Devotion in the Later Middle Ages* (Princeton: Princeton University Press, 2000); María-Helena Sánchez Ortega, *Pecadoras de verano, arrepentidas en invierno: El camino de la conversión femenina* (Madrid: Alianza, 1995).

15. See, for example, Bynum, *Holy Feast;* Catherine M. Mooney, ed., *Gendered Voices: Medieval Saints and Their Interpreters* (Philadelphia: University of Pennsylvania Press, 1999); Gabriella Zarri, "Living Saints: A Typology of Female Sanctity in the Early Sixteenth Century," in *Women and Religion in Medieval and Renaissance Italy,* ed. Daniel Bornstein and Roberto Rusconi (Chicago: University of Chicago Press, 1996; orig. essay publ. 1980), 219–303.

16. Patricia Ranft, *A Woman's Way: The Forgotten History of Women Spiritual Directors* (New York: Palgrave, 2000), 97–101; quotes at 99. For more on this relationship see Ute Stargardt, "Male Clerical Authority in the Spiritual (Auto)biographies of Medieval Holy Women," in *Women as Protagonists and Poets in the German Middle Ages: An Anthology of Feminist Ap-*

proaches to Middle High German Literature, ed. Albrecht Classen (Goppingen: Kummerle Verlag, 1991), 209–38; Dyan Elliott, "Dominae or Dominatae? Female Mysticism and the Trauma of Textuality," in *Women, Marriage, and Family in Medieval Christendom: Essays in Memory of Michael M. Sheehan, CSB,* ed. Constance M. Rousseau and Joel D. Rosenthal (Kalamazoo, Mich.: Medieval Institute Publications, 1998), 56–61; Dyan Elliott, "Authorizing a Life: The Collaboration of Dorothea of Montau and John Marienwerder," in Mooney, *Gendered Voices,* 168–91; John Coakley, *Draw Me After You: Clerics and Holy Women, 1150–1400* (New York: Columbia University Press, forthcoming), chap. 10.

17. Patricia Ranft, "A Key to Counter Reformation Activism: The Confessor-Spiritual Director," *Journal of Feminist Studies in Religion* 10 (1994): 9–23; Coakley, *Draw Me After You,* Introduction; Gabriella Zarri, "From Prophecy to Discipline, 1450–1650," in *Women and Faith: Catholic Religious Life in Italy from Late Antiquity to the Present,* ed. Lucetta Scaraffia and Gabriella Zarri (Cambridge, Mass.: Harvard University Press, 1999; orig. publ. 1994), 83–112.

18. Quoted in Friedrich von Hügel, *The Mystical Element of Religion as Studied in Saint Catherine of Genoa and Her Friends* (London: J. M. Dent, 1923; 1st ed. 1908), 1:157–58.

19. "[F]ue la primera vez que hablé con nuestra Santa . . . el modo de hablar, tan humilde y sinzero, tan lleno de amor de Dios y tan assentada virtud . . ." Miguel González Vaquero, *La muger fuerte, por otro título, La vida de Doña María Vela . . .* (Madrid, 1674; 1st ed. 1618), 141 r–v; "Pues digo que el primer día que hablé a V.M. . . . quedé con una satisfacción y dilatación de corazón, que no me conocía, por haber hallado lo que tanto deseaba, que era topar con alguna persona que tuviese experiencia de este trato interior . . ." Doña María Vela y Cueto, *Autobiografía y Libro de las Mercedes,* ed. Olegario González Hernández (Barcelona: Juan Flors, 1961), 352. In listing the uses of the verb "tratar" in his 1611 dictionary Sebastián de Covarrubias defined "tratar a uno" as "tener conocimiento con él y conversación" (to be acquainted with and have conversation with [a person]). I suggest that this interactive and conversational sense is embedded in María Vela's use of the phrase "trato interior." Sebastián de Covarrubias Orozco, *Tesoro de la lengua castellana o española,* ed. Felipe C. R. Maldonado and Manuel Camarero (Madrid: Editorial Castalia, 1995), 934.

20. On the problem of scrupulosity in confession in general see Tentler, *Sin and Confession,* 78–82. On female penitents as overly scrupulous, see, for example, Taylor, *Soldiers,* 129–30; Elliott, "Dominae or Dominatae?" 67; Haliczer, *Sexuality,* 33–35. Haliczer observes that confession "offered women some unique opportunities for self-expression and spiritual growth" and allowed a woman "to give voice to thoughts and feelings she probably could not express to anyone else, least of all her husband and family." He concludes that "[c]onfessional interaction, while inherently unequal, entailed an obligation on the part of the priest to listen to his female penitent, treat her with respect, and provide her with spiritual guidance" (34).

21. Cited and discussed in Elliott, "Dominae or Dominatae?" 47–77; quote at 67.

22. Elizabeth A. Clark, *Jerome, Chrysostom and Friends: Essays and Translations* (New York: Edwin Mellen Press, 1979), esp. pt. 2; Ranft, *Woman's Way,* 39–43; Carolyn Valone, "Roman Matrons as Patrons: Various Views of the Cloister Wall," in *The Crannied Wall: Women, Religion, and the Arts in Early Modern Europe,* ed. Craig A. Monson (Ann Arbor: University of Michigan Press, 1992), 49–72; Simon Ditchfield, "An Early Christian School of Sanctity in Tridentine Rome," in *Christianity and Community in the West: Essays for John Bossy,* ed. Simon Ditchfield (Aldershot, U.K.: Ashgate, 2001), 183–205. A good example of the artistic depiction of this theme is *Saint Jerome with Saint Paula and Saint Eustochium,* painted by Francisco de Zurbarán and his workshop between 1640 and 1650, now housed in the National Gallery of Art, Washington, D.C. This image may be viewed at: http://www.nga.gov/cgi-bin/pimage?41430+0+0+gg30.

23. See, for example, Nancy Caciola, *Discerning Spirits: Divine and Demonic Possession in the Middle Ages* (Ithaca: Cornell University Press, 2003).

24. Moshe Sluhovsky, "'Believe Not Every Spirit:' Possessed Women, Mysticism, and Discernment of Spirits in Early Modern Europe" (in progress), chap. 5.

25. Luis de la Puente, *Vida del Padre Baltasar Alvarez* (Madrid, 1615), 36v–37r. For the emphasis on confession and spiritual direction among Jesuits generally see Michael Maher, "Confession and Consolation: The Society of Jesus and Its Promotion of the General Confession," in *Penitence in the Age of Reformations*, ed. Katharine Jackson Lualdi and Anne T. Thayer (Aldershot, U.K.: Ashgate, 2000), 184–200.

26. Pierre Champion, in his biographical introduction to *The Spiritual Doctrine of Father Louis Lallemant of the Society of Jesus*, ed. Alan G. McDougall (Westminster, Md.: Newman Book Shop, 1946; orig. publ. 1694), 11–12.

27. *The Spiritual Direction of Saint Claude de la Colombière*, ed. and trans. Mother M. Philip (San Francisco: Ignatius Press, 1934), x. See also Georges Guitton, *Perfect Friend: The Life of Blessed Claude La Colombière, SJ, 1641–1682*, trans. William J. Young (St. Louis: Herder, 1956), chap. 26. He was beatified in 1929 and canonized in 1992.

28. The idea that the faithful ought to receive communion every eight days appears to have derived from the work by the early Christian writer Gennadius, *De ecclesiasticis dogmatibus*, long attributed to St. Augustine. Session 13, chap. 7 in *Canons and Decrees of the Council of Trent*, trans. H. J. Schroeder (Rockford, Ill.: Tan Books, 1978), 77.

29. Miri Rubin, *Corpus Christi: The Eucharist in Late Medieval Culture* (Cambridge: Cambridge University Press, 1991), 147–55.

30. Pedro de Ribadeneyra, *Vida de Doña Estefanía Manrique de Castilla* Biblioteca Nacional, Madrid MS 7421, n.d., 27v.

31. Brown, *Pastor and Laity*, 63–67, 277–78n152. For more visual representations of this open style of confession see, for example, the woodcut from the title page of *Somma dello Arciuescoue Antonino* (Florence, 1507), reproduced on the cover of Lualdi and Thayer, *Penitence in the Age of Reformations*, and illustrations reproduced in Myers, *"Poor, Sinning Folk,"* 50, 51, 68 (1445, 1495, c.1547).

32. Brown, *Pastor and Laity*, 63–67, 277–78n152; Richard Trexler, *Synodal Law in Florence and Fiesole, 1306–1518* (Vatican City: Biblioteca Apostolica Vaticana, 1971), 268: 62–65. Priests were also not to confess women at night. Randolph, "Regarding Women," 39. For a discussion of both sexual tensions and confessors' manuals in a somewhat later period see Rudolph M. Bell, "Telling Her Sins: Male Confessors and Female Penitents in Catholic Reformation Italy," in *That Gentle Strength: Historical Perspectives on Women in Christianity*, ed. Lynda L. Coon, Katherine J. Haldane, and Elisabeth W. Sommer (Charlottesville: University Press of Virginia, 1990), 118–33.

33. "Se sentaba en el confesionario público . . . a oír las confesiones de cuantos se querían ir a confesar con él .. . obra de grand caridad. . . ." Alonso Fernández de Madrid, *Vida de Fray Fernando de Talavera, Primer Arzobispo de Granada*, ed. Féliz G. Olmedo (Granada: Universidad de Granada, 1992; orig. publ. c.1530), 103–4. Covarrubias did not include the word "confesionario" in his 1611 dictionary.

34. See, for example, François Lebrun, "The Two Reformations: Communal Devotion and Personal Piety," in *A History of Private Life*, ed. Roger Chartier, trans. Arthur Goldhammer (Cambridge, Mass.: Harvard University Press, 1989; orig. publ. 1986), 3:75–80, and illustrations 68, 77, 78. See also illustration in Myers, *"Poor, Sinning Folk"* 138.

35. Luis de Granada, *Vida del Padre Maestro Juan de Avila* in *Vidas del Padre Maestro Juan de Avila*, ed. Luis Sala Balust (Barcelona: Juan Flors, 1964; orig. publ. 1588), 113–16; quote at

114: "Y entrada en el confesionario, comenzó a crujir el manto de tafetán que traía: por lo cual el padre le reprendió agramente, porque, viniendo a confesarse y llorar sus pecados, venía tan galana . . ."

36. François Lebrun's assertion that the confessional box "came into wide use in the sixteenth century" ("Two Reformations," 79) is not borne out by the work of other scholars. See Wietse de Boer, *The Conquest of the Soul: Confession, Discipline, and Public Order in Counter-Reformation Milan* (Leiden: Brill, 2001), 84–125; Myers, *"Poor, Sinning Folk"* 185–203; Haliczer, *Sexuality,* chap. 2.

37. See, for example, Adelina Sarrión Mora, *Sexualidad y confesión: La solicitación ante el Tribunal del Santo Oficio (siglos XVI–XIX)* (Madrid: Alianza, 1994); Juan Antonio Alejandre, *El veneno de Dios: La Inquisición de Sevilla ante el delito de solicitación en confesión* (Madrid: Siglo Veintiuno, 1994); Haliczer, *Sexuality;* Jorge René González Marmolejo, "Clérigos solicitantes, perversos de la confesión," in *De la santidad a la perversión, O de porqué no se cumpla la ley de Dios en la sociedad novohispana,* ed. Sergio Ortega (Mexico City: Grijalbo, 1985), 239–52; de Boer, *Conquest,* 30–32, 97–100; Giovanna Paolin, "Confessione e confessori al femminile: monache e direttori spirituali in ambito veneto tra '600 e '700," in *Finizione e santità tra medievo ed età moderna,* ed. Gabriella Zarri (Turin: Rosenberg and Sellier, 1991), 366–88.

38. On pilgrimages, shrines, and hermitages see, for example, Philip M. Soergel, *Wondrous in His Saints: Counter-Reformation Propaganda in Bavaria* (Berkeley: University of California Press, 1993), chap. 1; Francisco Losa, *La Vida que Hizo el Siervo de Dios Gregorio López, en algunas lugares de esta Nueva España . . .* (Mexico City: Juan Ruiz, 1613), 37r–40v. On confessing members of the nobility in their private chapels see, for example, Ribadeneyra *Vida de Doña Estefanía Manrique de Castilla,* 26r; Jason K. Nye, "Johannes Uhl on Penitence: Sermons and Prayers of the Dean of Rottweil, 1579–1602," in Lualdi and Thayer, *Penitence in the Age of Reformations,* 156.

39. De la Puente, *Vida del Padre Baltasar Alvarez,* 36v–37r.

40. Pedro de Ribadeneyra, *Vida del Padre Ignacio de Loyola* in *Historias de la Contrarreforma,* ed. Eusebio Rey (Madrid: Editorial Católica, 1945; orig. publ. 1583), 366–80.

41. See, for example, Ulrike Strasser, "Bones of Contention: Cloistered Nuns, Decorated Relics, and the Contest over Women's Place in the Public Sphere of Counter-Reformation Munich," *Archive for Reformation History* 90(1999): 255–88; Elizabeth A. Lehfeldt, "Discipline, Vocation, and Patronage: Spanish Religious Women in a Tridentine Microclimate," *Sixteenth Century Journal* 30, no. 4 (1999): 1009–30; Alison Weber, "Spiritual Administration: Gender and Discernment in the Carmelite Reform," *Sixteenth Century Journal* 31, no. 1 (2000): 123–46; Silvia Evangelisti, "'We do not have it, and we do not want it': Women, Power, and Convent Reform in Florence," *Sixteenth Century Journal* 34, no. 3 (2003): 677–700.

42. Michel de Certeau, "Introduction" to Jean-Joseph Surin, *Correspondance,* ed. Michel de Certeau (Paris: Desclée de Brouwer, 1966), 56–66. See also Adriano Prosperi, "Spiritual Letters," in Scaraffia and Zarri, *Women and Faith,* 113–28.

43. See, for example, Tentler, *Sin and Confession,* chap. 3; R. Po-Chia Hsia, *The World of Catholic Renewal, 1540–1770* (Cambridge: Cambridge University Press, 1998), 198–200. For a more balanced view of confessors' manuals see Lu Ann Homza, *Religious Authority in the Spanish Renaissance* (Baltimore: Johns Hopkins University Press, 2000), chap. 5. I first discussed the cases that follow in Jodi Bilinkoff, "Confession, Gender, Life-Writing: Some Cases (Mainly) from Spain," in Lualdi and Thayer, *Penitence in the Age of Reformations,* 169–83.

44. Juan Bernique, *Idea de Perfección, y Virtudes. Vida de . . . Catalina de Jesús y San Francisco* (Alcalá de Henares, 1693). There were other cases in which priests, if not actually abusive, were very controlling of female penitents. See, for example, María-Helena Sánchez Ortega, *Con-*

fesión y trayectoria femenina: Vida de la Venerable Quintana (Madrid: CSIC, 1996), 253–59, 267–71; Rodrigo Cánovas, "Ursula Suárez (Monja Chilena, 1666–1749): La autobiografía como penitencia," *Revista Chilena de Literatura* 35(1990): 97–115.

45. Luisa Ciammitti, "One Saint Less: The Story of Angela Mellini, a Bolognese Seamstress (1667–17[?])," in *Sex and Gender in Historical Perspective*, ed. Edward Muir and Guido Ruggiero (Baltimore: Johns Hopkins University Press, 1990; orig. essay publ. 1979), 141–76.

46. Ibid. A Spanish Carmelite friar was seen prostrating himself before the *beata* Francisca López (1570–1650), asking for her blessing and declaring that "after the Passion of Our Lord and the favor of Our Lady, it was by her help that he hoped to be saved." This is one of several cases of women "blessing" priests cited in Donald H. Marshall, "Frequent and Daily Communion in the Catholic Church of Spain in the Sixteenth and Seventeenth Centuries" (Ph.D. diss., Harvard University, 1952), 168–70. For Paola Antonia Negri (1508–55), revered as "madre divina" or "madre maestra" by a coterie of "figliuli spirituali" that included priests, see, for example, Zarri "Living Saints," 231.

47. "Habiéndome dado Su Majestad un Padre Espiritual, de que yo he tenido muy grande necesidad . . . para que me ayudase y enseñase en el trato más interior a que estaba llamada . . . hizo gran provecho en mi alma, en muy breve espacio . . ." Elías Gómez Domínguez, *Beata Mariana de Jesús, Mercedaria Madrileña* (Rome: Instituto Histórico de la Orden de la Merced, 1991). This book includes a transcription of Mariana's autobiography, 86–141; quotes at 98–99. Pedro de San Cecilio, *Anales del Orden de Descalzos de Nuestra Señora de la Merced . . .* (Barcelona, 1669), 1, pt. 1:267. For the suppression of *beatas* in Seville in this same period see Mary Elizabeth Perry, *Gender and Disorder in Early Modern Seville* (Princeton: Princeton University Press, 1990) 103–5.

48. San Cecilio, 1, pt. 2:233–34; Jodi Bilinkoff, "A Saint for a City: Mariana de Jesús and Madrid, 1565–1624," *Archive for Reformation History* 88 (1997): 322–37. Mariana de Jesús and Juan Bautista del Santísimo Sacramento also collaborated in the enterprise of life-writing, as I discuss in chapter 3.

49. There is an extensive literature on Augustine's *Confessions* and their influence on the genre of autobiography. See, for example, Karl Joachim Weintraub, *The Value of the Individual: Self and Circumstance in Autobiography* (Chicago: University of Chicago Press, 1978), chap. 2.

50. On this point see Coakley's introduction to *Draw Me After You* and Mooney's introduction to *Gendered Voices*.

51. Prologue to *The Book of Her Life* in *The Collected Works of St. Teresa of Avila*, trans. Kieran Kavanaugh and Otlilio Rodríguez (Washington, D.C.: Institute of Carmelite Studies, 1976–80), 1:32. I use throughout the standard form of citing Teresa's works, listing chapters and paragraphs.

52. Scholars of Hispanic literature have been especially active in this field. For the case of Teresa of Avila in particular see Rosa Rossi, *Teresa of Avila: Biografía de una escritora* (Barcelona: Icaria, 1984; orig. publ. 1983); Alison Weber, *Teresa of Avila and the Rhetoric of Femininity* (Princeton: Princeton University Press, 1990). See also Isabelle Poutrin, *Le voile et la plume: Autobiographie et sainteté féminine dans l'Espagne moderne* (Madrid: Casa de Velázquez, 1995); Kristine Ibsen, *Women's Spiritual Autobiography in Colonial Spanish America* (Gainesville: University Press of Florida, 1999); Kathleen Ann Myers, *Neither Saints Nor Sinners: Writing the Lives of Women in Spanish America* (New York: Oxford University Press, 2003). Sonja Herpoel, by contrast, places more emphasis on the repressive aspects of the genre: *A la zaga de Santa Teresa: Autobiografías por mandato* (Amsterdam: Rodopi, 1999).

53. John Coakley, "Friars as Confidants of Holy Women in Medieval Dominican Hagiography," in *Images of Sainthood in Medieval Europe*, ed. Renate Blumenthal-Kosinski and Timea Szell

(Ithaca: Cornell University Press, 1991), 222–46, and now see his introduction to *Draw Me After You*.

54. For what follows I am heavily indebted to Coakley, "Friars as Confidants" and *Draw Me After You*, chap. 9. Also extremely helpful is the work of Karen Scott; see, for example, "Catherine of Siena, 'Apostola,'" *Church History* 61 (1992): 34–46; "Urban Spaces, Women's Networks, and the Lay Apostolate of Catherine Benincasa," in *Creative Women in Medieval and Early Modern Italy: A Religious and Artistic Renaissance*, ed. E. Ann Matter and John Coakley (Philadelphia: University of Pennsylvania Press, 1994) 105–19; "Mystical Death, Bodily Death: Catherine of Siena and Raymond of Capua on the Mystic's Encounter with God," in Mooney, *Gendered Voices*, 136–67.

55. Coakley, *Draw Me After You*, chap. 9.

56. Ibid.

57. For discussion and references see chapter 5.

Chapter 2. How to Be a Counter-Reformation Hagiographer

1. Peter Burke, "How to Be a Counter-Reformation Saint," in *Religion and Society in Early Modern Europe*, ed. Kaspar von Greyerz (London: Allen and Unwin, 1984), 45–55, quote at 49.

2. Ibid., 53. There is an extensive literature on sainthood, particularly for the pre-1500 period. Frequently cited general studies include Peter Brown, *The Cult of the Saints: Its Rise and Function in Latin Christianity* (Chicago: University of Chicago Press, 1981); André Vauchez, *Sainthood in the Later Middle Ages*, trans. Jean Birrell (Cambridge: Cambridge University Press, 1997; orig. publ. 1988); Donald Weinstein and Rudolph M. Bell, *Saints and Society: The Two Worlds of Western Christendom, 1000–1700* (Chicago: University of Chicago Press, 1982); Richard Kieckhefer, *Unquiet Souls: Fourteenth-Century Saints and Their Religious Milieu* (Chicago: University of Chicago Press, 1984); Caroline Walker Bynum, *Holy Feast and Holy Fast: The Religious Significance of Food to Medieval Women* (Berkeley: University of California Press, 1987); Aviad Kleinberg, *Prophets in Their Own Country: Living Saints and the Making of Sainthood in the Later Middle Ages* (Chicago: University of Chicago Press, 1992). For the post-1500 period, see Weinstein and Bell, *Saints and Society*; Gabriella Zarri, "Living Saints: A Typology of Female Sanctity in the Early Sixteenth Century," in *Women and Religion in Medieval and Early Modern Italy*, ed. Daniel Bornstein and Roberto Rusconi (Chicago: University of Chicago Press, 1996; orig. essay publ. 1980), 219–303; Kenneth L. Woodward, *Making Saints: How the Catholic Church Determines Who Becomes a Saint, Who Doesn't, and Why* (New York: Simon and Schuster, 1990). There are numerous studies of individual figures and geographical regions.

3. I am using the term "saints" here to mean all those regarded as saintly or exemplary in their own times, not just those who were officially canonized. Burke recognizes this broader definition as well, referring to "informally chosen holy people," "unofficial saints," and "local cults." *How to Be a Counter-Reformation Saint*, 45, 47–48. Among the relatively few studies that have treated hagiographers as a group, see Thomas Heffernan, *Sacred Biography: Saints and Their Biographers in the Middle Ages* (New York: Oxford University Press, 1988); José Luis Sánchez Lora, *Mujeres, conventos y formas de la religiosidad barroca* (Madrid: FUE, 1988); John Coakley, "Friars as Confidants of Holy Women in Medieval Dominican Hagiography," in *Images of Sainthood in Medieval Europe*, ed. Renate Blumenfeld-Kosinski and Timea Szell (Ithaca: Cornell University Press, 1991), 222–46; John Coakley, *Draw Me After You: Clerics and Holy Women, 1150–1400* (New York: Columbia University Press, forthcoming); Catherine M. Mooney, ed., *Gendered Voices: Medieval Saints and Their Interpreters* (Philadelphia: University of Pennsylvania Press, 1999).

4. I use here the English translation of 1619: *The Life of the Holy Maid and Venerable Mother Suor Maria Maddalena de Patsi* . . . (Cologne? 1619), 2. This is a facsimile edition in the series *English Recusant Literature, 1558–1640*, ed. D. M. Rogers (Menston, U.K.: Scolar Press, 1970). "Il sommo Dio si è sempre mostratò e si và mostrando maraviglioso ne' suoi santi; acciòchè in ogni secolo si truovi . . . á nostri tempi á apparito mirabile in Suor Maria Maddalena . . . semplicemente si descrivera la vita e la morte sua, assinchè, si come ella disiderò tutti possano, in quello specchio di bontà rimarando, infiammarsi di que el celeste fuoco, che del continuo abbruciò il suo purissimo cuore." Vincenzio Puccini, *Vita della Veneranda Madre Suor M. Maddalena de' Pazzi Fiorentina* (Florence, 1611; 1st ed. 1609),1.

5. "[P]ara que ninguno desconfie de su Misericordia, por muchas, gravísimas y feas que sean sus cuitas." Quoted in María-Helena Sánchez Ortega, *Confesión y trayectoria femenina: Vida de la Venerable Quintana* (Madrid: CSIC, 1996), 211.

6. To cite just a few examples: *Tesoro del Carmelo escondido . . . Vida . . . de la Venerable Madre Isabel de Jesús* . . . (Madrid, 1685), concludes with a collection of the sermons in Isabel's honor given by the book's compiler, Manuel de Paredes, as well as other clerics. This is available on microfiche: *Escritoras españolas: 1500–1900* (Madrid: Chadwyck-Healey, 1991–92), libro 22. Marcos Torres included a letter from the Bishop of Málaga thanking him for delivering the sermon at the funeral of María de Pol. Marcos Torres, *[N]oticias . . . de la vida y virtudes . . . de Doña María de Pol, su madre* (Málaga? 1660). For Mariana de Jesús of Quito (d. 1645) as the subject of both sermons and hagiographies by various confessors see note 8. For this sort of preaching generally see, for example, Frederick J. McGinness, *Right Thinking and Sacred Oratory in Counter-Reformation Rome* (Princeton: Princeton University Press, 1995).

7. André Duval, *La Vie admirable de la Bienhereuse Soeur Marie de l'Incarnation . . . appelée dans le monde Mademoiselle Acarie* (Paris: Librairie Victor Lecoffre, 1893; orig. publ. 1621). "Et semble que la France a plus d'interest en cela que le reste de la Chrestienté, pource qu'estant en plusieurs lieux pleine d'un grand nombre d'heretiques, il est à presumer que par le lecture de cette vie ils demeureront confus, ne voyant aucun de mesme parmy soy honoré de grands miracles, comme a esté celle de qui nous escrivons; de sorte que peut-estre quelques uns d'entre eux pourront se ranger sous les enseignes de l'Eglise . . . ," xxii.

8. "[D]espertar con su exemplo a las Señoras, que estan entretenidas con los regalos y baxezas de esta vida." Pedro de Ribadeneyra, "Vida de Doña Estefanía Manrique de Castilla" (c. 1606), Biblioteca Nacional, Madrid (BNM), MS 7421. Jodi Bilinkoff, "The Many 'Lives' of Pedro de Ribadeneyra," *Renaissance Quarterly* 52(1999): 185–89. In a similar vein, Alonso de Rojas, lauding the ascetic Mariana de Jesús, exhorted "Learn, girls of Quito, from your fellow countrywoman, [to prefer] holiness over beauty, virtues over ostentation." Quoted in Ronald J. Morgan, "'Just like Rosa': History and Metaphor in the *Life* of a Seventeenth-Century Peruvian Saint," *Biography* 21(1998): 283.

9. *Tesoro del Carmelo escondido* 742.

10. Puccini, *Vita della Veneranda*, 2.

11. See *Tesoro del Carmelo escondido*, for example, throughout the unpaginated prologue, and 741–43, 745. For further discussion of this imagery see Sherry M. Velasco, *Demons, Nausea, and Resistance in the Autobiography of Isabel de Jesús (1611–1682)* (Albuquerque: University of New Mexico Press, 1996), 26–28. This metaphor of "bringing to light" previously unknown lives was utilized frequently by hagiographers. See, for example, *Opere spirituali della reverenda . . . Battista da Genova . . . con la vita della medesima trascritta dal . . . Dionisio da Piacenza . . . hor prima dato in luce* . . . (Verona, 1602). Cited in the "Reportorio dei testi a stampa," in *Donna, disciplina, creanza cristiana dal XV al XVII secolo*, ed. Gabriella Zarri (Rome: Edizioni di Storia e Letteratura, 1996), 694.

12. "Car la Vie de cette excellente Religieuse que je donne au public est rare et extraordinaire . . ." *La Vie de la Venerable Mere Marie de l'Incarnation* . . . (Paris, 1677), I–ii. In like manner, the Jesuit Paul Ragueneau explained to the dedicatee of his 1671 *Life* of Catherine de Saint Augustin that "this work that I present to you contains something that is as extraordinary as it is little known to the people of this world" ("l'Ouvrage que je vous presente a quelque chose de si extraordinaire & de si peu connu des gens du monde . . ."). Paul Ragueneau, *La Vie de la Mere Catherine de Saint Augustin, Religieuse Hospitaliere de la Misericorde de Quebec en la Nouvelle-France* (Paris, 1671).

13. "[S]e expone a censura de sospechoso lo que en los Padres alaba el hijo por apasionado . . . siendo mi sacerdocio llave para desencerrarle . . ."; "V. M. es muy hijo de tal Madre, como hijo tenía mas frecuentes asistencias, y como confesor tendría mas interior noticia que ninguno, y así executará en el estado que profesa . . . y satisfacción a la obligación de su sangre. . . ." Torres, *[N]oticias*, 1–2. There are other cases of clerics being ordered to write exemplary lives by diocesan or, more commonly, monastic superiors, usually with the goal of recording the institutional history of their order as well as lauding an individual member.

14. "[L]as razones que motivaron al Author a sacar a luz esta historia . . . Estrechísima es la obligación . . . que para honrar y venerar a los padres, executa a los hijos. La luz de la razon lo dicta, leyes humanos lo persuaden, y preceptos Divinos lo confirman." Juan Bernique, *Idea de Perfección, y Virtudes. Vida de la V.M. y Sierva de Dios Catalina de Jesús y San Francisco* (Alcalá de Henares, 1693).

15. "Raccolto dai divoti religiosi (suo Confessore e un figliulo suo spirituale)." Quoted in Friedrich von Hügel, *The Mystical Element in Religion as Studied in Saint Catherine of Genoa and Her Friends* (London: J.M. Dent, 1923; 1st ed. 1908), 1:415.

16. For the much-debated composition and publication history of these texts see von Hügel, 1:407ff. In his introduction to the most recent English edition Serge Hughes takes issue with von Hügel. Catherine of Genoa, *Purgation and Purgatory, The Spiritual Dialogue* (New York: Paulist Press, 1979), 1–67. A similar case is that of Paola Antonia Negri (1508–55), whose coterie of "figliuli spirituali" revered her as their "madre divina" or "madre maestra." After Negri's death some of her followers collected and published her letters, along with an account of her life. Adriano Prosperi, "Dalle 'divine madri' ai 'padri spirituali,'" in *Women and Men in Spiritual Culture, XIV–XVII Centuries: A Meeting of South and North*, ed. Elisja Schulte van Kessel (The Hague: Netherlands Government Printing Office, 1986), 71–90; Adriano Prosperi, "Spiritual Letters," in *Women and Faith: Catholic Religious Life in Italy from Late Antiquity to the Present*, ed. Lucetta Scaraffia and Gabriella Zarri (Cambridge: Harvard University Press, 1999; orig. publ. 1994): 113–28; Andrea Erba, "Il 'caso' di Paola Antonia Negri nel Cinquecento italiano," in van Kessel, *Women and Men in Spiritual Culture* 193–211. Zarri, "Living Saints," 231.

17. The effect that the older man had upon his protégé comes through more clearly in the original French: "un autre saint homme, que la reconnaissance demande que nous fassions aussi connaître à son tour. C'est le Père Vincent Huby, qui, par le pouvoir qu'il avait sur mon esprit, m'a engagé à entreprendre les petits ouvrages . . ." *The Spiritual Doctrine of Father Louis Lallemant of the Society of Jesus* (Westminster, Md.: The Newman Book Shop, 1946), vii, 24. *La Vie et La Doctrine Spirituelle du Père Louis Lallemant de la Compagnie de Jésus* (Paris: Desclée de Brouwer, 1959), 41–42, 69. For the general ambiance among French Jesuits of the time see Michel de Certeau, *The Mystic Fable*, trans. Michael B. Smith (Chicago: University of Chicago Press, 1992; orig. publ. 1982), 1:260–70. See the same author's introduction to Jean-Joseph Surin, *Correspondance*, ed. Michel de Certeau (Paris: Desclée de Brouwer, 1966), esp. 56–66, for the formation of the "cult" of Surin. Another such case, this time among Span-

ish Jesuits, is that of Pedro de Ribadeneyra, with regard to Ignatius Loyola, and of Cristóbal López, with regard to Ribadeneyra. Bilinkoff, "Many 'Lives'" 180, 184–85, 190–91.

18. "La divina Providencia que quiso autorizar y honrar esta ciudad de Avila con tanta nobleza de linajes, para que de ella naciesen hombres valerosos . . . quiso también enriquecerla en nuestros tiempos de mujeres fuertes . . . del espíritu . . ." I use here the edition published in Madrid in 1674: Miguel González Vaquero, *La muger fuerte . . . La vida de D. Maria Vela . . .*, 1r–v. As Richard Kagan points out, works "celebrating, and indeed, magnifying, the importance of the home town" were extremely popular in Spain at this time. "Clio and the Crown: Writing History in Habsburg Spain," in *Spain, Europe and the Atlantic World: Essays in Honour of John H. Elliott*, ed. Richard L. Kagan and Geoffrey Parker (Cambridge: Cambridge University Press, 1995), 73–99. For an example outside Spain see McGinness, *Right Thinking*, 175, for early seventeenth-century sermons in honor of Santa Francesca Romana that also glorified the city of Rome.

19. "[E]t priveroit-on la France d'un tres grand honneur, et la ravaleroit-on par ce moyen au dessous des autres nations, qui ont esté en ce siecle favorisées du Ciel des Saincts fort illustres; comme Italie de sainct Charles Borromée, et l'Espagne du bien-heureux Ignace, fondateur de l'Order de la Compagnie de Jesus, et la bien-heureuse mere Terese." Duval, *La Vie admirable*, xxii.

20. "[E]sta República, . . . debe estar gozosa, porque la ilustró esta sierva de Dios con su asistencia . . . el sacrificio sagrado ofrecido por la salud de vuestra Patria . . ." Quoted in Morgan, "'Just like Rosa,'" 285.

21. As Ronald Morgan comments, "writing the life of Mariana de Jesús becomes [for Morán] a method of celebrating the merits of Quito." Ibid., 278–79, 292–93. A number of recent studies consider the role of saints in the formation of Creole identity in colonial Spanish America. See, for example, Teodoro Hampe Martínez, *Santidad e identidad criolla: Estudio del proceso de canonización de Santa Rosa* (Cuzco: Centro de Estudios Regionales Andinos "Bartolomé de las Casas," 1998); Antonio Rubial García, *La santidad controvertida: Hagiografía y conciencia criolla alrededor de los venerables no canonizados de Nueva España* (Mexico City: Fondo de Cultura Económica, 1999); Kathleen Ann Myers, "'Redeemer of America': Rosa de Lima (1586–1617), the Dynamics of Identity and Canonization," in *Colonial Saints: Discovering the Holy in the Americas, 1500–1800*, ed. Allan Greer and Jodi Bilinkoff (New York: Routledge, 2003), 251–75; Ronald J. Morgan, *Spanish American Saints and the Rhetoric of Identity, 1600–1810* (Tucson: University of Arizona Press, 2002).

22. Jesuit General Francis Borgia ordered Pedro de Ribadeneyra to write the life of Ignatius Loyola: *Vida del Padre Ignacio de Loyola, fundador de la religión de la Compañía de Jesús* (Madrid, 1586), 3v. General Claudio Aquaviva likewise commissioned Sebastiano Berretari to write the life of Jose de Ancheta: *Vida del Padre Joseph de Ancheta de la Compañía de Jesús, y Provincial del Brasil* (Barcelona, 1622), preface. Discalced Carmelite authorities appointed Alonso de la Madre de Dios as both biographer of John of the Cross and procurator of his cause for canonization: *Vida, virtudes y milagros del santo padre Fray Juan de la Cruz* (Madrid: Editorial de Espiritualidad, 1989; orig. publ. c.1630), 39–41. Confessor-hagiographers who also testified at hearings or were otherwise involved in canonization proceedings include Julián de Avila (Teresa of Avila), André Duval (Barbe Acarie), Francisco Losa (Gregorio López), and Alonso de la Madre de Dios (John of the Cross).

23. Bilinkoff, "Many 'Lives.'" Ribadeneyra also wrote his own autobiography.

24. See the introduction by Guglielmo M. di Agresti to Serafino Razzi, *Vita di Santa Caterina de' Ricci* (Florence: Olschki, 1965; orig. publ. 1594). "Reportorio," 654–57. As a "figliulo spirituale" of Caterina, Razzi both gave and received spiritual direction in this relationship. Anna

Scattigno, "'Carissimo figliolo in Cristo.' Direzione spirituale e mediazone sociale nell'epistolario di Caterina de' Ricci (1542–1590)," in *Ragnatele di rapporti: Patronage e reti di relazione nella storia delle donne,* ed. Lucia Ferrante, Maura Palazzi, and Gianna Pomata (Turin: Rosenberg and Sellier, 1988), 219–39. A somewhat different but no less interesting case is that of the pious layman Miguel Batista de Lanuza, who, between 1638 and 1659 wrote the lives of at least six Spanish Discalced Carmelite nuns. Isabelle Poutrin, *Le voile et la plume: Autobiographie et sainteté féminine dans l'Espagne moderne* (Madrid: Casa de Velázquez, 1995) 217, 228, 258–59, 439.

25. Puccini, *Vita della Veneranda,* 251–55. Cepari wrote at least two other lives besides those of Gonzaga and Ricci. "Reportorio," 487. Serafino Razzi's brother, the Camaldolese monk Silvano Razzi, was also an active hagiographer. In addition to the lives of individuals he published the popular six-volume *Delle vite delle donne illustri per santita* between 1595 and 1606. "Reportorio," 657–58.

26. "[A] la manera que el Padre Fray Raimundo de Capua, Confesor que fue de la bienaventurada Santa Catalina de Sena . . . lo mismo se ve y leemos en otras muchas Crónicas y Historias." Quoted in Elías Gómez Domínguez, *Beata Mariana de Jesús, mercedaria madrileña* (Rome: Instituto Histórico de la Orden de la Merced, 1991), 87–88. Intriguingly, during the same years in which he translated Raymond of Capua's *Legenda Maior* into Castilian, Antonio de la Peña fervently promoted his penitent, María de Santo Domingo, like Catherine a charismatic Dominican tertiary of humble birth. In his introduction to the translation he defended the practice of narrating the lives of saintly women. *La vida de la bienaventurada sancta Caterina de Sena* (Alcalá de Henares, 1511). Jodi Bilinkoff, "A Peasant Visionary and Her Audience in Early Sixteenth-Century Spain," *Studia Mystica* 18 (1997): 36–59.

27. Male promoters explicitly compared their penitents with Catherine of Siena (and implicitly, themselves with Raymond of Capua) in the cases of Maria Maddalena de' Pazzi, Catherine of Genoa, María Vela, Catherine de Saint Augustin, Mariana de Jesús (of Madrid), Mariana de Jesús (of Quito), Catalina de Jesús y San Francisco, and Caterina de' Ricci discussed above. To this list we may add Rose of Lima (d. 1617) and the Portuguese holy woman Isabel de Miranda (d. 1610), just to show the extraordinary breadth and longevity of this cultural construct. See Kathleen Ann Myers, *Neither Saints Nor Sinners: Writing the Lives of Women in Spanish America* (New York: Oxford University Press, 2003), chap. 1; Maria de Lurdes Correia Fernandes, "A construção da santidade nos finais do século XVI. O caso de Isabel de Miranda, tecedeira, viúva e 'santa' (c. 1539–1610)," in *Actas do Colóquio Internacional Piedade Popular: Sociabiladades, representações, espiritualidades* (Lisbon: Centro de História da Cultura/Terramar, 1999), 243–72.

28. "Siendo yo de edad nueve o diez años me mando leyese en presencia de mis hermanas la vida de la V. Señora Doña María de Pol, escrita por el Padre Marcos de Torres, S.J., hijo suyo, y admirando yo el misterio de que un hijo suyo oviese sido el escritor de las virtudes de su madre, llamandome con grazejo repetidas vezes su historiador, y aun quando me advertia tibio en los estudios, estimulaba mi floxedad, diziendome: buena traza llevas de ser mi Coronista . . . [this book] ha dispuesto el Cielo, acaso por dar cumplimiento a esta profecia." Bernique, "Prólogo al Lector," in *Idea de Perfección,* n.p.

29. "Estando un día, despues de comulgar, recogida . . . me dixo Su Magestad 'Hija, di a tu Confesor, que escriva tu vida' . . . Pero que no determinaba a hazerlo [write her life], por falta de talento, y de tiempo, y la mucha dificultad que tenia, en escrivir." Sánchez Ortega, *Confesión,* 272, 274; see also discussion 271–85. For an overview of the debates over the proper "discernment of spirits" that embroiled Teresa of Avila and so many other religious women see Alison P. Weber, "Between Ecstasy and Exorcism: Religious Negotiation in Sixteenth-Cen-

tury Spain," *Journal of Medieval and Renaissance Studies* 23 (1993): 221–34. See also Anne Jacobson Schutte, *Aspiring Saints: Pretense of Holiness, Inquisition, and Gender in the Republic of Venice, 1618–1750* (Baltimore: Johns Hopkins University Press, 2001), chap. 3.

30. "Conozco mi ignorancia, tibieza, y falta de experiencia, especialmente en estas materias." Noriega authored at least one other hagiography and, according to some sources, was an avid student of history. Sánchez Ortega, *Confesión*, 52; see also 37–44, 50–58, 276–85.

31. "Voy poniendo y refiriendo aquí como me voy acordando habérmelo dicho esta Sierva de Dios, preguntándole algunas cosas para gloria de Dios, como su confesor . . ." Gómez Domínguez, *Beata Mariana de Jesús*, 125; "Muchas vezes estava yo mirando en ella . . ." González Vaquero, *La muger fuerte*, 17v–18r. From at least the thirteenth century on, the imperative of testifying to a deceased penitent's saintly virtues in effect exempted confessors from maintaining the "seal of confession." Alexander Murray, "Confession as a Historical Source in the Thirteenth Century," in *The Writing of History in the Middle Ages: Essays Presented to Richard William Southern*, ed. R. H. C. Davis and J. M. Wallace-Hadrill (Oxford: Oxford University Press, 1981), 275–322, esp. 283.

32. "[A]yiendome dicho y avisado de ello primero día del mes de Enero del año de mil y seiscientos y setenta y seis . . . que he visto complidas al pie de la letra . . ." *Tesoro del Carmelo escondido*, "Prólogo"; "Y aunque es mucho lo que en este punto dexó dictado, todavia me persuado, fue sin comparación mucho mas, lo que ella misma no supo dezir." Sánchez Ortega, Confesión, 279. Or could it be that she chose not to reveal certain things to Noriega?

33. Rubial García, *La santidad controvertida*, 93–128.

34. I treat the relationship between Losa and López briefly in "Navigating the Waves (of Devotion): Toward a Gendered Analysis of Early Modern Catholicism," in *Crossing Boundaries: Attending to Early Modern Women*, ed. Jane Donawerth and Adele Seeff (Newark, Del.: University of Delaware Press, 2000), 161–72, and more extensively in "Francisco Losa and Gregorio López: Spiritual Friendship and Identity Formation on the New Spain Frontier," in Greer and Bilinkoff, *Colonial Saints*, 115–28.

35. Francisco Losa, *La vida que Hizo el Siervo de Dios Gregorio Lopez, en algunas lugares de esta Nueva España* . . . (Mexico City: Juan Ruiz, 1613). For English quotations I use the translation made in Paris, 1638: *The Life of Gregory Lopes that Great Servant of God* . . . This facsimile edition is available as volume 3 in the series *English Recusant Literature, 1558–1640* (Menston, U.K.: Scolar Pres, 1969) 240–42. See also Losa, *Vida*, 1r–v, 4r, 8r–v, 9r–v, 116v–19v; *Life of Gregory Lopes*, 101–2, 165–66. Rubial, noticing how Losa was able to recall specific dates "con gran exactitud," suggests that he carried with him "un diario." Rubial García, *La santidad controvertida*, 101.

36. Luis de la Puente, *Vida maravillosa de la Venerable Virgen Doña Marina de Escobar* . . . (Madrid: Francisco Nieto, 1665); Maria de Lurdes Correia Fernandes, "Uma clarissa ilustre do século XVI: Ana Ponce de León, Condessa de Féria e monja de Santa Clara de Montilla," in *Las Clarisas en España y Portugal, Actas del Congreso Internacional*, ed. José Martí Mayor and María del Mar Graña Cid (Madrid: Archivos e Historia, 1994), 1:331–40; Scattigno, "'Carissimo figuliolo in Cristo,'" 219–20. Timoteo de' Ricci was Caterina's uncle.

37. Bernique, Prólogo, in *Idea de Perfección*; Torres, *[N]oticias*, 6.

38. González Vaquero, *La muger fuerte*, 45v. For the complex interactions between María Vela's various confessors and other clerical authorities, see Susan D. Laningham, "Gender, Body and Authority in a Spanish Convent: The Life and Trials of María Vela y Cueto, 1561–1621" (Ph.D. diss., University of Arkansas, 2001), chap.4.

39. "Dire la qualité de cette vision, si elle fut intellectuelle ou sensible, nous ne le pouvons pas, parce que son directeur le Père Dom Beaucousin était mort, il n'y a plus moyen de le

savoir. . . ." Duval, *La Vie admirable*, 120–21. The translation of this passage is that of Lancelot C. Sheppard in his *Barbe Acarie: Wife and Mystic* (New York: David McKay, 1953), 89–90. Duval did in fact consult previous confessors of Acarie, either in person or through their writings. See, for example, 97–98, 330–43, 365, 421, 509 (Beaucousin, while he was still alive). On Beaucousin and Acarie's circle generally see Barbara B. Diefendorf, *From Penitence to Charity: Pious Women and the Catholic Reformation in Paris* (New York: Oxford University Press, 2004), chap. 3. For other cases of confessor-hagiographers conferring with their predecessors see Ribadeneyra, *Vida de Doña Estefanía*, 2r, 15r; Puccini, *Vita della Veneranda*, 209, 248–49; Ragueneau, *La Vie de la Mere Catherine*, 356–58.

40. "[N]oticias administradoras de testigos de vista y de lo que por palabra y por escrito me ha participado. . . ." Bernique, Prólogo, in *Idea de Perfección*.

41. Losa, *Life of Gregory Lopes*, 141;, see also 111–12, 112–22, 143–49, 220–22, *Vida*, 1r–v, 4r, 8r, 22r; Rubial García, *La santidad controvertida*, 106–7. See also Ribadeneyra, *Vida de Doña Estefanía*, 2r–v, for his interviews with servants in Estefanía Manrique's household.

42. These *attestazioni* are transcribed and reproduced in facsimile in *Tutte le Opere di Santa Maria Maddalena de' Pazzi* (Florence: Centro Internazionale del Libro, 1960–67), 4:300–12, also 3:413ff. The depositions were to serve multiple purposes: to affirm the orthodoxy of Maria Maddalena's pronouncements and set the stage for beatification hearings, as well as to collect information later used in hagiographies.

43. Puccini, *Vita della Veneranda*, 7, 98–99; see also 9, 11, 28, 81. André Duval also collected testimonies from Acarie's convent sisters, although in a much less systematic way. Duval, *La Vie admirable*, 549–59, 580ff.

44. Losa, *Life of Gregory Lopes*, 178–79; see also 272–73; *Vida*, 4r–5r.

45. Bernique, Prólogo, in *Idea de Perfección*; Torres, *[N]oticias*, 117, also 147. For another instance of spiritual letters exchanged between mother and son, see *Marie de l'Incarnation: Entre mère et fils: le dialogue des vocations*, ed. Raymond Brodeur (Montréal: Les Presses de l'Université Laval, 2000).

46. Ribadeneyra, *Vida de Doña Estefanía*, 2r–v, 8v, 11v; *Tesoro del Carmelo escondido*, "Prólogo." The authorship of these poems is apparently in question. See Velasco, *Demons, Nausea, and Resistance*, 7–10. See also 69–79 for discussion of how Isabel, worried that her autobiographical writings could fall into the hands of the Inquisition, handed in each notebook to Paredes for safekeeping as she finished.

Chapter 3. Whose *Life* Is This Anyway?

1. *La Vie de la Venerable Mere Marie de l'Incarnation Premiere Superieur des Ursulines de la Nouvelle France* (Paris, 1677). I have used the facsimile edition produced at Solesmes in 1981. "Il y a plus d'un Autheur; il y en a deux, & l'un & l'autre étoient necessaires pour achever l'Ouvrage. Cette grande Servante de Dieu y a travaillé elle-méme, & son fils y a mis la derniere main, en forte neanmoins qu'il n'y parle que comme un écho qui répond à ce qu'elle dit par ses propres paroles . . ." ii. The translation of the first sentence of this passage is that of Natalie Zemon Davis in *Women on the Margins: Three Seventeenth-Century Lives* (Cambridge, Mass.: Harvard University Press, 1995), 104; the rest of the translation is my own. See also Davis's discussion 103–5.

2. *Vie de la Venerable Mere Marie*, xxxiv; "Car la Vie de cette excellente Religieuse que je donne au public est rare & extraordinaire . . . ," i–ii (emphasis added).

3. However, even this text raises questions of composition and genre. See Elizabeth Rhodes, "What's in a Name: On Teresa of Avila's *Book*," in *The Mystical Gesture: Essays on Medieval and Early Modern Spiritual Culture in Honor of Mary E. Giles*, ed. Robert Boenig (Aldershot,

U.K.: Ashgate, 2000), 79–106; Alison Weber, "The Three Lives of the *Vida:* The Uses of Convent Autobiography," in *Women, Texts and Authority in the Early Modern Spanish World,* ed. Marta V. Vicente and Luis R. Corteguera (Aldershot, U.K.: Ashgate, 2003), 107–25.

4. Thomas F. Mayer and D. R. Woolf discuss "mixtures," "overlaps," and the creation of "hybrid forms" in their introduction to *The Rhetorics of Life-Writing in Early Modern Europe: Forms of Biography from Cassandra Fedele to Louis XIV* (Ann Arbor: University of Michigan Press, 1995), 19. They echo the earlier assessment by Darcy Donahue that "[a]ccounts of the lives and saintly virtues of women religious are a kind of literary hybrid." "Writing Lives: Nuns and Confessors as Auto/Biographers in Early Modern Spain," *Journal of Hispanic Philology* 13 (1989): 231. For a discussion of "cooperative ventures" see Frank Tobin, "Henry Suso and Elsbeth Stagel: Was the *Vita* a Cooperative Effort?" in *Gendered Voices: Medieval Saints and Their Interpreters,* ed. Catherine M. Mooney (Philadelphia: University of Pennsylvania Press, 1999), 118. See also the contribution by Dyan Elliott, "Authorizing a Life: The Collaboration of Dorothea of Montau and John Marienwerder," 168–91; Isabel Barbeito Carneiro refers to the 1693 life of Catalina de Jesús y San Francisco as "una conmovedora combinación bio-autobiográfica" and "una entrañable juego literario" carried out between the holy woman and her biological son in *Mujeres del Madrid barroco: Voces testimoniales* (Madrid: horas y horas, 1992), 87. For "coupures et collages" see Isabelle Poutrin, *Le Voile et la plume: Autobiographie et sainteté féminine dans l'Espagne moderne* (Madrid: Casa de Velázquez, 1995), 269. Poutrin also speaks of "montages," 252, 269, and comments that "[l]e texte des *vies* résulte de multiples compromis entre les lois du genre littéraire . . ." 251.

5. Francisco Márquez Villanueva, "La vocación literaria de Santa Teresa," *Nueva Revista de Filología Hispánica* 32 (1983): 355–79; Rosa Rossi, *Teresa de Avila: Biografía de una escritora* (Barcelona: Icaria, 1984; orig. publ. 1983); Alison Weber, *Teresa of Avila and the Rhetoric of Femininity* (Princeton: Princeton University Press, 1990); Carole Slade, *St. Teresa of Avila: Author of a Heroic Life* (Berkeley: University of California Press, 1995).

6. "[Keeping a spiritual diary as ordered by her confessor] no me es de pequeño tormento, según la adversión que le tengo: y en escrebirle de nuevo me sacrifico, pues es como si saliera al suplicio o estuviera un martirio. No sé como escrebirle, padre mío; levántame esta penitencia y déme otra cualquiera." Quoted in Rodrigo Cánovas, "Ursula Suárez (Monja chilena, 1666–1749): La Autobiografía como penitencia," *Revista Chilena de Literatura* 35 (1990): 97–115; quote at 98. The stated disinclination toward writing did constitute something of a cliché in this period, but this does not mean that individuals did not actually experience these emotions. Suárez, who maintained complicated relations with a series of confessors, has recently begun to receive scholarly attention. See also María Inés Lagos, "Confessing to the Father: Marks of Gender and Class in Ursula Suárez's *Relación,*" *Modern Languages Notes* 110 (1995): 353–84; Kristine Ibsen, *Women's Spiritual Autobiography in Colonial Spanish America* (Gainesville: University Press of Florida, 1999), chap. 6; Kathleen Ann Myers, *Neither Saints Nor Sinners: Writing the Lives of Women in Spanish America* (New York: Oxford University Press, 2003), chap. 5.

7. *Vida de la Venerable Madre Isabel de Iesus, Recoleta Agustina en el Convento de San Juan Bautista de la Villa de Arenas. Dictada por ella misma y Añadido lo que falto de su Dichosa Muerte El P. Fr. Francisco Ignacio, Predicador de la Orden de N.P.S. Agustin, y su Confessor* (Madrid, 1675). This sort of collaboration could take place between male biographers and male subjects as well: thus the lay Jesuit Cristóbal López appended his reminiscences of his mentor Pedro de Ribadeneyra to the latter's autobiography, composed around 1611. See Jodi Bilinkoff, "The Many 'Lives' of Pedro de Ribadeneyra," *Renaissance Quarterly* 52 (1999): 180–96.

8. Elías Gómez Domínguez, *Beata Mariana de Jesús, Mercedaria Madrileña* (Rome: Instituto

Histórico de la Orden de la Merced, 1991). This book includes a transcription of Mariana's spiritual memoir 86–141; I will cite it as *Autobiography*.

9. Gómez Domínguez, *Beata Mariana*, 78–79; "[L]a causa del V.P. Fr. Juan Bautista del SSmo Sacramento . . ." (undated, late 18th century?), Archivo Histórico Nacional, Madrid (AHN), Clero leg. 4093. This document incorrectly lists his birth as 1548; Pedro de San Cecilio, *Annales del Orden de Descalzos de Nuestra Señora de la Merced* . . . (Barcelona, 1669), 1:219–361, for his encounter with the life of Diego Anadón, see 1:1194–96; Gregorio de San Miguel, "La vida del muy Venerable Padre Fr. Joan de S. Joseph" (c. 1638), Biblioteca Nacional, Madrid (BNM), MS 4441 22r–39v; Bruce Taylor, *Structures of Reform: The Mercedarian Order in the Spanish Golden Age* (Leiden: Brill, 2000).

10. Jodi Bilinkoff, "A Saint for a City: Mariana de Jesús and Madrid, 1565–1624," *Archive for Reformation History* 88 (1997): 322–37.

11. *Autobiography*, 87–88: "Toda la historia de la bienaventurada Angela de Foligno, la supo su Confesor, habiéndole oído de su propia boca; a la manera que el Padre Fray Raimundo de Capua, Confesor que fue de la bienaventurada Santa Catalina de Sena, y también, como se escribe la vida y milagros y revelaciones de la Beata Madre Teresa de Jesús . . . y lo mismo se puede referir de otras muchas vidas y revelaciones, especialmente la relación que de su santa vida dio la Venerable Madre Bautista Venancia, Genovesa, a su Confesor . . . [y] lo mismo se ve y leemos en otras muchas Crónicas y Historias." Juan Bautista may be referring to the popular *Vida* of Teresa of Avila by the Jesuit Francisco de Ribera published in Salamanca in 1590, one of several biographies composed by her former confessors. The learned Genoese nun Battista Vernazza, a close associate of Catherine of Genoa, lived from 1497 to 1587. Her *Opere spirituali* were published in Venice in 1588. To a second edition published in Verona in 1602 was appended "la vita della medisima trascritta dal m.r.p.d. Dionisio de Piacenza . . . hor primo dato in luce . . ." See the "Reportorio dei testi a stampa," included in *Donna, disciplina, creanza cristiana dal XV al XVII secolo*, ed. Gabriella Zarri (Rome: Edizioni di Storia e Letteratura, 1996), 693–94.

12. The use of authorizing precedents was quite common among male promoters of charismatic women. See, for example, the introduction to the Castilian edition of Raymond of Capua's biography of Catherine of Siena. This translation, by Antonio de la Peña, a confessor and staunch defender of the controversial *beata* María de Santo Domingo (d. c. 1524), is probably the text referred to by Juan Bautista. *La vida de la bienaventurada sancta Catalina de Sena* (Alcalá de Henares, 1511).

13. Gómez Domínguez, *Beata Mariana*, 78–85, 142–68. On the beatification of Mariana de Jesús see Lara Mary Diefenderfer, "Making and Unmaking Saints in Seventeenth-Century Madrid" (Ph.D. diss., University of Virginia, 2003).

14. Bilinkoff, "A Saint for a City."

15. *Autobiography*, 125

16. Ibid., 130: "[E]l haber yo tomado este trabajo de escribir aquí en suma algo de la vida y mercedes de esta Sierva de Dios ha sido con santos fines de la gloria de Nuestro Señor y ser su confesor también."

17. Ibid. 129: "[P]or ser muy enfermiza y tener muy a menudo grandes enfermedades, y de cincuenta años . . . y también lo digo porque yo que lo escribo soy viejo de sesenta años y dejándose para adelante podría ser no saberse tan gran misericordia."

18. Ibid., 130; text ends abruptly at 141.

19. Ibid, for example, 119, 125.

20. Ibid., 119–20; Carlos M. N. Eire, *From Madrid to Purgatory: The Art and Craft of Dying in Sixteenth-Century Spain* (Cambridge: Cambridge University Press, 1995), esp. bk. 1.

21. *Autobiography*, 124–26, 132. Francisco Ignacio claimed that the prayers of his holy penitent, Isabel de Jesús, brought rain as well. Both Mariana and Isabel lived in central Castile, a region still frequently plagued by drought.

22. Ibid., 98–102, 105, 113–14.

23. Ibid., 121–23. Juan Bautista also underscores Mariana's reception of the eucharist on a frequent, even daily, basis, a hallmark of Mercedarian spirituality in this period.

24. Electa Arenal, "The Convent as Catalyst for Autonomy: Two Hispanic Nuns of the Seventeenth Century," in *Women in Hispanic Literature: Icons and Fallen Idols*, ed. Beth Miller (Berkeley: University of California Press, 1983), 154. For Isabel's rhetorical use of terms such as "pastorcilla," Electa Arenal and Stacey Schlau, *Untold Sisters: Hispanic Nuns in Their Own Works* (Albuquerque: University of New Mexico Press, 1989), 199–200. This book includes excerpts of Isabel's *Life* in Spanish with English translation, 208–27. See also Sonja Herpoel, "L'analphabétisme contre le pouvoir: le témoignage d'Isabel de Jesús," *Bulletin Hispanique* 91 (1989): 395–408.

25. For biographical information see works cited above at note 24 as well as Sonja Herpoel, "Los auditorios de Isabel de Jesús," in *Estudios sobre escritoras hispánicas en honor de Georgina Sabat-Rivers*, ed. Lou Charnon-Deutsch (Madrid: Castalia, 1992), 128–41; Poutrin, *La Voile et la plume*, 312.

26. *Vida de la Venerable Madre Isabel de Iesus*. Francisco supplies a list of the bishops of Avila, clerics, and theologians who approved Isabel's spirit, and with whom he appears to have been familiar, 410–11. Isabelle Poutrin, *La Voile et la plume*, 312, assigns to the friar the family name "del Castillo" without citing sources. This name does not appear in the *Vida* and is not used by other scholars.

27. *Vida*, 157; Arenal and Schlau, *Untold Sisters*, 192–93.

28. *Vida*, 174, 196: "[T]u espiritu sea tan bueno como el de la Santa Madre Teresa de Iesus . . ."

29. Isabel hears God scold her for not obeying him and "manifestar . . . sus misericordias." Ibid., 4. In his unpaginated Prólogo and pages 397–98, Francisco Ignacio describes the process by which Isabel was directed to relate her life by her prioress and several confessors acting on orders from the bishop of Avila.

30. See Arenal and Schlau, *Untold Sisters*, 194–95, for an interesting discussion of the personal and textual relationship that developed between these two nuns. However, I cannot agree with their assertion that as "the transcriber of Isabel's visionary life, [Inés del Sacramento] was privy, in a way the priests and confessors could not be, to Madre Isabel's innermost thoughts and feelings," 194. My study of many cases in which religious women and priests maintain close relationships and reveal to one another their "innermost thoughts and feelings" prevents me from making such a categorical statement.

31. *Vida*, 399–400: "[This is Isabel's book] sin que una palabra se le aya añadido, ni quitado a sus escritos, porque no parecio decente con vana pulidez borrar lo sencillo de su estilo, no entrometer clausulas, explicaciones, ni notas en lo que Dios dicto a una rustica pastorcilla . . ."

32. Ibid., 399: "[L]a dichosa muerte . . . cosas que profetizo en su vida, y milagros que N.S. ha obrado por su medio."

33. Ibid., Prólogo. Arenal and Schlau discuss Isabel's social role as mediator and "neighborhood spiritual advisor," but likewise cite no instances of prophecy. *Untold Sisters*, 206–7. See also Herpoel, "L'analphabétisme," 396.

34. Eugenio Ayape, "Breve Noticia de las Monjas Agustinas Recoletas," *Recollectio* 2 (1979): 333–50. The Arenas house was the fourth convent of Augustinian Recollects to be founded. *Vida*, 121–27, 144–53. Isabel also made some useful connections with the Discalced Franciscan friars in Arenas, for whom she worked voluntarily, and with the uncle of her fellow nun and sec-

retary, Inés del Sacramento, a cleric responsible for issuing licenses to enter religious houses. Arenal, "The Convent as Catalyst," 158–59; Arenal and Schlau, *Untold Sisters,* 194.

35. *Vida,* Prólogo, 410: "[L]as mercedes y regalos que N.S. la hizo en su santa casa . . . la fundacion del Convento de Madres Recoletas de N.P. San Agustin de la Villa de Serradilla por aver profetizado esta Sierva de Dios muchos años antes" (emphasis added).

36. Ibid., 409–10: "Enterraronla con poca assistencia de gente, porque las Religiosas con el ahogo de la pena que les causo faltarles tan gran Sierva de Dios . . . a nadie avisaron, ni a los Religiosos del Convento de nuestro Padre San Agustin de dicha Villa dieron parte, que lo sintieron muchissimo. Recompensoselo Dios a otro dia, y los siguientes, porque acudio mucha gente, no solo de la Villa, sino tambien de la Comarca . . ."

37. Jodi Bilinkoff, *The Avila of Saint Teresa: Religious Reform in a Sixteenth-Century City* (Ithaca: Cornell University Press, 1989), 166–84, 194–96.

38. *Vida,* 211; Arcángel Barrado Manzano, *San Pedro de Alcántara (1499–1562): Estudio documentado y crítico de su vida* (Madrid: Editorial Cisneros, 1965).

39. *La Vie de la Venerable Mere Marie de l'Incarnation,* 736: "Une heure avant sa mort, elle versa trois ou quatre grosses larmes . . . Un peu aprés elle ouvrit doucement les yeux qu'elle avoit tenu fermez depuis quelques heures, comme pour dire le dernier adieu à ses cheres Soeurs . . . , puis elle les referma pour ne les plus ouvrir à la terre ny aux creatures. Enfin sur les six heures du soir . . . jettarit seulement deux petits soûpirs, elle rendit sa belle ame entre les bras de celuy aprés lequel elle avoit soûpiré toute sa vie. . . ."

40. For biographical information see Davis, *Women on the Margins,* 63–102; Anya Mali, *Mystic in the New World: Marie de l'Incarnation (1599–1672)* (Leiden: Brill, 1996); Marie-Florine Bruneau, *Women Mystics Confront the Modern World: Marie de l'Incarnation (1599–1672) and Madame Guyon (1648–1717)* (Albany: State University of New York Press, 1998), 33–122; Dominique Deslandres, "In the Shadow of the Cloister: Representations of Female Holiness in New France," in *Colonial Saints: Discovering the Holy in the Americas, 1500–1800,* ed. Allan Greer and Jodi Bilinkoff (New York: Routledge, 2003), 129–52; Dominique Deslandres, *Croire et faire croire: Les missions françaises au XVIIe siècle (1600–1650)* (Paris: Fayard, 2003), chaps. 23–24.

41. Davis, *Women on the Margins,* 103–7, 128–32; Guy-Marie Oury, *Dom Claude Martin: Le fils de Marie de l'Incarnation* (Solesmes: Abbey de Solesmes, 1983); Dom Chassy, "Recrutement et vocation chez les Bénédictins de St-Maur," in *La vocation religieuse et sacerdotale en France: XVII–XIX Siècles* (Angers: Université d'Angers, 1979), 41–49.

42. Davis, *Women on the Margins,* 103–4; Mali, *Mystic in the New World,* 56–89 (she uses the expression "emotional blackmail," 60); Bruneau, *Women Mystics,* 57–76.

43. John J. Sullivan, trans., *The Autobiography of Venerable Marie of the Incarnation, O.S.U.: Mystic and Missionary* (Chicago: Loyola University Press, 1964). Some selections from Marie's autobiography, as well as other writings, are also available in *Marie of the Incarnation: Selected Writings,* ed. Irene Mahoney (New York: Paulist Press, 1989). The Additions and last four chapters written by Claude Martin have, to my knowledge, never been translated into English.

44. Oury, *Dom Claude Martin,* 175–97; Jacques Lonsagne, "Introduction" to 1981 facsimile edition of *La Vie de la Venerable Mere Marie,* 7–23; Davis, *Women on the Margins,* 128–32. For other examples of editorial interventions in the writings of religious women by their spiritual directors see Julia Boss, "The Life and Death of Mother Marie de Saint Joseph," in *Religions of the United States in Practice,* ed. Colleen McDannell (Princeton: Princeton University Press, 2001) 1: 352; Kathleen A. Myers, "The Mystic Triad in Colonial Mexican Nuns' Discourse: Divine Author, Visionary Scribe, and Clerical Mediator," *Colonial Latin American Historical Review* 6 (1997): 479–524.

45. *Vie de la Venerable Mere Marie*, 725: "Ce n'est pas la Mere de l'Incarnation qui parle; la mort qui impose le silence aux plus grands Saints, luy va fermer la bouche . . ."

46. Ibid., 740: "Mais je dois en raporter icy de plus particuliers . . ." For further use of the term "particulier" and also "détail" see, for example, 748. Martin also intensifies this effect with frequent use of the third person impersonal form, for example, 736: "[C]ar on la vid encore en cet état porter d'une main tremblante son Crucifix à la bouche . . ." ("[O]ne could see her while still in that state [of ecstasy] carry in a trembling hand her crucifix to her mouth . . ."). Only on reflection does the reader realize that the "viewer" in this sentence could not have been Martin himself. For other examples of this sort, 727, 729, 731, 739.

47. Ibid., 740–44; for transcribed letter, 730: "[M]ais plûtot celles qui l'assistoient remarquoient . . ." See 733 for Jesuit *Relations*.

48. Ibid., for example, 727, 737, 745 (quotes from letter sent by Ursulines in Canada to the Jesuit Paul Ragueneau), 755: "[C]et écrit est tombé entre mes mains . . ."

49. Ibid., 751; "Je vous estime heureux, dit elle, de luy estre ce que vous êtes." Others may have been more reluctant informants. Martin quotes from a French nun "qui ne desire pas que son nom paroisse icy" ("who does not wish that her name appear here"). Oury, *Dom Claude Martin*, 176–77, states that Martin compiled "dossiers" of the materials sent to him by people with whom he corresponded.

50. *Vie de la Venerable Mere Marie*, 749–51.

51. Ibid., for example, 727, 757.

52. Ibid., 748, 753: "[U]ne sainte Thecle, dans le zele de la foy & de la conversion des infideles . . . une sainte Monique, dans les travaux où elle s'est exposée pour gagner à Dieu un fils qui étoit dans l'égarement . . ." Martin also includes saints Gertrude and "Leudivige" (Lidwige of Schiedam) in this list of holy predecessors. The reference to Augustine obviously held personal significance for Martin: interestingly, at the time he was preparing the *Vie* he was also supervising the Maurist edition of the church father's works. Oury, *Dom Claude Martin*, 153–74; Davis, *Women on the Margins*, 129–30. There were at least two other cases of clerical sons who wrote the lives of their exemplary mothers; both similarly made references to the Augustine-Monica relationship. Marcos Torres, *Noticias . . . de la vida y virtudes . . . de Da. María de Pol, su madre* (Málaga? 1660), 4–5, 100–105, 113; Juan Bernique, *Idea de Perfección, y Virtudes. Vida de . . . Catalina de Jesús y San Francisco* (Alcalá de Henares, 1693), prologue, 397–98.

53. *Vie de la Venerable Mere Marie*, 748: "Je passe sous silence les excessives penitences & mortifications . . . Je ne parlaray point pareillement de ses communications & unions intimes avec sa divine Majesté . . . Je laisse à parler plus en détail de ses graces gratuites . . ." See also 733, 749, 751. My thanks to Marjorie Woods for explaining this rhetorical device. For general discussion of Martin's style and concern for "politesse," see Davis, *Women on the Margins*, 128–32; Lonsagne, "Introduction," 11–14.

54. *Vie de la Venerable Mere Marie*, 744–45: "Il est vray qu'il n'appartient qu'au Vicaire de Jesus-Christ, de donner aux défunts le nom de saint par une declaration solemnelle & autentique que l'on appelle canonization, & que nul autre n'a le pouvoir de les declarer tels . . . qui puissent attirer la veneration publique des fideles." These procedures were institutionalized during the pontificate of Urban VIII (1623–44), the very years of Claude Martin's education and entrance into the priesthood. Kenneth L. Woodward, *Making Saints: How the Catholic Church Determines Who Becomes a Saint, Who Doesn't, and Why* (New York: Simon and Schuster, 1990) chap.2. Hereafter hagiographers often felt obliged to include a disclaimer of the sort offered by the Jesuit Pierre Champion: "And now, that I may comply with the decrees of Urban VIII and other Sovereign Pontiffs, I protest that as regards the Life of Fr. [Louis] Lallemant I ask from the reader but a human faith; and that in speaking of this Father as a

saintly man, I in no wise pretend to invest him with a title which it belongs only to the Apostolic See to give to those whom it judges worthy of it." *The Spiritual Doctrine of Father Louis Lallemant* (Westminster, Md.: The Newman Book Shop, 1946; orig. publ. 1694), viii.

55. *Vie de la Venerable Mere Marie*, 740–57. For a case study of canonization in the early modern period see Gillian T. W. Ahlgren, *Teresa of Avila and the Politics of Sanctity* (Ithaca: Cornell University Press, 1996), 148–56.

56. *Vie de la Venerable Mere Marie*, 756–57: "S'il est permis de juger de sa gloire par les vertus qu'elle a pratiquées, & de sa recompense par les services qu'elle a rendus à Dieu; l'on ne peut douter qu'elle ne soit élevée à un tres haut degré, & que sa recompense ne luy ait été donnée à la mesure des plus grands Saints . . . qu'il seroit difficile de trouver un moment en sa vie qui ait été vuide de merite." This ringing proclamation seems very poignant given that Marie de l'Incarnation was not declared Venerable until 1911 and Blessed until 1980. Despite the efforts of her many devotees, she has yet to attain the status of saint. Interestingly, Claude Martin acquired a reputation for holiness among his fellow French Benedictines and himself became the subject of hagiographical treatment. Edmond Martene, *La Vie du venerable pere Dom Claude Martin, religieux benedictin de la Congregation de S. Maur; Decedé en odeur de sainteté au Monastere de Mairmontier, le 9 du mois d'Aoust 1696* (Tours, 1697).

57. *The Life of the Holy and Venerable Mother Suor Maria Maddalena de Patsi . . . written in Italian by . . . Vincentio Puccini* (Cologne? 1619; facsimile edition, Menston, U.K.: Scolar Press, 1970), preface. This case offers another fascinating example of collaboration and genre-mixing, with Maria Maddalena, a team of nuns from her convent, and various clerics all participating in the production of this text. For the process of composition see the Introduction by Ermanno de SSmo Sacramento to *Tutte le Opere di Santa Maria Maddalena de'Pazzi* (Florence: Il Centro Internazionale del Libro, 1960), 1:39–63; Anna Scattigno, "Maria Maddalena de' Pazzi tra esperienza e modello," in Zarri, *Donna, disciplina,* 85–101. For analyses of her language see Giovanni Pozzi, *Le parole dell'estasi* (Milan: Adelphi, 1984); Armando Maggi, *Uttering the Word: The Mystical Performances of Maria Maddalena de' Pazzi, a Renaissance Visionary* (Albany: State University of New York Press, 1998).

58. Davis, *Women on the Margins*, 129–31; for a discussion of Jansenism see 113–14. The Spanish Jesuit Pedro de Ribadeneyra (1526–1611) was likewise concerned to disassociate his subject, a pious noblewoman, from the many suspicious *beatas* of her day and only cautiously cited prayers she had composed. See his "Vida de Doña Estefanía Manrique de Castilla" (c. 1606), Biblioteca Nacional, Madrid (BNM), MS 7421.

59. Poutrin, *La Voile et la plume*, 269–73.

60. Karen-Edis Barzman, "Gender, Religious Representation and Cultural Production in Early Modern Italy," in *Gender and Society in Renaissance Italy*, ed. Judith C. Brown and Robert C. Davis (London: Longman, 1998), 229–30. See also Ahlgren, *Politics of Sanctity*, 156–63; Donahue, "Writing Lives," 231–32; Kathleen Ann Myers, "Sor Juana y su mundo: La influencia mediativa del clero en las 'Vidas' de religiosos y monjas," *Revista de Literatura* 61 (1999): 35–59, and a thoughtful analysis by Asunción Lavrin, "La vida femenina como experiencia religiosa: biografía y hagiografía en Hispanoamérica colonial," *Colonial Latin American Review* 2 (1993): 27–51.

61. This concept was first developed by Sandra M. Gilbert and Susan Gubar in *The Madwoman in the Attic: The Woman Writer and the Nineteenth-Century Literary Imagination* (New Haven: Yale University Press, 1979). It has been applied more recently to the authorial activities of early-modern Hispanic nuns. See Arenal and Schlau, *Untold Sisters*, 7, 14; Alison Weber, "On the Margins of Ecstasy: María de San José as (Auto)Biographer," *Journal of the Institute of Romance Studies* 4 (1996): 251–68.

62. Quoted in Sullivan, *The Autobiography of Venerable Marie of the Incarnation*, 191. Charlevoix's *Vie de la Mère de l'Incarnation, institutrice & première superieure des Ursulines de la Nouvelle France* was published in Paris in 1724. For feelings of inadequacy and envy expressed by clerical promoters of holy women during the Middle Ages see John Coakley, "Friars as Confidants of Holy Women in Medieval Dominican Hagiography," in *Images of Sainthood in Medieval Europe*, ed. Renate Blumenfeld-Kosinski and Timea Szell (Ithaca: Cornell University Press, 1991), 222–46; John Coakley, "Gender and the Authority of Friars: The Significance of Holy Women for Thirteenth-Century Franciscans and Dominicans," *Church History* 60 (1991): 445–60.

63. For background see Bilinkoff, *Avila*, 184–99.

64. The relationship between María Vela and Miguel González Vaquero and the priest's style of spiritual direction are treated briefly in Jodi Bilinkoff, "Confessors, Penitents, and the Construction of Identities in Early Modern Avila," in *Culture and Identity in Early Modern Europe (1500–1800): Essays in Honor of Natalie Zemon Davis*, ed. Barbara B. Diefendorf and Carla Hesse (Ann Arbor: University of Michigan Press, 1993) 83–100. See also Donahue, "Writing Lives," 230–39; Poutrin, *La Voile et la plume*, 81–83. For a more detailed and nuanced analysis, Susan D. Laningham, "Gender, Body and Authority in a Spanish Convent: The Life and Trials of María Vela y Cueto, 1561–1621" (Ph.D. diss., University of Arkansas, 2001).

65. For the publication history of *La Muger Fuerte* and María Vela's writings see Poutrin, *La Voile et la plume*, 424, 442–43; Introduction by Olegario González Hernández to Doña María Vela y Cueto, *Autobiografía y Libro de las Mercedes* (Barcelona: Juan Flors, 1961); Introduction by Frances Parkinson Keyes to *The Third Mystic of Avila: The Self-Revelation of María Vela, a Sixteenth-Century Spanish Nun* (New York: Farrar, Straus and Cudahy, 1960). For letters exchanged between María Vela and her two brothers see Susan Laningham, "Making a Saint out of a Sibling," in *Thicker than Water: Sisters and Brothers in the Early Modern World*, ed. Naomi Yavneh and Naomi Miller (Aldershot, U.K.: Ashgate Press, forthcoming).

66. *La Muger Fuerte, Por Otro Titulo, La Vida de Doña María Vela . . . Escrita por el Doctor Miguel González Vaquero su Confessor . . .* (Madrid, 1674; 1st ed. 1618), 139r, 141v.

67. *Muger Fuerte*, 17v–18r: "Hasta aqui son palabras suyas, y salió tan bien con la doctrina, que no solo vivia olvidada de todo lo de la tierra, sino de si misma . . . Muchas vezes estava yo mirando en mi interior esto que voy escriviendo . . ." See also 31v, 56r–v, 119v. A similar case is that of the *Vida* of Doña Ana Ponce de León (in religion Ana de la Cruz) published by Martín de Roa in 1604. Ana's confessors had ordered her to keep a written record of the "particulares regalos" and "sentimientos espirituales" she had received from God; Roa then transcribed these first-person accounts in his biography. See Maria de Lurdes Correia Fernandes, "Uma Clarissa Ilustre do Século XVI: Ana Ponce de León, Condessa de Féria e Monja de Santa Clara de Montilla," in *Las Clarisas en España y Portugal, Actas del Congreso Internacional*, ed. José Martí Mayor and María del Mar Graña Cid (Madrid: Archivos e Historia, 1994). 1: 331–40.

68. Ibid., 43v: "El P. Salzedo la mandó . . . que escriviesse todas las mercedes sobrenaturales de revelaciones que nuestro Señor la avia hecho y las que fuesse recibiendo, cuyos originales tengo yo en mi poder, y dellos voy sacando para esta historia."

69. Ibid., 14v–15r, 43v, 53v, 58r–v, 194r. For Vaquero's use of letters to and by María Vela and other sources see, for example, 12r, 50v–51r, 136v–138v, 175v–176r. For his orders to her to write her *Vida*, 56r–v, 138v. The stated intention of religious women (and sometimes men) of burning their writings, of course, constituted something of a topos in this period.

70. Vaquero insists upon his penitent's exemplary humility—for example, ibid. 134v, 161v, 175v–176r—and reinforces this with terms such as "muestra" or "prueba" (demonstration, proof).

This was in fact a controversial point during María's lifetime, with many accusing her of pride and exhibitionism.

71. He recounts many of their conversations and personal encounters, for example, ibid. 18v–19r, 134v, 193v, 194v. In his *Life* of Catherine de Saint Augustin (discussed in note 75), Paul Ragueneau stresses that "she kept secret the ways with which God treated her and declared them only to those whose duty it was to know" ("Elle tient secretes les voyes de Dieu sur elle & ne les declaré qu'à ceux qui les doivent sçavoir") (notably Ragueneau himself), 332.

72. Guy-Marie Oury, *L'Itineraire Mystique de Catherine de Saint-Augustin* (Solesmes: Abbey de Solesmes, 1985), 8–9.

73. Jacques Bigot, *La Vie du Pere Paul Ragueneau de la Compagnie de Iesus Missionnaire du Canada* (undated, c. 1700). I have used the modern critical edition prepared by Guy Laflèche (Montreal: VLB, 1979); see also Laflèche's helpful introduction and appendices; Oury, *L'Itineraire*, 15–17.

74. Besides the biography by Oury, see Leslie Choquette's brief treatment of Catherine in "'Ces Amazones du Grand Dieu': Women and Mission in Seventeenth-Century Canada," *French Historical Studies* 17 (1992): 628–55; Allan Greer, "Colonial Saints: Gender, Race, and Hagiography in New France," *William and Mary Quarterly*, 3d ser., 57 (2000): 323–48; Jodi Bilinkoff, "Navigating the Waves (of Devotion): Toward a Gendered Analysis of Early Modern Catholicism," in *Crossing Boundaries: Attending to Early Modern Women*, ed. Jane Donawerth and Adele Seeff (Newark, Del.: University of Delaware Press, 2000), 161–72; Deslandres, "In the Shadow of the Cloister;" Deslandres, *Croire et faire croire*.

75. Paul Ragueneau, *La Vie de la Mere Catherine de Saint Augustin, Religieuse Hospitaliere de la Misericorde de Quebec en la Nouvelle-France* (Paris, 1671). I have used Microfiche #50849 produced by the CIHM/ICHM of Canada. My sincere thanks to the staff of Jackson Library at the University of North Carolina at Greensboro for locating and acquiring this microfiche for me, and to the National Humanities Center for assisting me in printing it out. The book was translated into Italian in the mid-eighteenth century. During the years that Ragueneau was back in France (1662–68) Catherine sent him yearly reports of the state of her soul. *Vie de la Mere Catherine*, 365–69.

76. *Vie de la Mere Catherine*, 1: "Cette Vie est composée presque toute entiere sur un journal, pris de certains papiers que ses Directeurs & Confesseurs luy avoient commandé d'écrire . . ." He reiterates this information throughout the text. See, for example, 72–74, 112, 303–6, 365–69. Oury describes the book as more of a collection of documents than a biography proper ("un recueil documentaire, plus qu'une biographie") and estimates that out of a total of 227 pages, 161 are made up entirely or in part of Catherine's own writings. *L'Itineraire*, 22; see also his comments at 148, 200. I am not sure to which edition Oury is referring, as the one I have consulted contains a total of 384 pages, but certainly his point about proportions is well taken.

77. For the composition of Catherine's *Journal* and Ragueneau's methods of editing see Oury, *L'Itineraire*, 10–13. He describes the *Journal* as a group of dated autobiographical fragments ("fragments autobiographiques datés"), 186. Ragueneau refers to his own editorial interventions on occasion; see, for example, *Vie de la Mere Catherine*, 9, 102–12, 350.

78. For a few cases in which Ragueneau makes comments on Catherine's words see ibid., 50–51, 105. See also Oury, *L'Itineraire*, 18.

79. *Vie de la Mere Catherine*, 136. Catherine's modern biographer, the Benedictine Guy-Marie Oury, concurs with this assessment, commmenting that "the quality of her description is astonishing" ("la qualité de la description est étonnante"). *L'Itineraire*, 120.

80. *Vie de la Mere Catherine*, 152. Note that Ragueneau includes himself within this listening audience.

81. Ibid., 364. Ragueneau reminds his readers of Catherine's youth throughout the text. This is a sentiment shared by Oury, who also makes numerous references to "the young nun" or "young nursing sister" and at times uses rather cloying and (probably unconsciously) condescending diminutive forms such as "cette petite soeur" (115) and "la petite religieuse" (169).

82. *Vie de la Mere Catherine*, 64: "Voicy une Histoire bien remarquable qu'elle écrit elle méme dans son Journal"; 89: "C'est le recit qu'elle en fait elle-méme."

83. At least fourteen chapters of the *Vie* are devoted wholly or in part to these topics. Ragueneau, however, never uses the term "possession" when referring to Catherine's many encounters with demons, preferring to make the theological distinction and speak instead of "obsession"; for example, 165, 170–75. Oury, *Itineraire*, 12, 179. There is a sizable literature on possession cases in early-modern France, particularly among nuns. See, for example, Moshe Sluhovsky, "A Divine Apparition or Demonic Possession? Female Agency and Church Authority in Demonic Possession in Sixteenth-Century France," *Sixteenth Century Journal* 27 (1996): 1036–52; Sluhovsky, "The Devil in the Convent," *American Historical Review* 107, no. 5 (2002): 1379–1411; Michel de Certeau, *The Possession at Loudon* (Chicago: University of Chicago Press, 2000; orig. publ. 1970).

84. *Vie de la Mere Catherine*, 369, "L'année suivante 1656 le méme Pere écrit encore assez amplement sur le mesme sujet. Je n'en mettray icy qu'une petite partie."

85. Ibid., 364: "Le Pere Ragueneau Jesuite étant descendu de la Mission des Hurons en l'année 1650, ne fut pas si-tôt arrivé à Quebec, qu'il se trouva engagé a prendre la direction de cette sainte Epouse de Jesus-Christ . . . il a eu le soin de sa conduite douze ans de suitte étant sur les lieux; & ayant été obligé de revenir en France en 1662 il a toûjours sceu du depuis par les Lettres qu'elle luy en écrivit jusques à la mort, tout son interieur."

86. Ibid., 352: "Ie ne puis plus fidelement rapporter icy les circonstances de sa Mort, qu'en les prenant de la lettre circulaire qu'en écrivit la Reverende Mere Marie de Saint Bonaventure de Iesus sa Superieure . . . Voicy comme elle en parle."

87. Ibid., no page number: "[J]e ne pouvois refuser à l'édification du public & à la consolation des bonnes ames, l'exemple d'une vie & d'une mort aussi pure & aussi precieuse devant Dieu, qu'est celle cy; dont j'ay été témoin à ma grande consolation l'espace de dix-huit ans, que Dieu m'a fait la grace de recevoir les communications qu'elle me donnoit par elle-méme de tout ce qui se passoit dans le plus secret de son ame, dont je benissois Dieu qui vraiement est admirable dans ses Saints."

88. Oury, *L'Itineraire*, 9, 23.

89. Ragueneau's account of the martyrdom of Brébeuf and other Jesuits in the *Relations* is available in English. See *Heroes of Huronia*, trans. Joseph Fallon (Fort Ste Marie, Ontario: The Martyrs Shrine, 1948). He retells the story in the *Vie de la Mere Catherine*, 170–82, one of the few places in the text where he speaks in a strong, authoritative narrative voice. He makes references to Brébeuf's relics, 361–62. For the literature of martyrdom and the uses of relics see Greer "Colonial Saints;" Julia Boss, "Writing a Relic: The Uses of Hagiography in New France," in Greer and Bilinkoff, *Colonial Saints*, 211–33.

90. Brébeuf was a native of Bayeux, the city in which Catherine made her religious profession, Oury, *L'Itineraire*, 152–54. For Catherine's mystical reception of the eucharist from Brébeuf see, for example, *Vie de la Mere Catherine*, 191. This motif goes way back in the history of Christian female mysticism. See Caroline W. Bynum, *Holy Feast and Holy Fast: The Religious Significance of Food to Medieval Women* (Berkeley: University of California Press, 1987), 48–69. Catherine did, of course, have a "real" confessor after Ragueneau's departure for France, the Jesuit Pierre Chatelain. She speaks warmly of Chatelain in the Journal entries transcribed in the *Vie*, and the priest provided Ragueneau with written documents and his own oral testimony after the nun's death.

91. *Vie de la Mere Catherine*, 115–18, 132–54, 182–218, 229–35, 247–99, 309–36, 343–52. Brébeuf is also mentioned in testimonies after Catherine's death, 382–83.

92. Jean de Brébeuf and the other Jesuit martyrs were finally beatified in 1925, canonized in 1930, and declared patron saints of Canada in 1940. Catherine de Saint Augustin was herself beatified in 1989.

93. *Vie de la Mere Catherine*, 384.

Chapter 4. Soul Mates

1. Two classic works that treat these issues for the early Christian period are Rosemary R. Ruether, "Misogynism and Virginal Feminism in the Fathers of the Church," in *Religion and Sexism: Images of Woman in the Jewish and Christian Traditions*, ed. Rosemary Radford Reuther (New York: Simon and Schuster, 1974), 150–83, and Elizabeth A. Clark, *Jerome, Chrysostom and Friends: Essays and Translations* (New York: Edwin Mellen Press, 1979), esp. pt. 2. Useful overviews that survey the whole Christian tradition may be found in Wendy M. Wright, *Bond of Perfection: Jeanne de Chantal and François de Sales* (New York: Paulist Press, 1985), 3–31, 104–17, and Patricia Ranft, *A Woman's Way: The Forgotten History of Women Spiritual Directors* (New York: Palgrave, 2000). There are numerous studies of friendship in the works and life experiences of particular Christian writers.

2. See, for example, R. Po-Chia Hsia, *The World of Catholic Renewal, 1540–1770* (Cambridge: Cambridge University Press) 198–200; Robin Briggs, *Communities of Belief: Cultural and Social Tensions in Early Modern France* (Oxford: Oxford University Press, 1989), chap.7.

3. *The Book of her Life*, 5:3, in *The Collected Works of St. Teresa of Avila*, trans. Kieran Kavanaugh and Otilio Rodríguez (Washington, D.C.: Institute of Carmelite Studies, 1976),1:46. See also 23:13–18, 24:1–5, 25:14–18, 26:3–4. and 30:13. For Spanish texts I have consulted Santa Teresa de Jesús, *Obras completas*, ed. Efrén de la Madre de Dios and Otger Steggink (Madrid: Editorial Católica, 1977).

4. *The Way of Perfection* 4:13, in *Collected Works*, 2:57. See also 4:14–16, 5:1–2. The right of Discalced Carmelite nuns to choose and change their confessors would come under attack after Teresa's death. Alison Weber, "Spiritual Administration: Gender and Discernment in the Carmelite Reform," *Sixteenth Century Journal* 31, no. 1 (2000): 123–46. See also Weber's introduction to María de San José, *For the Hour of Recreation*, trans. Amanda Powell (Chicago: University of Chicago Press, 2002). For the situation among various religious orders in Spain see Isabelle Poutrin, *Le voile et la plume: Autobiographie et sainteté féminine dans l'Espagne moderne* (Madrid: Casa de Velázquez, 1995), 115–19.

5. *The Autobiography of Saint Margaret Mary Alacoque*, trans. Sisters of the Visitation, Partridge Green (Rockford, Ill.: Tan Publishers, 1986), 77. "Et ma douleur était qu'au lieu de me retirer de la tromperie où je croyais d'être effectivement, ils m'y renfonçaient encore plus avant, tant mes confesseurs que les autres . . ." *Vie de Sainte Marguerite-Marie Alacoque ecrite par elle-même* (Paris: Gigord, 1934; orig. completed 1685), 84.

6. *The Third Mystic of Avila: The Self Revelation of María Vela, a Sixteenth Century Spanish Nun*, trans. Frances Parkinson Keyes (New York: Farrar, Straus and Cudahy, 1960), 86. This is a somewhat loose translation of the Spanish but accurately conveys the sense of María's narrative up to this point. The original text reads: "[Y] yo quedé tan cansada de Padres que no quise hablar en más." Doña María Vela y Cueto, *Autobiografía y Libro de las mercedes*, ed. Olegario González Hernández (Barcelona: Juan Flors, 1961), 352. For examples of Spanish American nuns and their difficulties with confessors see Kristine Ibsen, *Women's Spiritual Autobiography in Colonial Spanish America* (Gainesville: University Press of Florida, 1999), 28–32.

7. "Después que vine a la ciudad de Avila me confesé sana cuantas veces podía, y tenía cansados algunos conventos con mis importunos y prolijos ruegos que me confesasen." "Información

de la vida, muerte, y milagros de la Venerable María Díaz (c. 1600–23)," Avila, Archivo
Diocesano, códice 3.345. See also Gerardo de S. Juan de la Cruz, "María Díaz, llamada 'La esposa del Santísimo Sacramento,'" *El Monte Carmelo* 17 (1915): 166–70; Jodi Bilinkoff, *The
Avila of Saint Teresa: Religious Reform in a Sixteenth-Century City* (Ithaca: Cornell University Press, 1989), 96–106.

8. "No te canses, que yo seré tu maestro." Quoted in Una Carmelita Descalza del Convento de
Santiago, *Una mística gallega en el siglo XVIII: La Venerable Madre María Antonia de Jesús* (La
Coruña: Galicia Editorial, 1991), 57. This echoes the famous experience of Teresa of Avila,
who heard God tell her "Don't be sad, for I shall give you a living book." *Book of Her Life*
26:5. Teresa's writings would heavily influence María Antonia. After she was widowed the
gallega became a nun in the order founded by Teresa.

9. *Mística gallega*, 67–72. Some of her letters to Castro have been transcribed in an appendix,
309–18. See also the "Relación de los padres y directores espirituales con quienes se confesó
y comulgó la Madre María Antonia de Jesús" that a later confessor ordered the nun to compose. The text is included in María Antonia de Jesús, *Edificio espiritual* (Santiago de Compostela: Bibliófilos Gallegos, 1954), 29–39.

10. Other cases include María Quintana (1648–1734), María-Helena Sánchez Ortega, *Confesión
y trayectoria femenina: Vida de la Venerable Quintana* (Madrid: CSIC, 1996), 240–41, 248–50;
Isabel de Jesús (1586–1648), *Vida de la Venerable Madre Isabel de Iesus, Recoleta Agustina . . .*
(Madrid: Viuda de Francisco Nieto, 1675), 53, 58, 157–74); Barbe Acarie (1566–1618), who,
while still a devout married woman, both toured various religious houses in Paris and invited
clerics to her home, André Duval, *La vie admirable de la Bienheureuse Soeur Marie de l'Incarnation . . .* (Paris: Librairie Victor Lecoffre, 1893; orig. publ. 1621) 102ff; Lancelot C. Sheppard, *Barbe Acarie, Wife and Mystic* (New York: David McKay, 1953), 65–81; and Catalina de
Jesús y San Franciso (1639–77), Juan Bernique, *Idea de perfección, y virtudes. Vida de . . .
Catalina de Jesús y San Francisco . . .* (Alcalá de Henares: Francisco García Fernández, 1693),
55–62. This chapter is entitled "Busca confesor a quien entregar la nave de su conciencia para
la dirección y govierno de su espiritu."

11. Pedro de San Cecilio, *Anales del Orden de Descalzos de Nuestra Señora de la Merced . . .*
(Barcelona, 1669), 1:233–34.

12. "Dieu fait des graces à qui il veut, & quand il veut, & si quelquefois il se fait voir aux femmes
plûtôt qu'aux hommes, c'est souvent un manquement d'humilité en nous . . ." Paul Ragueneau, *La vie de la Mere Catherine de Saint Augustin . . .* (Paris, Florentin Lambert, 1671), 10–
15; quote at 11. Similar points were made by supporters of María de Santo Domingo (d. c.
1524). Jodi Bilinkoff, "Establishing Authority: A Peasant Visionary and Her Audience in Early
Sixteenth-Century Spain," *Studia Mystica* 18 (1997): 49–52.

13. Coakley develops this theme in several essays—for example, "Friars, Sanctity, and Gender:
Mendicant Encounters with Saints, 1250–1325," in *Medieval Masculinities: Regarding Men in
the Middle Ages*, ed. Clare A. Lees (Minneapolis: University of Minnesota Press, 1994), 91–
110—and in his book *Draw Me After You: Clerics and Holy Women, 1150–1400* (New York:
Columbia University Press, forthcoming).

14. Luisa Ciammitti, "One Saint Less: The Story of Angela Mellini, a Bolognese Seamstress
(1667–17[?])," in *Sex and Gender in Historical Perspective*, ed. Edward Muir and Guido Ruggiero (Baltimore, Md.: Johns Hopkins University Press, 1990; orig. essay publ. 1979), 141–
76. The Poor Clare Battista da Varano reported that Fra Pietro da Mogliano was initially "inspired" to hear her confession; they subsequently maintained a close relationship. Battista da
Varano, *My Spiritual Life*, trans. Joseph Berrigan (Toronto: Peregrina Publishing, 1986; orig.
publ. 1491), 46–48.

15. "Dia da Conceição foi o primeiro em que me confessou e logo senti desusados efeitos, assim na comoção interior e abalo com as suas palavras, como na confiança com que lhe descobri minhas misérias, que conforme o meu génio foi coisa bem sobrenatural . . . quisesse ele pelo amor de Deus ser guia de minha alma, a que ele respondeu que o mesmo desejava de me pedir." Antónia Margarida de Castelo Branco, *Autobiografia, 1652–1717*, ed. João Palma-Ferreira (Lisbon: Imprensa Nacional, 1983), 184. This passage comes from a chapter titled "Deu-me Deus Padre espiritual e do que por ordem sua obrei."

16. Luis de la Puente, *Vida del Padre Baltasar Alvarez* (Madrid, 1615), 39v. Alvarez was a native of Alhama, near Granada.

17. Benjamin A. Ehlers, "Christians and Muslims in Valencia: The Archbishop Juan de Ribera (1532–1611) and the Formation of a 'Communitas Christiana'" (Ph.D. diss., Johns Hopkins University, 1999), 97–103; quotes at 97, 103; Ehlers, "Catholic Reform as Process: The Archbishop Juan de Ribera (1532–1611) and the Colegio de Corpus Christi, Valencia," *Archive for Reformation History* 95 (2004): 186–209. See also Francisco Pons Fuster, *Místicos, beatas y alumbrados: Ribera y la espiritualidad valenciana del s. XVII* (Valencia: Institució Valenciana D'Estudis i Investigació, 1991), 143–75. After Agullona's death Ribera commissioned his own confessor to write the *beata's* life and wrote an introduction for the book. Jaime Sanchis, *La venerable setabense Margarita Agullona Terciaria Franciscana* (Valencia, 1607). My thanks to Benjamin Ehlers for providing me with this reference.

18. "Pues digo que el primer día que hablé a V.M. me cuadró tanto su espíritu y quedé con una satisfacción y dilatación de corazón, que no me conocía, por haber hallado lo que yo tanto deseaba, que era topar con alguna persona que tuviese experiencia de este trato interior y oración sobrenatural . . ." Vela, *Autobiografía*, 355. This is my translation; the one offered by Keyes in *Third Mystic*, 91, while more tepid, still carries an erotic charge.

19. "[F]ue la primera vez que hablé con nuestra Santa y aunque avia tratado almas muy aventajadas hallé aquí tanto que me causó notable confusión . . . el modo de hablar, tan humilde y sinzero, tan lleno de amor de Dios y tan assentada virtud . . . pareciendome que se le avian de seguir a mi alma muchas ganancias . . ." Miguel González Vaquero, *La muger fuerte, por otro titulo, La vida de Doña María Vela . . .* (Madrid, 1674; 1st ed., 1618), 141r–v.

20. Mary Luti, "'A Marriage Well Arranged': Teresa of Avila and Fray Jerónimo Gracián de la Madre de Dios," *Studia Mystica* 12 (1989): 32–46; quotes at 34–35. Gracián used similarly emotional language when recalling his "íntima amistad" with Teresa in the autobiography he composed in dialogue form around 1609. Jerónimo Gracián de la Madre de Dios, *Peregrinación de Anastasio*, ed. Giovanni Maria Bertini (Barcelona: Juan Flors, 1966), 266–67. Earlier in her life Teresa had been quite fond of a Dominican confessor, García de Toledo. After the friar asked her to commend him in her prayers, Teresa beseeched "'Lord, You must not deny me this favor,'" adding, "'See how this individual is fit to be our friend.'" *Book of Her Life* 34: 6–8.

21. Quoted in Jesús G. Lunas Almeida, *La historia del señorío de Valdecorneja en la parte referente a Piedrahita* (Avila: Senén Martín, 1930), 175. Jodi Bilinkoff, "Charisma and Controversy: The Case of María de Santo Domingo," in *Spanish Women in the Golden Age: Images and Realities*, ed. Magdalena S. Sánchez and Alain Saint-Saëns (Westport, Conn.: Greenwood Press, 1996), 23–35.

22. Other cases of women and priests conversing while traveling include Barbe Acarie and André Duval and Jeanne de Chantal and François de Sales. See, for example, Duval, *Vie admirable*, 31; Wright, *Bond of Perfection*, 53–54.

23. *Mística gallega*, 113–14, 121–22. Priests sometimes reported premonitions too. When Jacques Gallemant was nine or ten years old, he had a chance encounter with a little girl of about four.

He heard an interior voice assure him of her future saintliness and "put that beautiful soul in his charge." When, twenty-seven years later, he met Barbe Acarie, he immediately recognized her as the "beautiful soul," and she recognized him as "the one through whom God would teach her the true way." Gallemant eventually became one of Acarie's spiritual directors and helpers in her mission to bring the Discalced Carmelite order to France. Placide Gallemant, *La vie du venerable prestre de J.C. Jacques Gallemant* . . . (Paris, 1663), 15–16, 51–52. My thanks to Barbara Diefendorf for providing me with this anecdote.

24. *The Letters of St. Margaret Mary Alacoque,* trans. Clarence A. Herbst (Rockford, Ill.: Tan Books, 1997), 212; *Autobiography of Saint Margaret Mary Alacoque,* 93; "Et lorsque ce saint homme vint ici, comme il parlait à la Communauté, j'etendis intérieurement ces paroles: 'Voilà celui que je t'envoie.'" *Vie de Sainte Marguerite-Marie Alacoque,* 107. Georges Guitton, *Perfect Friend: The Life of Blessed Claude La Colombière, S.J. (1641–1682),* trans. William J. Young (St. Louis: B. Herder, 1956), 133–44. María Vela first met, then received divine endorsement of, her new confessor, Miguel González Vaquero. When she asked in prayer whether she should offer the priest her special obedience, she heard God reply with a scriptural quotation: "This is my beloved Son, in whom I am well pleased: hear ye him" (Matthew 17:5), words she understood to refer to Vaquero. *Autobiografía,* 355; *Third Mystic,* 92.

25. Wright, *Bond of Perfection,* 34.

26. Ibid., 34–36. "Dieu, ce me semble, m'a donné à vous; je m'en assure toutes les heures plus fort. C'est tout ce que je vous puis dire; recommandez-moi à votre bon Ange." François de Sales, *Correspondance: Les lettres d'amitié spirituelle,* ed. André Ravier (Paris: Desclée de Brouwer, 1980), 153.

27. Wright, *Bond of Perfection,* 122. See also Wright's analysis of Sales's language and theology, 117–27. Unfortunately, most of Chantal's letters to Sales are no longer extant. "[D]ès le commencement que vous conférâtes avec moi de votre intérieur Dieu me donna un grand amour de votre esprit. Quand vous vous déclarâtes à moi plus particulièrement, ce fut un lien admirable à mon âme pour chérir de plus en plus la vôtre . . . Mais maintenant, ma chère Fille, il y est survenu une certaine qualité nouvelle qui ne se peut nommer, ce me semble; mais seulement son effet est une grande suavité intérieure que j'ai à vous souhaiter la perfection de l'amour de Dieu et les autres bénédictions spirituelles . . . Chaque affection a sa particulière différence d'avec les autres; celle que je vous ai a une certaine particularité qui me console infiniment, et, pour dire tout, qui m'est extrêmement profitable. Tenez cela pour une très veritable vérité et n'en doutez plus." Sales, *Correspondance,* 165–66. This use of providential and eroticized language can also be found in the rather unusual case of a priest bonding with a male penitent. In his 1613 *Life* of the hermit Gregorio López, Francisco Losa insisted that "from the first time I visited him . . . it pleased God out of his mercy to give me such a care of Gregory that if it was necessary to do something for him, never so hard, I should not have stuck upon it . . . [T]o say in a word, from the time I knew him until he died in my company . . . methought I could have been content to have been his slave . . ." I examine this text in Jodi Bilinkoff, "Francisco Losa and Gregorio López: Spiritual Friendship and Identity Formation on the New Spain Frontier," in *Colonial Saints: Discovering the Holy in the Americas, 1500–1800,* ed. Allan Greer and Jodi Bilinkoff (New York: Routledge, 2003), 115–28.

28. Quoted in Friedrich von Hügel, *The Mystical Element of Religion as Studied in Saint Catherine of Genoa and Her Friends* (London: J.M. Dent, 1923; 1st ed. 1908), 1:157–58. For cloistered nuns, especially after the stricter measures of the Council of Trent were put into place, this ability to make visual contact with a spiritual advisor was severely curtailed. Yet this did not prevent religious women and their confessors from developing intimate relationships. As the Ursuline Marie de Saint Joseph (d. 1652) once told a priest, for the purposes of conversation

"she needed only ears to hear him speak, and a tongue to answer him." Julia Boss, "The Life and Death of Mother Marie de Saint Joseph," in *Religions of the United States in Practice*, ed. Colleen McDannell (Princeton: Princeton University Press, 2001) 1:355–56. And, as we have seen, many priests and nuns expressed their feelings toward one another in letters.

29. "[S]i estuviesse con las personas más principales del mundo, y con la misma Reyna . . . las dexaba a todas para confessarla a ella, tanta era la pureza y gracia que descubría en su bendita alma, y lo que estimava su trato." Quoted in Pons Fuster, *Místicos*, 170.

30. "Dieu m'a fait la grace de recevoir les communications qu'elle me donnoit par elle-méme de tout ce qui se passoit dans le plus secret de son ame, dont je benissois Dieu qui vraiment est admirable dans ses Saints." Ragueneau, *Vie de la Mere Catherine*. José Esteban Noriega also expressed gratitude for having had the opportunity to direct and be edified by María Quintana, recalling "quantos tuvimos la ocasión afortunada de tratar con intimidad especialmente en los ultimos años de su vida, a esta criatura." Sánchez Ortega, *Confesión*, 279.

31. "El amor que tienes a tu Confesor, no es malo, ni en el me desagradas; antes me das mucho gusto, porque es lo mismo que quererme a Mi: y esse amor te lo doy." Sánchez Ortega, *Confesión*, 282–83; see 276–85 for a discussion of Quintana's relationships with her confessors generally.

32. Allan Greer, *Mohawk Saint: Catherine Tekakwitha and the Jesuits* (New York: Oxford University Press, 2004), chap.1. Francisco Losa went so far as to resign his position at the Cathedral of Mexico City to devote himself to the physical needs of Gregorio López (d. 1596). Bilinkoff, "Francisco Losa and Gregorio López, 118–20."

33. *Third Mystic*, 103–4. For analyses of both Vela's relationship with Vaquero and the ways in which she and others understood her body see Susan D. Laningham, "Gender, Body and Authority in a Spanish Convent: The Life and Trials of María Vela y Cueto, 1561–1621" (Ph.D. diss., University of Arkansas, 2001).

34. "Apretaronme tanto estos trabajos que para comulgar necesitaba de muchos mandatos del Confesor. . . . necesitaba de la asistencia de mi Confesor todos los dias, por mis muchos escrupulos no pudiendo hacerlo por la trabizon de la lengua, suspension de sentidos, sin poderme mover, afligida de dolores y valdada de pies y manos, con que le era fuerça a mi Confesor el asistirme, para que hiciese algo." Bernique, *Idea de Perfección*, 142. Severe somatic responses of this type, usually related to reception of the eucharist, were fairly common among religious women. See also Sherry M. Velasco, *Demons, Nausea, and Resistance in the Autobiography of Isabel de Jesús, 1611–1682* (Albuquerque: University of New Mexico Press, 1996). For cases from an earlier period see Caroline W. Bynum, "Fast, Feast, and Flesh: The Religious Significance of Food to Medieval Women," *representations* 11 (1985): 1–25, esp. 17–18.

35. Isabel de Jesús, *Vida de la Venerable Madre*, 411–12. This ancedote was recounted by Isabel's last confessor, Francisco Ignacio, in the section he composed and appended to the nun's memoir.

36. "[S]iendo mi salud desmedrada, mis años sobre sessenta y dos, entonses temí maior desasón de salud. Todo esto comuniqué a Gerónima como a mi hija . . . díjele a Gerónima pidiese a Dios. . . ." Olmos recalled this episode in a preface to the nun's memoir. Jerónima Nava y Saavedra, *Autobiografía de una monja venerable*, ed. Angela Inés Robledo (Cali: Universidad del Valle, 1994; orig. publ. 1727), 50–51.

37. " . . . V.M se determinó a decirla una misa por mí y ofrecer su salud por la mía. Oyeron a Vuestra Merced y dióle muy gran calentura. Yo mejoré tres o cuatro días y luego volvió el trabajo . . . volvíme al Señor, suplicándose que no pasase su mal de V.M. adelante, pues no pasaba mi paz; y así lo hizo Su Majestad mejorando a V.M. aunque estuvo quince días sin poderme

ver, y yo los llevé . . . sin comulgar, que esto en estando V.M. ausente no lo podía hacer . . ." Vela, *Autobiografía*, 368. Vaquero recounted another occasion, when he had to travel to Madrid for a cure for "una grave enfermedad del pecho" (heart problems?). María had just spent a five- or six-month period free from illness and demonic attack, but as soon as her confessor left town, her bodily torments resumed. *La muger fuerte*, 188v.

38. There were, of course, cases of confessors who coerced female penitents into having sex with them, an infraction that aroused the wrath of ecclesiatical authorities. These cases do not tend to involve relationships of spiritual direction and mutual friendship of the sort I have been describing. There is a substantial literature on *solicitantes* (priests who solicited sexual favors during confession) and their prosecution by the inquisitions of the Hispanic world. See, for example, Adelina Sarrión Mora, *Sexualidad y confesión: La solicitación ante el Tribunal del Santo Oficio (siglos XVI–XIX)* (Madrid: Alianza, 1994); Juan Antonio Alejandre, *El veneno de Dios: La Inquisición de Sevilla ante el delito de solicitación en confesión* (Madrid: Siglo Veintiuno, 1994); Stephen Haliczer, *Sexuality in the Confessional: A Sacrament Profaned* (New York: Oxford University Press, 1996); Jorge René González Marmolejo, "Clérigos solicitantes, perversos de la confesión," in *De la santidad a la perversión, O de porqué no se cumpla la ley de Dios en la sociedad novohispana*, ed. Sergio Ortega (Mexico City: Grijalbo, 1985), 239–52; Ibsen, *Women's Spiritual Autobiography*, 32–39. Wietse de Boer surveys some of the literature on clerical solicitation in Italy in *The Conquest of the Soul: Confession, Discipline, and Public Order in Counter-Reformation Milan* (Leiden: Brill, 2001), 30–32, 97–100. See also Giovanna Paolin, "Confessione e confessori al femminile: monache e direttori spirituali in ambito veneto tra '600 e '700," in *Finzione e santità tra medievo ed età moderna*, ed. Gabriella Zarri (Turin: Rosenberg and Sellier, 1991), 366–88.

39. Wright *Bond of Perfection*, 102, 123–24. After a tentative start to their relationship, Fra Pietro da Mogliano, "loved me with a holy and spiritual love beyond any he had for any other spiritual daughter he had in this world," Battista da Varano insisted, adding "I know this for a certainty." *My Spiritual Life*, 47–48.

40. Quoted in Electa Arenal and Stacy Schlau, *Untold Sisters: Hispanic Nuns in Their Own Works* (Albuquerque: University of New Mexico Press, 1989), 224.

41. Examples include Teresa of Avila, Maria Maddalena de'Pazzi, María Vela, and Margaret Mary Alacoque. For medieval women's experience of mystical marriage with Christ see, for example, André Vauchez, *Sainthood in the Later Middle Ages*, trans. Jean Birrell (Cambridge: Cambridge University Press, 1997; orig. publ. 1988), 376–85; Caroline Walker Bynum, *Holy Feast and Holy Fast: The Religious Significance of Food to Medieval Women* (Berkeley: University of California Press, 1987) 131, 174–75, 246–51; John Coakley, "A Marriage and Its Observer: Christine of Stommeln, the Heavenly Bridegroom, and Friar Peter of Dacia," and Karen Scott, "Mystical Death, Bodily Death: Catherine of Siena and Raymond of Capua on the Mystic's Encounter with God," in *Gendered Voices: Medieval Saints and Their Interpreters*, ed. Catherine M. Mooney (Philadelphia: University of Pennsylvania Presss, 1999), 99–117, 136–67.

42. *Spiritual Testimonies* 35, 36 in *Collected Works* vol. 1. See also 38, 39. The intense relationship between Teresa and Gracián was not without its strains, however. For their occasional "spats," Teresa's efforts to defend Gracián to others, etc. see Luti, "A Marriage Well Arranged." In his memoir Gracián repeated Teresa's account of their mystical "betrothal" but also alluded to some of their arguments, *Peregrinación de Anastasio*, 260–63.

43. "Une fois qu'il vint dire la sainte messe à notre église, Notre-Seigneur lui fit de très grandes grâces et à moi aussi. Car lorsque je m'approchai pour le recevoir par la sainte communion, il me montra son sacré Coeur comme une ardente fournaise, et deux autres qui s'y allaient unir

et abîmer, me disant: 'C'est ainsi que mon pur amour unit ces trois coeurs pour toujours.' Et après, il me fit entendre que cette union était toute pour la gloire de son sacré Coeur, dont il voulait que je lui découvrise les trésors, afin qu'il en fit connaître et en publiât le prix et l'utilité; et que pour cela il voulait que nous fussions comme frère et soeur, également partagés de biens spirituels." *Vie de Sainte Marguerite-Marie Alacoque*, 110–11. I have rendered this translation, with aid from that offered in *Autobiography of Saint Margaret Mary Alacoque*, 95–96. See also *Letters of St. Margaret Mary Alacoque*, 243, and Colombière's London retreat of 1677 in Claude de la Colombière, *Spiritual Direction*, trans. Mother M. Philip (San Francisco: Ignatius Press, 1998) 20–22. As Raymond Jonas has noted, Margaret Mary Alacoque belonged to the religious order, the Visitation Sisters, founded by Jeanne de Chantal and François de Sales, and may well have been familiar with their rhetorical styles and theological positions. *France and the Cult of the Sacred Heart: An Epic Tale for Modern Times* (Berkeley: University of California Press, 2000), 13–33. For the tradition of heart imagery in medieval devotional writing and especially art, see Jeffrey F. Hamburger, *Nuns as Artists: The Visual Culture of a Medieval Convent* (Berkeley: University of California Press, 1997). Wendy Wright has recently discussed Margaret Mary's experience of exchanging her heart with that of Christ in the context of this tradition but does not mention de la Colombière: "Inside My Body Is the Body of God: Margaret Mary Alacoque and the Tradition of Embodied Mysticism," in *The Mystical Gesture: Essays on Medieval and Early Modern Spiritual Culture in Honor of Mary E. Giles*, ed. Robert Boenig (Aldershot, U.K.: Ashgate, 2000), 185–92.

44. For a good overview of the meanings and hagiographical uses of "the good death" see Carlos M. N. Eire, *From Madrid to Purgatory: The Art and Craft of Dying in Sixteenth-Century Spain* (Cambridge: Cambridge University Press, 1995) esp. 371–78.

45. "Toutes les soeurs en furent grandement attristées . . . Je tâchai de les consoler du mieux que je pus, bien que pour moi j'eusse autant qu'elles besoin de consolation." Duval, *Vie admirable*, 304–17; quote at 314. For more on Acarie and Duval and their years of collaboration see Barbara B. Diefendorf, *From Penitence to Charity: Pious Women and the Catholic Reformation in Paris* (New York: Oxford University Press, 2004), chap. 3.

46. "[P]erdió la habla, cosa de media hora antes de espirar, pero siempre ayudándose como podia a ir diziendo conmigo, hasta que llegó el dichoso punto que tenia tan deseado; pagandola Dios a toda su voluntad con feliz muerte los trabajos de tan santa vida." *La muger fuerte*, 193v–96r; quote at 195v–96r.

47. "El dolor de su falta atravesó mi corasón; de suerte que fue menester, para poder salir del monasterio, aun confortarme; y acompañándome parte de la comunidad de dichas religiosas . . . hasta la puerta, les dije estas palabras: 'Señoras Vuesas [sic] Reverensias se an de servir de averme por escusado en la assistensia al entierro de el cuerpo de Gerónima, quando les consta lo que me atormentado la pesadumbre de su fallesimiento.'" Nava y Saavedra, *Autobiografía de una monja venerable* 31–35, quote at 33. Ibsen *Women's Spiritual Autobiography*, 44–45. Naturally women grieved for their spiritual directors too. The death of Pietro da Mogliano, Battista da Varano recalled, "almost tore me from myself." *My Spiritual Life*, 59–61. She later wrote an account of the friar's "good death" for the consolation of Elisabetta Montefeltro-Gonzaga, the Duchess of Urbino and another of Mogliano's spiritual daughters. "Del Felice Transito del Beato Pietro da Mogliano" (1491) in Camilla Battista da Varano, *Le Opere Spirituali*, ed. Giacomo Boccanera (Jesi: Scuola Tipografica Francescana, 1958), 70–111.

48. Vincenzo Puccini, *The Life of the Holy and Venerable Mother Suor Maria Maddalena de Patsi [sic]* (Cologne? 1619) (Menston, U.K.: Scolar Press, 1970), 274–88; quotes at 278, 288. "No userò molte parole, per che me ancora trovandomi in questa valle di lagrime te degni di pre-

garo l'eterno Dio, confidandomi in quello, che ammistrandomi nella tua malattia i santisimi sacramenti, mi promettisi sovente con isuegliata carità . . ." *Vita della Veneranda Madre Suor M. Maddalena de' Pazzi Fiorentina* (Florence, 1611; 1st ed. 1609), 1:109.

49. "E tu, beata madre e diletta sposa di Giesù, che hora ti truovi . . . a godere la gloria de i beati in cielo et il premio delle tue honorate fatiche e santi meriti . . . priega, in charità, per la mia salute e buona fine. Amen." Serafino Razzi, *Vita di Santa Caterina de' Ricci*, ed. Guglielmo M. di Agresti (Florence: Olschki, 1965; orig. publ. 1594), 307–9; quote at 309. Agresti, in his introductory study, reproduces a pen-and-ink drawing that accompanies a manuscript in the library of the University of Bologna. He speculates that it depicts "il sole [S. Caterina?] che ilumina due città [Firenze e Prato], con un frate orante [Razzi?]." The sun appears to have the face of a woman in a nun's wimple. The illustration is placed between xviii and xix.

50. See the previous chapter for a discussion of the relationship between Catherine and Brébeuf and its rhetorical uses by Paul Ragueneau. See also Allan Greer, "Colonial Saints: Gender, Race, and Hagiography in New France," *William and Mary Quarterly*, 3d ser., 57 (2000): 323– 48. Other cases of women mystics who described postmortem encounters with spiritual directors include Teresa of Avila and Francisca Llopis. See, for example, *The Book of Her Life* 36:20–21 (Pedro de Alcántara), 38:13 (Pedro Ibáñez). Antonio Panes, *Chronica de la Provincia de San Juan Bautista . . . de Nuestro Seraphica Padre San Francisco* (Valencia, 1665–66) 2:770–73 (Jerónimo Simón). For background on this last pair see Pons Fuster, *Místicos*, 49– 96.

51. See, for example, Thomas N. Tentler, *Sin and Confession on the Eve of the Reformation* (Princeton: Princeton University Press, 1977), 70–82; Frederick J. McGinness, "*Roma Sancta* and the Saint: Eucharist, Chastity, and the Logic of Catholic Reform," *Historical Reflections/ Reflexions Historiques* 15 (1988): 96–116; Miri Rubin, *Corpus Christi: The Eucharist in Late Medieval Culture* (Cambridge: Cambridge University Press, 1991), esp. 147–55; Haliczer *Sexuality* ch.2, Michael Maher, "Confession and Consolation: The Society of Jesus and Its Promotion of the General Confession," in *Penitence in the Age of Reformations*, ed. Katharine Jackson Lualdi and Anne T. Thayer (Aldershot, U.K.: Ashgate, 2000), 184–200.

52. Session 13, chap. 7 in *Canons and Decrees of the Council of Trent*, trans. H.J. Schroeder (Rockford, Ill.: TAN Books, 1978), 77. See also André Duval, *Des sacrements au concile de Trente* (Paris: Editions du Cerf, 1985), chap.4.

53. McGinness "*Roma Sancta*," 105. For other regions of Europe see de Boer *Conquest of the Soul*, 77–79; W. David Myers, "*Poor, Sinning Folk*": *Confession and Conscience in Counter-Reformation Germany* (Ithaca: Cornell University Press,1996), 144–62.

54. "In the interpretation of communion there were two ideas at work, often at variance: first, that Christ himself was present at the altar, with all the implications which this had for the handling of the eucharist and for the exclusivity of access to it; and secondly, that the eucharist was necessary and useful, that it could do good and was powerful, thus creating a potential entry into lives, minds and aspirations. The first could exert pressure leading to infrequent and awesome communion, and the second made it a desired object and locus of power which was tantalisingly offered and longingly pursued." Rubin, *Corpus Christi*, 150.

55. For example, a Jesuit writing from Burgos in 1557 reported that on Sundays and Holy Days "a great multitude of women burning with divine love [for communion and confession] fills our chapel," and that "fervor for the Blessed Sacrament is immense, especially among the women." Men, however, "are not at all well disposed toward us, with a few exceptions . . ." Cited in Donald H. Marshall, "Frequent and Daily Communion in the Catholic Church of Spain in the Sixteenth and Seventeenth Centuries" (Ph.D. diss., Harvard University, 1952), 29–31. See also Julián Zarco Cuevas, *España y la comunión frecuente y diaria en los siglos XVI*

y XVII (El Escorial: La Ciudad de Dios, 1913); Myers, *"Poor, Sinning Folk,* 35; Haliczer, *Sexuality,* chap. 2.

56. Bynum, *Holy Feast and Holy Fast.*

57. Haliczer, *Sexuality,* 33. See also Mary Elizabeth Perry, *Gender and Disorder in Early Modern Seville* (Princeton: Princeton University Press, 1990), 98–99.

58. Baltasar Alvarez, *Escritos espirituales,* ed. Camilo María Abad and Faustino Boado (Barcelona: Juan Flors, 1961), 151: "No gastar tiempo con mujeres . . . en visitas y por carta . . . aplicarse más al trato de hombres, donde hay menos peligro y más fructo . . ."

59. Quoted in Marshall, "Frequent and Daily Communion," 128.

60. *La muger fuerte* (1627), 28v–30r. In a similar vein, Marcos Torres used the metaphor of hunger to describe the spiritual longings of the married María de Pol, who, "para satisfacer a la hambre que a este pan soberano la tiraba . . . tomó el medio de comulgar cada día espiritualmente . . ." After she was widowed her confessor allowed her to receive communion every eight days. Marcos Torres, "[N]oticias] . . . de la vida y virtudes . . . de Da. María de Pol, su madre," (Málaga? 1660), 44, 90.

61. Examples include Isabel de Jesús, Catalina de Jesús y San Francisco, and Francisca Llopis. See *Vida de la Venerable Madre Isabel de Iesus,* 58; Bernique, *Idea de perfección,* 45–47; Panes, *Chronica de la Provincia de San Juan Bautista,* 759–66.

62. Examples include Maria Maddalena de' Pazzi, Estefanía Manrique de Castilla, Marie de l'Incarnation, María Quintana, and Isabel de Jesús. See Puccini, *The Life of the Holy and Venerable Mother,* 8, 11, 13–14; Pedro de Ribadeneyra, "Vida de Doña Estefania Manrique de Castilla"(c. 1606), Biblioteca Nacional, Madrid (BNM), MS 7421 12v–13r, 27v; Claude Martin, *La vie de la Venerable Mere Marie de l'Incarnation* (Paris, 1677, facsimile ed. 1981), 731, 756; Natalie Zemon Davis, *Women on the Margins: Three Seventeenth Century Lives* (Cambridge, Mass.: Harvard University Press, 1995) 290–91, note 239; Sánchez Ortega, *Confesión,* 260; Isabel de Jesús, *Vida de la Venerable Madre,* 123.

63. André Duval explicitly contrasts Barbe Acarie, with her desire for communion and firm belief that the consecrated host is truly the body of Christ, with the "heretics" so rampant in the France of their day, *Vie admirable,* 319–20. See also Benjamin Ehlers's discussion in "Catholic Reform as Process" of Archbishop Juan de Ribera and his efforts to promote both the cult of the local holy woman Margarita Agullona and sacramental piety in late-sixteenth-century Valencia.

64. These attitudes are surveyed in the works on soliciting confessors listed in note 38 above. See also Colleen Seguin, "Ambiguous Liaisons: Women's Relationships with their Confessors in Early Modern England," *Archive for Reformation History* 95 (2004): 156–85; R. N. Swanson, "Angels Incarnate: Clergy and Masculinity from Gregorian Reform to Reformation," in *Masculinity in Medieval Europe,* ed. D. M. Hadley (London: Longman, 1999), 160–77.

Chapter 5. Reading Habits

1. Several recent works feature transcriptions and studies of convent chronicles. see, for example, Manuel Ramos Medina, *Místicas y Descalzas: Fundaciones Femeninas Carmelitas en la Nueva España* (Mexico City: CONDUMEX, 1997); Elisa Sampson Vera Tudela, *Colonial Angels: Narratives of Gender and Spirituality in Mexico, 1580–1750* (Austin: University of Texas Press, 2000); Charlotte Woodford, *Nuns as Historians in Early Modern Germany* (Oxford: Oxford University Press, 2002); K. J. P. Lowe, *Nuns' Chronicles and Convent Culture in Renaissance and Counter-Reformation Italy* (Cambridge: Cambridge University Press, 2003). For preaching on the saints in this period see, for example, Frederick J. McGinness, *Right Thinking and Sacred Oratory in Counter-Reformation Rome* (Princeton: Princeton University Press, 1995).

2. The scholarly literature on the impact of printing is immense; for a good overview see Roger Chartier, *The Order of Books: Readers, Authors and Libraries between the Fourteenth and Eighteenth Centuries* (Cambridge: Cambridge University Press 1994; orig. publ. 1992).

3. "Reportorio," in *Donna, disciplina, crean*͡*a cristiana dal XV al XVII secolo: Studi e testi a stampa,* ed. Gabriella Zarri (Rome: Edizioni di Storia e Letteratura, 1996), 407–797.

4. Ottavio Gondi, *Vita della beata Angela Bresciana* . . . (Brescia, 1600, 1605, 1619, 1620; Venice, 1618; Bologna, 1638); Giacomo Grassetti, *Vita della B. Caterina di Bologna* . . . (Bologna, 1610, 1620, 1630, 1639, 1652, 1654); Cattaneo Marabotto [and Vernazza, Ettore], *Libro della vita mirabile et dottrina santa della b.Caterina da Genova* (Genoa, 1551, 1667, 1681; Florence, 1568, 1580, 1589; Venice, 1590, 1601, 1615; Naples, 1645); Vincenzio Puccini, *Vita della Madre Suor Maria Maddalena de' Pa*͡*i Fiorentina* . . . (Florence, 1609, 1611, 1621, 1639; Milan, 1615; Rome, 1629; Venice, 1642, 1666, 1671, 1675; Naples, 1652).

5. Raimundus de Vineis, *Vita e miracoli della serafica santa Caterina da Siena* (Florence, 1477; Milan 1486, 1489, 1490; Siena, 1524 (2); Venice 1556, 1561, 1562, 1578, 1579, 1580, 1583, 1584, 1587, 1591, 1597, 1600, 1603, 1604, 1608 (2), 1612, 1617; plus two editions without place or date). For the original composition of this text see Karen Scott, "Mystical Death, Bodily Death: Catherine of Siena and Raymond of Capua on the Mystic's Encounter with God," in *Gendered Voices: Medieval Saints and Their Interpreters,* ed. Catherine M. Mooney (Philadelphia: University of Pennsylvania Press,1990), 136–67. For its influence see note 42.

6. Isabelle Poutrin, *Le voile et la plume: Autobiographie et sainteté féminine dans l'Espagne moderne* (Madrid: Casa de Velázquez, 1995), especially her bibliographical appendixes, 283–467. José Luis Sánchez Lora, *Mujeres, conventos y formas de la religiosidad barroca* (Madrid: FUE, 1988), 359–401, for publication statistics and trends. See 403–53 for his discussion of hagiography as the literary form par excellence of the Spanish Baroque.

7. Antonio Daza, *Historia, Vida, Milagros, Extasis y Revelaciones de la Bienaventurada Virgen Santa Juana de la Cru*͡ . . . (Madrid, 1610, 1614; Zaragoza, 1611; Valladolid, 1611; Lérida, 1617); Miguel González Vaquero, *La Muger Fuerte . . . La Vida de Doña María Vela* . . . (Madrid, 1618 (2), 1674; Barcelona, 1627, 1640). Both these texts were translated and published in Italy too, the Daza text in Padua, 1619, and González Vaquero in Milan, 1622 and 1632. Poutrin mentions a 1635 Milanese edition as well, but this is not listed in "Reportorio."

8. Henri-Jean Martin, *Livre, pouvoirs et société a Paris au XVIIe siècle* (Geneva: Droz, 1999), 1: 154–60. Other general discussions of French hagiographical texts and their readers include Henri Bremond, *A Literary History of Religious Thought in France* (London: Society for Promoting Christian Knowledge, 1928–36), 1:193–204; 2:3–5; Albrecht Burkardt, "Reconnaissance et dévotion: Les vies des saints et leurs lectures au début du XVIIe siècle a travers les procès de canonisation," *Revue d'histoire moderne et contemporaine* 43 (1996): 214–33.

9. See Martin *Livre,* 2:1070, for graphs. On *Lives* of exemplary women published in France see François Lebrun, "A corps perdu: Les biographies spirituelles féminines du XVIIe siècle" *Le temps de la réflexion* 7 (1986): 389–408; Lebrun, "Mutations de la notion de martyre au XVIIe siècle d'après les biographies spirituelles féminines," in *Sainteté et martyre dans les religions du Livre,* ed. Jacques Marx (Brussels, Université de Bruxelles, 1989), 77–90; Elizabeth Rapley, *The Dévotes: Women and Church in Seventeenth-Century France* (Montreal and Kingston: McGill-Queen's University Press, 1990); Barbara B. Diefendorf, *From Penitence to Charity: Pious Women and the Catholic Reformation in Paris* (New York: Oxford University Press, 2004).

10. On life-writing and hagiography in Portugal see, for example, Isabel Morujão, *Contributo para uma bibliografia cronológica da literatura monástica feminina portuguesa dos séculos XVII e XVIII* (Lisbon: Universidade Católica Portuguesa, 1995); Maria de Lurdes Correia Fernandes, *A bib-*

lioteca de Jorge Cardoso (d. *1669*), autor do '*Agiológio Lusitano*': Cultura, erudição e sentimento religioso no Portugal moderno (Porto: Universidade do Porto, 2000); and the same author's introduction to her edition of Fr. Luís dos Anjos, *Jardim de Portugal, em que se da noticia de algunas Sanctas, & outras molheres illustres em virtude* . . . (1626) (Porto: Campo das Letras, 1999),9–29.

11. "Reportorio" 2434–49; Martin, *Livre*, 1:20, 158; Diefendorf, *From Penitence to Charity*, Introd., chap 3. The *Life* of Teresa of Avila was also translated into Dutch between 1608 and 1610 and into English in 1611. See Cordula van Wyhe, "Cloistered Court Ladies: Teresian Routes to Sanctity in Seventeenth-Century Flanders" (paper presented at the international conference "Female Monasticism in Early Modern Europe," Wolfson College, Cambridge University, July 2003); Claire Walker, *Gender and Politics in Early Modern Europe: English Convents in France and the Low Countries* (Houndmills, U.K.: Palgrave Macmillan, 2003), 152. Francisco de Ribera's biography of Teresa, first published in Salamanca in 1590, was also quickly translated and enjoyed considerable popularity throughout Europe during the seventeenth century. In a diary she maintained in the 1630s at the request of her confessor, the Flemish nun Margaret of the Mother of God recalled how an early employer, an aristocratic woman, had translated for her a biography of Teresa of Avila (most likely Ribera's), rendering the text from Spanish into Flemish. Reading this book made such a strong impression upon the young woman that she resolved to enter the Discalced Carmelite convent in Brussels. My thanks to Cordula van Wyhe for sharing this anecdote with me.

12. I have compiled these somewhat rough—and undoubtedly conservative—figures by consulting the following works: Electa Arenal and Stacey Schlau, *Untold Sisters: Hispanic Nuns in Their Own Works* (Albuquerque: University of New Mexico Press, 1989; Kathleen A Myers and Amanda Powell, eds., *A Wild Country Out in the Garden: The Spiritual Journals of a Colonial Mexican Nun* (Bloomington: Indiana University Press, 1999); Kristine Ibsen, *Women's Spiritual Autobiography in Colonial Spanish America* (Gainesville: University Press of Florida, 1999); Sampson Vera Tudela, *Colonial Angels;* Ronald J. Morgan, *Spanish American Saints and the Rhetoric of Identity, 1600–1810* (Tucson: University of Arizona Press, 2002).

13. These likewise rough estimates on New France were derived from the following works Rapley, *Dévotes;* Leslie Choquette, "'Ces Amazones du Grand Dieu': Women and Mission in Seventeenth-Century Canada," *French Historical Studies* 17(1992): 627–55; Allan Greer, "Colonial Saints: Gender, Race, and Hagiography in New France," *William and Mary Quarterly*, 3d ser., 57 (2000): 323–48; Dominique Deslandres, "In the Shadow of the Cloister: Representations of Female Holiness in New France," in *Colonial Saints: Discovering the Holy in the Americas, 1500–1800*, ed. Allan Greer and Jodi Bilinkoff (New York: Routledge, 2003), 129–52.

14. The anonymous English translator of Vincenzio Puccini's biography of Maria Maddalena de' Pazzi dedicated this work to "the Right Honorable and Most Reverend Ladie, the Ladie Mary Percy, la abbesse of the English religious of the holy order of S. Benet at Our Blessed Ladyes of the Assumption in Bruxells." He notes, however, that she had already read the book "in the originall tongue." *The Life of the Holy and Venerable Mother Suor Maria Maddalena de Patsi* [*sic*] (Cologne? 1619), Epistle Dedicatory, 2r–3v. This text is available as volume 33 in the series *English Recusant Literature, 1558–1640*, ed. D. M. Rogers (Menston, U.K.: Scolar Press, 1970). See also Walker, *Gender and Politics*, chap 5. For Francisca Josepha de Castillo and her reading of Pazzi's *Life* see note 55 below.

15. According to the "Reportorio," at least nine hagiographies, sermons, and panegryrics dedicated to Rose of Lima were published in Italy during the seventeenth century. These included

Serafino Bertolini's *La rosa peruana, overo vita della sposa di Christo suor Rosa di Santa Maria* . . . , first published in Rome in 1666 and reprinted in Rome and Padua in 1669 and 1671. For Quito's *beata* Mariana de Jesús and her use of Rose of Lima as a model see Morgan, *Spanish American Saints,* chap. 5.

16. Allan Greer, "Iroquois Virgin: The Story of Catherine Tekakwitha, in New France and New Spain," in *Colonial Saints,* 235–50; Greer, *Mohawk Saint: Catherine Tekawitha and the Jesuits* (New York: Oxford University Press, 2005).

17. *Life* 1:1 in *The Collected Works of St. Teresa of Avila,* trans. Kieran Kavanaugh and Otilio Rodríguez (Washington, D.C.: Institute of Carmelite Studies, 1976), 1:33. For Spanish texts I have consulted Santa Teresa de Jesús, *Obras completas,* ed. Efrén de la Madre de Dios and Otger Steggink (Madrid: Editorial Católica, 1977); Jeanne-Marie Guyon, *La vie par elle-même et autres écrits biographiques,* ed. Dominique Tronc (Paris: Honoré Champion, 2001; orig. publ. 1720), 127; Battista da Varano, *My Spiritual Life,* trans. Joseph Berrigan (Toronto: Peregrina Publishing, 1986; orig. publ. 1491), 20–21.

18. *The Autobiography of Saint Margaret Mary Alacoque,* trans. Sisters of the Visitation (Rockford, Ill.: TAN Books, 1986), 35–36; *Vie de Saint Marguerite-Marie Alacoque écrite par elle-même* (Paris: Gigord, 1934; orig. completed 1685) 25: "Et comme je ne lisais guère d'autre livre que la Vie des Saints, je disais en l'ouvrant: il m'en faut chercher une bien aisée à imiter, afin que je puisee faire comme elle a fait, pour devenir sainte comme elle"; *Obras completas de la Madre Francisca Josepha de la Concepción de Castillo,* ed. Dario Achury Valenzuela (Bogotá: Banco de la República, 1968; orig. completed c. 1715), 1: 5: "Leía mi madre los libros de santa Teresa de Jesús, y sus *Fundaciones,* y a mí me daba un tan grande deseo de ser como una de aquellas monjas . . ."

19. "En aquel tiempo fue Dios servido que me llevasen el libro de doña María Vela; y oyendo los muchos trabajos que padeció, la tuve mucha envidia, y con grandes ansias decía en mi corazón: bien pasaría yo todos estos trabajos con la gracia del Señor." Quoted in Poutrin, *Voile et la plume,* 82 n40. For other readers of Vaquero's text, 81–83.

20. On group readings of the *Life* of Teresa of Avila, see André Duval, *La vie admirable de la Bienheureuse Soeur Marie de l'Incarnation . . . appelée dans la monde Mademoiselle Acarie* (Paris: Librairie Victor Lecoffre, 1893; orig. publ. 1621), xvii–xix. For group readings of the *Life* of Mariana de San José, see Myers and Powell, *Wild Country,* 307–16.

21. For the case of Teresa Mir see James A. Amelang, "Los usos de la autobiografía: monjas y beatas en la Cataluña moderna," in *Historia y Género: Las mujeres en la Europa moderna y contemporánea,* ed. James A. Amelang and Mary Nash (Valencia: Edicions Alfons el Magnànim, 1990), 197–98. For Marie de l'Incarnation see Natalie Zemon Davis, *Women on the Margins: Three Seventeenth-Century Lives* (Cambridge, Mass.: Harvard University Press, 1995), 68. For Margarita Escobar y Villalba see Poutrin, *Voile et la plume,* 82n39.

22. Miguel González Vaquero, *La muger fuerte, por otro título, La vida de Doña María Vela* (Madrid: Imprenta Real, 1674; 1st ed. 1618), 119v–120v, where Vaquero relates how he shared with his penitent his copy of the just-published *Life* of Gregorio López by Francisco Losa. For cases of clerics sharing their books with female penitents in colonial Peru see Nancy E. van Deusen, "Circuits of Knowledge among Lay and Religious Women in Early Seventeenth-Century Peru" (paper presented at the Twelfth Berkshire Conference on the History of Women, Storrs, Conn., June 2002).

23. The Portuguese friar Brás Soares read the *Lives* of Catherine of Siena, Teresa of Avila, and other figures to his unlettered penitent Isabel de Miranda. Maria de Lurdes Correia Fernandes, "A construção da santidade nos finais do século XVI: O caso de Isabel de Miranda, tecedeira, viúva e 'santa' (ca. 1539–1610)," in *Actas do Colóquio Internacional Piedade Popular:*

Sociabilidades, representações, espiritualidades (Lisbon: Centro de História da Cultura/ Ter-ramar, 1999), 243–72, esp. 248, 257–58.

24. Una Carmelita Descalza del Convento de Santiago, *Una mística gallega en el siglo XVIII: La Venerable Madre María Antonia de Jesús* (La Coruña: Fundación "Pedro Barrié de la Maza, Conde de Fenosa," 1991), 53, quoting from local beatification hearings initiated soon after her death in 1760: "Tomando un librito lo abrió por las primeras hojas y leyó 'Amor de Dios' y así fue leyendo en él de corrido, entiendo perfectamente el sentido de lo que leía . . . el Señor le había concedido el favor de aprender a leer, sin otro maestro que El." She likewise claimed the sudden ability to write, 67–69. The earlier Discalced Carmelite Ana de San Bartolomé (1549–1626) insisted that through the intercession of Teresa of Avila she had learned to write in one day. Alison Weber, "The Partial Feminism of Ana de San Bartolomé," in *Recovering Spain's Feminist Tradition*, ed. Lisa Vollendorf (New York: Modern Languages Association, 2001), 73.

25. *Una mística gallega*, 67.

26. *Life* 9:7, *Collected Works*, 1:72. For a cogent analysis of Teresa's use of Augustine's *Confessions* see Carole Slade, *St. Teresa of Avila: Author of a Heroic Life* (Berkeley: University of California Press, 1995), esp. chap 3.

27. Jerónima Nava y Saavedra, *Autobiografía de una monja venerable*, ed. Angela Inés Robledo (Cali: Ediciones Universidad del Valle, 1994; orig. completed 1727), 97–98, "E sido afision-adísima a los santos que se an señalado en yr por el camino del amor de Dios. Y como el glo-rioso santo San Francisco de Sales tanto encarga en sus obras el que amemos a Dios, le e tenido, desde que supe esto, grande afecto al santo y sus dulsísimas y claras doctrinas . . . A esto tam-bién me tiene redusida mi confesor, que es amantísimo del amor de Dios y siempre me lo en-carga . . ." Maria Maddalena de'Pazzi, according to her biographer, took Diego de Alcalá (d. c. 1463; canonized 1588) as her "particular Patron," and once fell into a rapture while "read-ing the life of St. Diego, to whom she was devoted." Puccini, *Vita della Madre Suor Maria Maddalena*, 127, 139. According to her fellow Ursuline Marie de l'Incarnation, after reading the life of Francis Xavier, to whom she had been "especially devoted since her childhood . . . because of his zeal in converting nations to the Faith of Jesus Christ," Marie de Saint Joseph resolved to become a missionary in Canada. Julia Boss, "The Life and Death of Mother Marie de Saint Joseph," in *Religions of the United States in Practice*, ed. Colleen McDannell (Prince-ton: Princeton University Press, 2001),1:355.

28. Clare of Assisi was understandably popular among Franciscan nuns and tertiaries. She was evoked by, among others: Battista da Varano, Catalina de Jesús y San Francisco, Jerónima Nava y Saavedra, and Francisca Josepha de Castillo. Pierre Acarie had the *Life* of Angela of Foligno translated from Latin into French for his pious young wife, Barbe. Duval, *Vie ad-mirable*, 26–28. See also Lancelot C. Sheppard, *Barbe Acarie, Wife and Mystic* (New York: David McKay, 1953), 25. Francisca Josepha de Castillo recalled that as a girl she learned to re-cite the divine office for no other reason than "having read in the life of Saint Mary Magda-lene, that she was carried seven times up to heaven by the angels, in imitation of the seven canonical hours" ("aunque no tenía más noticia que haber leído en la vida de santa María Mag-dalena, que era llevada por los angeles siete veces al cielo, a imitación de las siete horas canóni-cas"). *Obras Completas de la Madre Francisca Josepha*, 1:16–17. The Colombian may have read this account in the *Flos Sanctorum* or another popular collection of saints' lives.

29. *Autobiography of Saint Margaret Mary Alcoque*, 97–98; *Vie de Saint Marguerite-Marie Ala-coque*, 113–14, "[I]l lui voulait donner la même récompense qu'à sainte Claire de Monte-falco . . ." See the previous chapter for a discussion of Margaret Mary's experience of the exchange of hearts and her relationship with her confessor, Claude de la Colombière. For

Clare of Montefalco and her cult see André Vauchez, *Sainthood in the Later Middle Ages*, trans. Jean Birrell (Cambridge: Cambridge University Press 1997; orig. publ. 1988), 348–53; Katherine Park, "Relics of a Fertile Heart: The 'Autopsy' of Clare of Montefalco," in *The Material Culture of Sex, Procreation, and Marriage in Premodern Europe*, ed. Anne L. McClanan and Karen Rosoff Encarnación (New York: Palgrave, 2002), 115–33.

30. Antonio de la Peña is an example of an author who cited Old Testament figures such as Deborah and Judith; see the prologue to his Spanish translation of Raymond of Capua, *La vida de la bienaventurada Sancta Caterina de Sena* [*sic*] (Alcalá de Henares, 1511). De la Peña was, at the time, the confessor and principal promoter of the Castilian *beata* María de Santo Domingo. For the use of early Christian and medieval figures such as Thecla and Lidwige of Schiedam, see the discussion of Claude Martin's *La Vie de la Venerable Mere Marie de l'Incarnation* (Paris, 1677), in chapter 3. Genealogies of illustrious men can be traced to Roman historians such as Plutarch. Used in medieval hagiographies, the genre nevertheless underwent a revival in the Renaissance, with Giovanni Boccaccio composing the first such history dedicated exclusively to women. See Guido A. Guarino's useful introduction to his translation of Boccaccio's *De Claris Mulieribus* (1362). *Concerning Famous Women* (New Brunswick: Rutgers University Press, 1963). Many hagiographers, such as Claude Martin, received humanistic training and would have been familiar with this text.

31. Serafino Razzi, *Vita di Santa Caterina de' Ricci*, ed. Guglielmo M. di Agresti (Florence: Olschki, 1965; orig. publ. 1594), 301–6: "Della comparazione di questa Serva di Dio con alcune altre vergini piu' antiche;" "per grazia del suo benedetto Giesù, che communica i suoi doni come, quando et a cui gli piace"; Paul Ragueneau, *La Vie de la Mere Catherine de Saint Augustin, Religieuse Hospitaliere de la Misericorde de Quebec en la Nouvelle France* (Paris: Florentin Lambert, 1671), 10–15: "Dieu fait des graces à qui il veut, & quand il veut; & si quelquefois il se fait voir aux femmes plûtôt qu'aux hommes, c'est souvent un manquement d'humilité en nous . . ." Isabelle Poutrin has also noticed this use of "précédents utiles" by hagiographers of exemplary women. *Voile et la plume*, 256–57.

32. For the use of Jerome and Paula see, for example, Juan Bernique, *Idea de Perfección, y Virtudes. Vida de . . . Catalina de Jesús y San Francisco* (Alcalá de Henares: Francisco García Fernández, 1693), prologue; Martín de Roa, *Vida de doña Ana Ponce de León . . .* (1604, 1615), cited in Maria de Lurdes Correia Fernandes, "Uma clarissa ilustre do século XVI: Ana Ponce de León, Condessa de Féria e monja de Santa Clara de Montilla," in *Las Clarisas en España y Portugal, Actas del Congreso Internacional*, ed. José Martí Mayor and María de Mar Graña Cid (Madrid: Archivos e Historia, 1994), 1:335. For the use of Augustine and Monica see chapter 3, note 52. For hagiographers' self-identification with Raymond of Capua see chapter 2, notes 26–27. After citing John Chrysostom's encomium on St. Paul, the Carmelite Friar Alonso de la Madre de Dios likened his subject, John of the Cross, to the famous apostle, thus by implication comparing himself with Chrysostom. Alonso de la Madre de Dios, *Vida, virtudes y milagros del Santo Padre Fray Juan de la Cruz* (Madrid: Editorial de Espiritualidad, 1989; orig. publ. c.1630), 39–41.

33. María-Helena Sánchez Ortega, *Confesión y trayectoria femenina: Vida de la Venerable Quintana* (Madrid: CSIC, 1996), esp. 211–30. Sánchez Ortega has also traced the general history of the cult of Mary Magdalene and its association with female sexuality, in *Pecadoras en verano, arrepentidas de invierno: El camino de la conversión femenina* (Madrid: Alianza, 1995). See also Katherine L. Jansen, *The Making of the Magdalen: Preaching and Popular Devotion in the Later Middle Ages* (Princeton: Princeton University Press, 2000), chaps. 5–6.

34. Quoted in Sánchez Ortega, *Confesión*, 237, 246–47: "Tambien dormi . . . por estos tiempos en una Cavalleriza sin puerta . . . despues de haver estado algun tiempo de rodillas como acos-

tumbaba, se me aparecio Santa Gertrudis (a quien yo he querido mucho desde niña) vestida de Monja Benita, muy hermosa, como estaba en el mundo . . . me quedo de la referida vision de Santa Gertrudis, en lo exterior, compostura, y en lo interior, devocion, inclinacion a todo lo bueno, en un total aborrecimiento a lo malo, que es pecado." For Gertrude the Great see Caroline Walker Bynum, "Women Mystics in the Thirteenth Century: The Case of the Nuns of Helfta," in her *Jesus as Mother: Studies in the Spirituality of the High Middle Ages* (Berkeley: University of California Press, 1982), 186–209.

35. Ragueneau, *Vie de la Mere Catherine*, 11.
36. Puccini, *Vita della Madre Suor Maria Maddalena*, 29–30.
37. Anna Scattigno, "Maria Maddalena de'Pazzi, tra esperienza e modello," in Zarri, *Donna, disciplina*, 87–89. For other examples of holy women in northern Italian cities see Gabriella Zarri, "Living Saints: A Typology of Female Sanctity in the Early Sixteenth Century," in *Women and Religion in Medieval and Renaissance Italy*, ed. Daniel Bornstein and Roberto Rusconi (Chicago: University of Chicago Press, 1996; orig. essay publ. 1980), 219–303.
38. Capocchi died in 1581, just a few months before Maria Maddalena entered the convent. Puccini, *Vita della Madre Suor Maria Maddalena*, 30; Scattigno "Maria Maddalena," 87–89. Serafino Razzi, *Seconda parte delle vite de' santi, e beati dell'ordine de'frati predicatori* . . . (Florence, 1588); Silvano Razzi, *Delle vite delle donne illlustri per santità* . . . (Florence, 1595–1606).
39. Ragueneau, *Vie de la Mere Catherine*, 249–50. On this occasion Catherine also prayed, as she often did, to the martyred missionary Jean de Brébeuf, another Norman.
40. *Ibid.*, 30–31: "Un Prédicateur Missionaire [Eudes?] que conduisoit pour lors une vertueuse fille, nommée Marie des Vallées de Coutance, luy dit vers ce temps-là, qu'infailliblement elle seroit Religieuse; & ce fut sans doute par l'entremise de cette bonne Ame, à laquelle on l'avoir recommandée."
41. Guy-Marie Oury, *L'itineraire mystique de Catherine de Saint-Augustin* (Solesmes: Abbey de Solesmes, 1985), 178–79: "[P]arce qu'elle sent une parenté entre ses propres épreuves et ce qu'elle connaît de la vie de la 'Sainte de Coutances' . . . l'analogie . . . conduit l'hospitalière à regarder la Sainte de Coutances comme un modèle et un protecteur céleste." On the relationship between Marie des Vallées and Jean Eudes see the introduction to *Bérulle and the French School: Selected Writings*, ed. William M. Thompson (New York: Paulist Press, 1989), 19–22.
42. I realize that Catherine of Siena can be considered a "medieval" saint. For analytical purposes, however, I include her in this cohort of "modern" saints, given her 1461 canonization and the extraordinary popularity of Raymond of Capua's *Legenda Maior* as a printed text and in vernacular translations. On Catherine's influence on later spiritual women, especially in Italy and Spain, see Zarri "Living Saints;" John Coakley, "Friars as Confidants of Holy Women in Medieval Dominican Hagiography," in *Images of Sainthood in Medieval Europe*, ed. Renate Blumenfeld-Kosinski and Timea Szell (Ithaca: Cornell University Press, 1991), 234–46; Alvaro Huerga, *Santa Catalina de Siena en la historia de la espiritualidad hispana* (Rome, 1969); Gillian T. W. Ahlgren, "Ecstasy, Prophecy, and Reform: Catherine of Siena as a Model for Holy Women of Sixteenth-Century Spain," in *The Mystical Gesture: Essays on Medieval and Early Modern Spiritual Culture in Honor of Mary E. Giles*, ed. Robert Boenig (Aldershot, U.K.: Ashgate: 2000), 53–65. Teresa's immense influence on Spanish and Spanish American religious women has been amply documented. See, for example, Poutrin, *Voile et la plume*, 76–79; Arenal and Schlau, *Untold Sisters*, 8–11, Myers and Powell, *Wild Country*, 304–16; Ibsen, *Women's Spiritual Autobiography*, esp. chap. 3; Sonja Herpoel, *A la zaga de Santa Teresa: Autobiografías por mandato* (Amsterdam: Rodopi, 1999), chap. 1. For Teresa's influence in France see works cited in notes 8 and 9.

43. *Las obras de . . . Sor Teresa de Jesús María [1592–c.1642]*, ed. Manuel Serrano y Sanz (Madrid: Gil Blas, 1921), 3–9: "Cuando yo entré monja me llamaba María . . . y después, por devoción de nuestra Madre Santa Teresa, me pusieron este nombre cuando profesé . . ." After her mother was widowed she too became a Discalced Carmelite nun, but entered a different convent. One of her two brothers became a Discalced Carmelite friar, the other a Jesuit priest.

44. One might make the same observation regarding northern Italian, especially Tuscan, women who cited Catherine of Siena, such as Maria Maddalena de'Pazzi (Florence), Caterina de'Ricci (Prato) and Caterina Fieschi Adorna (Catherine of Genoa).

45. "Yo no conocí ni vi a la Madre Teresa de Jesús mientras estuvo en la tierra; mas agora que vive en el cielo la conozco y veo casi siempre en dós imagines vivas que nos dejó de sí, que son sus hijas y sus libros . . ." Luis de León, *Obras completas castellanas*, ed. Félix García (Madrid: Editorial Católica, 1977), 1:904. Examples of Spanish Discalced Carmelites include Teresa de Jesús María (note 43); María Antonia de Jesús (note 24); and Isabel de Jesús, see Sherry M. Velasco, *Demons, Nausea, and Resistance in the Autobiography of Isabel de Jesús, 1611–1682* (Albuquerque: University of New Mexico Press, 1996). For Discalced Carmelite nuns in Mexico, Ramos Medina, *Místicas y Descalzas*. For nuns in Flanders, van Wyhe, "Cloistered Court Ladies."

46. On the acquaintance of María de San José (1656–1719) with the *Life* of Mariana de San José (1568–1638) see Myers and Powell, *Wild Country*, 309–16. The Mexican nun would have been reading Luis Muñoz, *Vida de la Venerable M. Mariana de San Ioseph. Fundadora de la Recolección de las Monjas Augustinas . . .* (Madrid, 1645). For this text, which includes Mariana's own autobiographical writings, see Poutrin, *Voile et la plume*, 338–39.

47. For the use of Catherine of Siena by Italian Dominicans see works by Zarri and Coakley, cited in note 42. She was also an important model for the Peruvian tertiary Rose of Lima (1586–1617). Morgan, *Spanish American Saints*, chap.4; Kathleen A. Myers, *Neither Saints Nor Sinners: Writing the Lives of Women in Spanish America* (New York: Oxford University Press, 2003), chap. 1.

48. For Teresa de Jesús María see note 43; for Francisca Josepha de Castillo, note 18; for Teresa Mir, note 21. Isabelle Poutrin, "Juana Rodríguez, una autora mística olvidada (Burgos, siglo XVII)," in *Estudios sobre escritoras hispánicas en honor de Georgina Sabat-Rivers*, ed. Lou Charnon-Deutsch (Madrid: Castalia, 1992), 269–70. Juana's convent sisters recalled, "Si saben, o han oído decir, que en la niñez . . . dio Nuestro Señor maravillosas señales de su futura santidad . . . que santa Teresa de Jesús (que estaba a la sazón en esta ciudad a la fundación del convento de sus Monjas), tomándole en brazos, y bendiciéndola, dijo a sus Padres tuviesen mucho cuidado con aquella niña, porque Dios había de obrar muchas maravillas en ella." See also 275–76.

49. Ursula Suárez, *Relación autobiográfica*, ed. Mario Ferreccio Podestá (Santiago de Chile: Universidad de Concepción, 1984; orig. completed c. 1730), 230: "[D]estas dos siervas de Dios gustaba yo leer sus vidas, y tenía deseos de ser como ellas . . ."

50. Ibsen *Women's Spiritual Autobiography*, 122: "Although she credits the spiritual writings of María de la Antigua and Marina Escobar as her primary literary models, Ursula's textual self bears little similarity to the hagiographic paradigm." María Inés Lagos, "Confessing to the Father: Marks of Gender and Class in Ursula Suárez's *Relación*," *Modern Language Notes* 110 (1995): 371: "She mentions having read [these] two nuns' lives . . . but she does not seem to have followed these models." For a thoughtful analysis of Ursula's interactions with these texts see Rodrigo Cánovas, "Ursula Suárez (Monja Chilena, 1666–1749): La autobiografía como penitencia," *Revista Chilena de Literatura* 35 (1990): esp. 108–15. Ursula would have

seen Luis de la Puente, *Vida maravillosa de la Venerable Virgen Doña Marina de Escobar* (Madrid, 1665; second part publ. by Andrés Pinto Ramírez, 1673).

51. Suárez, *Relación autobiográfica*, 214–15. For biographical details see sources cited above and also Myers, *Neither Saints Nor Sinners*, chap. 5. For María de la Antigua, Poutrin, *Voile et la plume*, 162–63, 327. Ursula would have read María's *Desengaño de Religiosas y almas que tratan de Virtud* (Seville, 1678). The Spanish nun also spent some time among the Mercedarians, who later claimed her as their own, but during Ursula's lifetime she was being heavily promoted by the Franciscans, who reopened beatification hearings in 1671.

52. Velasco, *Demons, Nausea, and Resistance*, 70–71.

53. Antónia Margarida de Castelo Branco, *Autobiografia, 1652–1717*, ed. João Palma-Ferreira (Lisbon: Imprensa Nacional, 1983), 187: "[T]omei esta Santa por mestra espiritual e várias vezes tenho experimentado o seu favor em muitas coisas que se não remediaram por via natural."

54. Duval, *Vie admirable*, 118–31. Diefendorf, *From Penitence to Charity*, chap. 3.

55. *Obras completas de la Madre Francisca Josepha*, 1:138: "Parecíame que la santa Magdalena de Pasis [sic], mi madre y mi señora, se llegaba amorosamente a mi alma, y se unía su espiritú con el mío, con un abrazo y unión muy estrecha e íntima, alentándome y consolándome." See also 67, 95. The Colombian most likely read the *Vida de la Bienaventurada y Extática Virgen María Magdalena de Pazzi, Florentina . . . Traducida de lengua toscana por Fr. Juan de Leçana . . .* , published in Zaragoza in 1650, and reprinted in Madrid in 1664 and 1669, the year of Pazzi's canonization. José Simón Díaz, "Hagiografías individuales publicadas en español de 1480 a 1700," *Hispania Sacra* 30, nos. 59–60 (1977): 42. She copied this or another *Life* of Pazzi into one of the devotional books she owned. Kathryn Joy McKnight, *The Mystic of Tunja: The Writings of Madre Castillo, 1671–1742* (Amherst: University of Massachusetts Press, 1997), 159.

Conclusion

1. See, for example, Michel Verdon, "Virgins and Widows: European Kinship and Early Christianity," *Man*, New Series, 23, no. 3 (1988): 488–505.

2. For the debate over nomenclature see John W. O'Malley, *Trent and All That: Renaming Catholicism in the Early Modern Era* (Cambridge, Mass.: Harvard University Press, 2000).

3. *Obras completas de la Madre Francisca Josepha de la Concepción de Castillo*, ed. Dario Achury Valenzuela (Bogotá: Banco de la República, 1968; orig. completed c. 1715), 1:5.

4. Isabelle Poutrin, *Le voile et la plume: Autobiographie et sainteté féminine dans l'Espagne moderne* (Madrid: Casa de Velázquez, 1995), 435–53; see also graph 352, which shows that the number of autobiographies composed by women declined after 1735 as well. For the Spanish American colonies, see, for example, the bibliographical sources cited in Kristine Ibsen, *Women's Spiritual Autobiography in Colonial Spanish America* (Gainesville: University Press of Florida, 1999) and in Asunción Lavrin and Rosalva Loreto López, eds., *Monjas y beatas: La escritura femenina en la espiritualidad barroca novohispana, siglos XVII y XVIII* (Puebla: Universidad de las Américas-Puebla, 2002). Standard sources on printed hagiographies of women in early-modern Italy and France all end around 1700; see chapter 5 for a more extended discussion and estimated figures.

5. There is a large literature on Jansenism in seventeenth- and eighteenth-century Europe. Helpful summaries of the issues are provided in R. Po-Chia Hsia, *The World of Catholic Renewal, 1540–1770* (Cambridge: Cambridge University Press, 1998), chap. 13; Robert Bireley, *The Refashioning of Catholicism, 1450–1700* (Washington, D.C.: Catholic University of America

Press, 1999), chap. 8; Michael A. Mullett, *The Catholic Reformation* (London: Routledge, 1999) chap. 5. See also William Doyle, *Jansenism: Catholic Resistance to Authority from the Reformation to the French Revolution* (New York: St. Martin's Press, 2000).

6. Dale Van Kley, *The Jansenists and the Expulsion of the Jesuits from France, 1757–1765* (New Haven: Yale University Press, 1975); William J. Callahan and David Higgs, eds., *Church and Society in Catholic Europe of the Eighteenth Century* (Cambridge: Cambridge University Press, 1979); Mario Rosa, *Settecento religioso: Politica della regione e religione del cuore* (Venice: Marsilio, 1999), esp. chaps. 2, 9.

7. The phrase "ecclesiastical civil war" is Mullett's, *Catholic Reformation*, 166. Cardinal Bona's remark is quoted in Elizabeth Rapley, *A Social History of the Cloister: Daily Life in the Teaching Monasteries of the Old Regime* (Montreal and Kingston: McGill-Queen's University Press, 2001), 66.

8. See, for example, Hsia, *World*, 206–9.

9. Daniella J. Kostroun, "Undermining Obedience in Absolutist France: The Case of the Port Royal Nuns, 1609–1709" (Ph.D. diss., Duke University, 2000).

10. It would also be interesting to examine the effect on Catholic religious life of political struggles in the American colonies in precisely this period, notably France's loss of Canada to the British after the Seven Years' War in 1763.

11. *The Way of Perfection* 3:5, in *The Collected Works of St. Teresa of Avila*, trans. Kieran Kavanaugh and Otilio Rodríguez (Washington, D.C.: Institute of Carmelite Studies, 1976–1985), 2:49–50. Jodi Bilinkoff, "Woman with a Mission: Teresa of Avila and the Apostolic Model," in *Modelli di santità e modelli di comportamento: Contrasti, intersezioni, complementarità*, ed. Guilia Barone, Marina Caffiero and Francesco Scorza Barcellona (Turin: Rosenberg and Sellier, 1994), 295–305.

12. See, for example, Jo Ann Kay McNamara, *Sisters in Arms: Catholic Nuns Through Two Millennia* (Cambridge, Mass.: Harvard University Press, 1996), chap. 16; Elizabeth Rapley, *The Dévotes: Women and Church in Seventeenth-Century France* (Montreal and Kingston: McGill-Queen's University Press, 1990); Rapley, *Social History of the Cloister;* Patricia Ranft, "A Key to Counter Reformation Women's Activism: The Confessor-Spiritual Director," *Journal of Feminist Studies in Religion* 10 (1994):9–23. For the Daughters of Charity in particular see Susan E. Dinan, "Confraternities as a Venue for Female Activism during the Catholic Reformation," in *Confraternities and Catholic Reform in Italy, France and Spain,* ed. John Patrick Donnelly and Michael W. Maher (Kirksville, Mo.: Thomas Jefferson University Press, 1999), 191–214.

13. Olwen Hufton, "The French Church," in Callahan and Higgs, *Church and Society,* 21. She continues: "Practical and pragmatic, popular attitudes in the eighteenth century towards the religious life were shaped by the aid it afforded in the here and now. This was an important aspect of the laicization of social attitudes."

14. William J. Callahan comments that in Spain during the eighteenth century the "vast majority of nuns lived in contemplative communities" and that "in general active work [in nursing and charitable endeavors] was not common." "The Spanish Church," in Callahan and Higgs, *Church and Society,* 44. The century did see an expansion of teaching orders for women, however. See Pilar Foz y Foz, "Los monasterios de la enseñanza y la educación de la mujer en España e Iberoamérica," in *I Congreso Internacional del Monacato Femenino en España, Portugal y América, 1492–1992* (León: Universidad de León, 1993), 1:67–84.

15. "The Development of the Individual" is the title of part 2 of Burckhardt's classic *The Civilization of the Renaissance in Italy,* first published in 1860. Thomas Heller and David Wellberry state as one of scholars' "general assumptions" that "some form of individualism—

broadly conceived as the view that the individual human subject is a maker of the world we inhabit—has been a key factor in the life of the West for the last five hundred years." Introduction to *Reconstructing Individualism: Autonomy, Individuality, and the Self in Western Thought,* ed. Thomas C. Heller, Morton Sosna, and David E. Wellberry (Stanford: Stanford University Press, 1986), 1–15; quote at 1.

16. Natalie Zemon Davis, "Boundaries and the Sense of the Self in Sixteenth-Century France," in Heller, Sosna, and Wellberry, *Reconstructing Individualism,* 53–63; quote at 53.

✺ SELECTED BIBLIOGRAPHY

Primary Sources

Spain

Alonso de la Madre de Dios. *Vida, virtudes y milagros del santo padre Fray Juan de la Cruz*. Madrid: Editorial de Espiritualidad, 1989; orig. publ. c. 1630.

Alvarez, Baltasar. *Escritos Espirituales*. Edited by Camilo María Abad and Faustino Boado. Barcelona: Juan Flors, 1961.

Bernique, Juan. *Idea de Perfección, y Virtudes. Vida de . . . Catalina de Jesús y San Francisco*. Alcalá de Henares, 1693.

Fernández de Madrid, Alonso. *Vida de Fray Fernando de Talavera, Primer Arzobispo de Granada*. Edited by Féliz G. Olmedo. Granada: Universidad de Granada, 1992; orig. publ. c. 1530.

González Vaquero, Miguel. *La muger fuerte, por otro título, La vida de Doña María Vela . . .* Madrid 1618, 1674.

Gracián, Jerónimo. *Peregrinación de Anastasio*. Edited by Giovanni Maria Bertini. Barcelona: Juan Flors, 1966; orig. publ. c. 1609.

"Información de la vida, muerte, y milagros de la Venerable María Díaz." Archivo Diocesano, Avila. Códice 3.345.

Isabel de Jesús. *Tesoro del Carmelo escondido . . . Vida. . . . de la Venerable Madre Isabel de Jesús . . .* Madrid, 1685.

Isabel de Jesús. *Vida de la Venerable Madre Isabel de Iesus . . . Dictada por ella misma y Añadido lo que faltó de su Dichosa Muerte*. Madrid, 1675.

María Antonia de Jesús. *Autobiography* (c. 1750). Excerpted in *Una mística gallega en el siglo XVIII: La Venerable Madre María Antonia de Jesús*, by Una Carmelita Descalza del Convento de Santiago. La Coruña: Galicia Editorial, 1991.

———. *Edificio Espiritual*. Santiago de Compostela: Bibliófilos Gallegos, 1954.

Mariana de Jesús. *Autobiography* (c. 1615). In *Beata Mariana de Jesús, Mercedaria Madrileña*, by Elías Gómez Domínguez. Rome: Instituto Histórico de la Orden de la Merced, 1991.

Noriega, José Esteban. *La Pecadora arrepentida. Vida y conversión de la Venerable María del Santísimo Sacramento, Llamada la Quintana* (1737). Excerpted in *Confesión y trayectoria femenina: Vida de la Venerable Quintana*, by María-Helena Sánchez Ortega. Madrid: CSIC, 1996.

Panes, Antonio. *Chronica de la Provincia de San Juan Bautista . . . de Nuestro Seraphica Padre San Francisco*. 2 vols. Valencia, 1665–66.

Pedro de San Cecilio. *Anales del Orden de Descalzos de Nuestra Señora de la Merced . . .* 2 vols. Barcelona, 1669.

Peña, Antonio de la. Introduction to his translation of *La vida de la bienaventurada sancta Caterina de Sena, by Raymond of Capua.* Alcalá de Henares, 1511.

Puente, Luis de la. *Vida del Padre Baltasar Alvarez.* Madrid, 1615.

———. *Vida maravillosa de la Venerable Virgen Doña Marina de Escobar . . .* Madrid: Francisco Nieto, 1665.

Ribadeneyra, Pedro de. "Vida de Doña Estefanía Manrique de Castilla." Biblioteca Nacional, Madrid. MS 7421.

———. *Vida del Padre Ignacio de Loyola, fundador de la religión de la Compañía de Jesús.* Madrid, 1583, 1586.

Teresa of Avila. *The Collected Works of St. Teresa of Avila.* Translated by Kieran Kavanaugh and Otilio Rodríguez. Washington, D.C.: Institute of Carmelite Studies, 1976–80.

———. *Obras completas.* Edited by Efrén de la Madre de Dios and Otger Steggink. Madrid: Editorial Católica, 1977.

Teresa de Jesús María. *Las obras de . . . Sor Teresa de Jesús María [1592–c. 1642].* Edited by Manuel Serrano y Sanz. Madrid: Gil Blas, 1921.

Torres, Marcos. *[N]oticias . . . de la vida y virtudes . . . de Doña María de Pol, su madre.* Málaga? 1660.

Vela y Cueto, María. *Autobiografía y Libro de las Mercedes.* Edited by Olegario González Hernández. Barcelona: Juan Flors, 1961.

———. *The Third Mystic of Avila: The Self-Revelation of María Vela, a Sixteenth-Century Spanish Nun.* Translated by Frances Parkinson Keyes. New York: Farrar, Straus and Cudahy, 1960.

Vidas del Padre Maestro Juan de Avila. Edited by Luis Sala Balust. Barcelona: Juan Flors, 1964.

Spanish America

Castillo, Francisca Josepha de. *Obras completas de la Madre Francisca Josepha de la Concepción de Castillo.* Edited by Dario Achury Valenzuela. Bogotá: Banco de la República, 1968; orig. completed c. 1715.

Losa, Francisco. *The Life of Gregory Lopes that Great Servant of God . . .* Menston, U.K.: Scolar Press, 1969; orig. publ. Paris, 1638.

———. *La Vida que Hizo el Siervo de Dios Gregorio López, en algunas lugares de esta Nueva España . . .* Mexico City: Juan Ruiz, 1613.

María de San José. *Autobiographical Writings.* Excerpted in *A Wild Country Out in the Garden: The Spiritual Journals of a Colonial Mexican Nun,* edited and translated by Kathleen A. Myers and Amanda Powell. Bloomington: Indiana University Press, 1999.

Nava y Saavedra, Jerónima. *Autobiografía de una monja venerable.* Edited by Angela Inés Robledo. Cali: Universidad del Valle, 1994; orig. publ. 1727.

Suárez, Ursula. *Relación autobiográfica.* Edited by Mario Ferreccio Podestá. Santiago de Chile: Universidad de Concepción, 1984; orig. completed c. 1730.

France and New France

Alacoque, Margaret Mary. *The Autobiography of Margaret Mary Alacoque.* Translated by Sisters of the Visitation, Partridge Green. Rockford, Ill.: Tan Publishers, 1986.

———. *The Letters of St. Margaret Mary Alacoque.* Translated by Clarence A. Herbst. Rockford, Ill.: Tan Publishers, 1954.

———. *Vie de Sainte Marguerite-Marie Alacoque écrite par elle-même.* Paris: Gigord, 1934; orig. completed 1685.

Bigot, Jacques. *La vie du Pere Paul Ragueneau de la Compagnie de Iesus Missionaire du Canada.* Edited by Guy Laflèche. Montreal: VLB, 1979; orig. publ. c. 1700.

Colombière, Claude de la. *The Spiritual Direction of Saint Claude de la Colombière.* Edited and translated by Mother M. Philip. San Francisco: Ignatius Press, 1934.

Duval, André. *La Vie admirable de la Bienhereuse Soeur Marie de l'Incarnation . . . appelée dans le monde Mademoiselle Acarie.* Paris: Librairie Victor Lecoffre, 1893; orig. publ. 1621.

Guyon, Jeanne-Marie. *La vie par elle-même et autres écrits biographiques.* Edited by Dominique Tronc. Paris: Honoré Champion, 2001; orig. publ. 1720.

Lallemant, Louis. *The Spiritual Doctrine of Father Louis Lallemant of the Society of Jesus.* Edited by Alan G. McDougall. Westminster, Md.: Newman Book Shop, 1946.

——. *La Vie et La Doctrine Spirituelle du Père Louis Lallemant de la Compagnie de Jésus.* Paris: Desclée de Brouwer, 1959; orig. publ. 1694.

Marie de l'Incarnation. *The Autobiography of Venerable Marie of the Incarnation, O.S.U: Mystic and Missionary.* Translated by John J. Sullivan. Chicago: Loyola University Press, 1964.

——. "Life of Marie de Saint Joseph." In Julia Boss, "The Life and Death of Mother Marie de Saint Joseph." In *Religions of the United States in Practice,* edited by Colleen McDannell, 1:347–65. Princeton: Princeton University Press, 2001.

——. *La Vie de la Venerable Mere Marie de l'Incarnation Premiere Superieur des Ursulines de la Nouvelle France.* Paris, 1677; facsimile ed., Solesmes, 1981.

Ragueneau, Paul. *La Vie de la Mere Catherine de Saint Augustin, Religieuse Hospitaliere de la Misericorde de Quebec en la Nouvelle-France.* Paris, 1671.

——et al. *Heroes of Huronia.* Translated by Joseph Fallon. Fort Ste Marie, Ontario: The Martyrs Shrine, 1948.

Sales, François de. *Correspondance: Les lettres d'amitié spirituelle.* Edited by André Ravier. Paris: Desclée de Brouwer, 1980.

Surin, Jean-Joseph. *Correspondance.* Edited by Michel de Certeau. Paris: Desclée de Brouwer, 1966.

Italy

Pazzi, Maria Maddalena de. *Tutte le Opere di Santa Maria Maddalena de' Pazzi.* 4 vols. Florence: Centro Internazionale del Libro, 1960–67.

Puccini, Vincenzio. *The Life of the Holy Maid and Venerable Mother Suor Maria Maddalena de Patsi . . .* Edited by D. M. Rogers. Menston, U.K.: Scolar Press, 1970; orig. publ. Cologne? 1619.

——. *Vita della Veneranda Madre Suor M. Maddalena de' Pazzi Fiorentina.* Florence, 1609, 1611.

Razzi, Serafino. *Vita di Santa Caterina de' Ricci.* Edited by Guglielmo M. di Agresti. Florence: Olschki, 1965; orig. publ. 1594.

Varano, Battista da. *My Spiritual Life.* Translated by Joseph Berrigan. Toronto: Peregrina Publishing, 1986; orig. publ. 1491.

——. *Le Opere Spirituali.* Edited by Giacomo Boccanera. Jesi: Scuola Tipografica Francescana, 1958.

Portugal

Berretari, Sebastiano. *Vida del Padre Joseph de Anchieta de la Compañía de Jesús, y Provincial de Brasil.* Barcelona, 1622.

Castelo Branco, Antónia Margarida de. *Autobiografia, 1652–1717.* Edited by João Palma-Ferreira. Lisbon: Imprensa Nacional, 1983.

Luís dos Anjos. *Jardim de Portugal, em que se da noticia de algunas Sanctas, & outras molheres ilustres em virtude . . .* Edited by Maria de Lurdes Correia Fernandes. Porto: Campo das Letras, 1999; orig. publ. 1626.

Schroeder, H. J., trans. *Canons and Decrees of the Council of Trent.* Rockford, Ill.: Tan Books, 1978.

SECONDARY SOURCES

Ahlgren, Gillian T. W. "Ecstasy, Prophecy, and Reform: Catherine of Siena as a Model for Holy Women of Sixteenth-Century Spain." in *The Mystical Gesture: Essays on Medieval and Early Modern Spiritual Culture in Honor of Mary E. Giles,* edited by Robert Boenig, 53–65. Aldershot, U.K.: Ashgate, 2000.

———. *Teresa of Avila and the Politics of Sanctity.* Ithaca: Cornell University Press, 1996.

Alejandre, Juan Antonio. *El veneno de Dios: La Inquisición de Sevilla ante el delito de solicitación en confesión.* Madrid: Siglo Veintiuno, 1994.

Amelang, James A. "Los usos de la autobiografía: monjas y beatas en la Cataluña moderna." In *Historia y Género: Las mujeres en la Europa moderna y contemporánea,* edited by James A. Amelang and Mary Nash, 191–212. Valencia: Edicions Alfons el Magnànim, 1990.

Arenal, Electa. "The Convent as Catalyst for Autonomy: Two Hispanic Nuns of the Seventeenth Century." In *Women in Hispanic Literature: Icons and Fallen Idols,* edited by Beth Miller, 147–83. Berkeley: University of California Press, 1983.

Arenal, Electa, and Stacey Schlau. *Untold Sisters: Hispanic Nuns in Their Own Works.* Albuquerque: University of New Mexico Press, 1989.

Barbeito Carneiro, Isabel. *Mujeres del Madrid barroco: Voces testimoniales.* Madrid: horas y horas, 1992.

Barzman, Karen-Edis. "Gender, Religious Representation and Cultural Production in Early Modern Italy." In *Gender and Society in Renaissance Italy,* edited by Judith C. Brown and Robert C. Davis, 213–33. London: Longman, 1998.

Bell, Rudolph. "Telling Her Sins: Male Confessors and Female Penitents in Catholic Reformation Italy." In *That Gentle Strength: Historical Perspectives on Women in Christianity,* edited by Lynda L. Coon, Katherine J. Haldane, and Elisabeth W. Sommer, 118–33. Charlottesville: University of Virginia Press, 1990.

Benvenuti Papi, Anna. *"In Castro Poenitentiae:" Santità e Società Femminile nell'Italia Medievale.* Rome: Herder, 1990.

Bilinkoff, Jodi. *The Avila of Saint Teresa: Religious Reform in a Sixteenth-Century City.* Ithaca: Cornell University Press, 1989.

———. "Charisma and Controversy: The Case of María de Santo Domingo." In *Spanish Women in the Golden Age: Images and Realities,* edited by Magdalena S. Sánchez and Alain Saint-Saëns, 23–35. Westport: Conn.: Greenwood Press, 1996.

———. "Confession, Gender, Life-Writing: Some Cases (Mainly) from Spain." In *Penitence in the Age of Reformations,* edited by Katharine Jackson Lualdi and Ann T. Thayer, 169–83. Aldershot, U.K.: Ashgate, 2000.

———. "Confessors, Penitents, and the Construction of Identities in Early Modern Avila." In *Culture and Identity in Early Modern Europe (1500–1800): Essays in Honor of Natalie Zemon Davis,* edited by Barbara B. Diefendorf and Carla Hesse, 83–100. Ann Arbor: University of Michigan Press, 1993.

———. "Francisco Losa and Gregorio López: Spiritual Friendship and Identity Formation on the New Spain Frontier," in *Colonial Saints: Discovering the Holy in the Americas, 1500–1800,* edited by Allan Greer and Jodi Bilinkoff, 115–28. New York: Routledge, 2003.

———. "The Many 'Lives' of Pedro de Ribadeneyra." *Renaissance Quarterly* 52 (1999): 180–96.

———. "Navigating the Waves (of Devotion): Toward a Gendered Analysis of Early Modern Catholicism." In *Crossing Boundaries: Attending to Early Modern Women,* edited by Jane Donawerth and Adele Seeff, 161–72. Newark, Del.: University of Delaware Press, 2000.

———. "A Peasant Visionary and Her Audience in Early Sixteenth-Century Spain." *Studia Mystica* 18 (1997): 36–59.

——. "A Saint for a City: Mariana de Jesús and Madrid, 1565–1624." *Archive for Reformation History* 88 (1997): 322–37.

Biller, Peter, and A. J. Minnis, eds. *Handling Sin: Confession in the Middle Ages.* Woodbridge, U.K.: York Medieval Press, 1998.

Bireley, Robert. *The Refashioning of Catholicism, 1450–1700.* Washington, D.C.: Catholic University of America Press, 1999.

Boenig, Robert, ed. *The Mystical Gesture: Essays on Medieval and Early Modern Spiritual Culture in Honor of Mary E. Giles.* Aldershot, U.K.: Ashgate, 2000.

Boss, Julia. "Writing a Relic: The Uses of Hagiography in New France." In *Colonial Saints: Discovering the Holy in the Americas, 1500–1800,* edited by Allan Greer and Jodi Bilinkoff, 211–33. New York: Routledge, 2003.

Bremond, Henri. *A Literary History of Religious Thought in France.* 3 vols. London: Society for Promoting Christian Knowledge, 1928–36.

Brown, D. Catherine. *Pastor and Laity in the Theology of Jean Gerson.* Cambridge: Cambridge University Press, 1987.

Brown, Peter. *The Cult of the Saints: Its Rise and Function in Latin Christianity.* Chicago: University of Chicago Press, 1981.

Bruneau, Marie-Florine. *Women Mystics Confront the Modern World: Marie de l'Incarnation (1599–1672) and Madame Guyon (1648–1717).* Albany: State University of New York Press, 1998.

Burkardt, Albrecht. "Reconnaissance et dévotion: Les vies des saints et leurs lectures au début du XVIIe siècle a travers les procès de canonization." *Revue d'histoire moderne et contemporaine* 43 (1996): 214–33.

Burke, Peter. "How to Be a Counter-Reformation Saint." In *Religion and Society in Early Modern Europe,* edited by Kaspar von Greyerz, 45–55. London: Allen and Unwin, 1984.

Bynum, Caroline Walker. "Fast, Feast, and Flesh: The Religious Significance of Food to Medieval Women." *representations* 11 (1985): 1–25.

——. *Holy Feast and Holy Fast: The Religious Significance of Food to Medieval Women.* Berkeley: University of California Press, 1987.

Caciola, Nancy. *Discerning Spirits: Divine and Demonic Possession in the Middle Ages.* Ithaca: Cornell University Press, 2003.

Callahan, William J., and David Higgs, eds. *Church and Society in Catholic Europe of the Eighteenth Century.* Cambridge: Cambridge University Press, 1979.

Cánovas, Rodrigo. "Ursula Suárez (Monja Chilena, 1666–1749): La autobiografía como penitencia." *Revista Chilena de Literatura* 35 (1990): 97–115.

Charnon-Deutsch, Lou, ed. *Estudios sobre escritoras hispánicas en honor de Georgina Sabat-Rivers.* Madrid: Castalia, 1992.

Choquette, Leslie. "'Ces Amazones du Grand Dieu': Women and Mission in Seventeenth-Century Canada." *French Historical Studies* 17 (1992): 628–55.

Ciammitti, Luisa. "One Saint Less: The Story of Angela Mellini, a Bolognese Seamstress (1667–17[?])." In *Sex and Gender in Historical Perspective,* edited by Edward Muir and Guido Ruggiero, 141–76. Baltimore: Johns Hopkins University Press, 1990; orig. essay 1979.

Coakley, John. *Draw Me after You: Clerics and Holy Women, 1150–1400.* New York: Columbia University Press, forthcoming.

——. "Friars as Confidants of Holy Women in Medieval Dominican Hagiography." In *Images of Sainthood in Medieval Europe,* edited by Renate Blumenthal-Kosinski and Timea Szell, 222–46. Ithaca: Cornell University Press, 1991.

——. "Friars, Sanctity, and Gender: Mendicant Encounters with Saints, 1250–1325." In *Medieval Masculinities: Regarding Men in the Middle Ages,* edited by Clare A. Lees, 91–110. Minneapolis: University of Minnesota Press, 1994.

168   SELECTED BIBLIOGRAPHY

———. "Gender and the Authority of Friars: The Significance of Holy Women for Thirteenth-Century Franciscans and Dominicans." *Church History* 60 (1991): 445–60.

———. "A Marriage and Its Observer: Christine of Stommeln, the Heavenly Bridegroom, and Friar Peter of Dacia," In *Gendered Voices: Medieval Saints and Their Interpreters*, edited by Catherine M. Mooney, 99–117. Philadelphia: University of Pennsylvania Press, 1999.

Correia Fernandes, Maria de Lurdes. *A biblioteca de Jorge Cardoso (d. 1669), autor do 'Agiológio Lusitano': Cultura, erudição e sentimento religioso no Portugal moderno.* Porto: Universidade do Porto, 2000.

———. "Uma clarissa ilustre do século XVI: Ana Ponce de León, Condessa de Féria e monja de Santa Clara de Montilla." In *Las Clarisas en España y Portugal, Actas del Congreso Internacional*, edited by José Martí Mayor and María del Mar Graña Cid, 1:331–40. Madrid: Archivos e Historia, 1994.

———. "A construção da santidade nos finais do século XVI. O caso de Isabel de Miranda, tecedeira, viúva e 'santa' (c. 1539–1610)." In *Actas do Colóquio Internacional Piedade Popular: Sociabiladades, representações, espiritualidades*, 243–72. Lisbon: Centro de História da Cultura / Terramar, 1999.

Davis, Natalie Zemon. "Boundaries and the Sense of the Self in Sixteenth-Century France." In *Reconstructing Individualism: Autonomy, Individuality, and the Self in Western Thought*, edited by Thomas C. Heller, Morton Sosna, and David E. Wellbery, 53–63. Stanford: Stanford University Press, 1986.

———. *Women on the Margins: Three Seventeenth-Century Lives.* Cambridge, Mass.: Harvard University Press, 1995.

De Boer, Wietse. *The Conquest of the Soul: Confession, Discipline, and Public Order in Counter-Reformation Milan.* Leiden: Brill, 2001.

Deslandres, Dominique. *Croire et faire croire: Les missions françaises au XVIIe siècle (1600–1650).* Paris: Fayard, 2003.

———. "In the Shadow of the Cloister: Representations of Female Holiness in New France." In *Colonial Saints: Discovering the Holy in the Americas, 1500–1800*, edited by Allan Greer and Jodi Bilinkoff, 129–52. New York: Routledge, 2003.

Diefenderfer, Lara Mary. "Making and Unmaking Saints in Seventeenth-Century Madrid." Ph.D. diss., University of Virginia, 2003.

Diefendorf, Barbara B. *From Penitence to Charity: Pious Women and the Catholic Reformation in Paris.* New York: Oxford University Press, 2004.

Dinan, Susan E. "Confraternities as a Venue for Female Activism during the Catholic Reformation." In *Confraternities and Catholic Reform in Italy, France, and Spain*, edited by John Patrick Donnelly and Michael W. Maher, 191–214. Kirksville, Mo.: Thomas Jefferson University Press, 1999.

———. "Spheres of Female Religious Expression in Early Modern France." In *Women and Religion in Old and New Worlds*, edited by Susan E. Dinan and Debra Meyers, 71–92. New York: Routledge, 2001.

Ditchfield, Simon. "An Early Christian School of Sanctity in Tridentine Rome." In *Christianity and Community in the West: Essays for John Bossy*, edited by Simon Ditchfield, 183–205 Aldershot, U.K.: Ashgate, 2001.

Donahue, Darcy. "Writing Lives: Nuns and Confessors as Auto / Biographers in Early Modern Spain." *Journal of Hispanic Philology* 13 (1989): 230–39.

Donnelly, John Patrick, and Michael W. Maher, eds. *Confraternities and Catholic Reform in Italy, France, and Spain.* Kirksville, Mo.: Thomas Jefferson University Press, 1999.

Doyle, William. *Jansenism: Catholic Resistance to Authority from the Reformation to the French Revolution.* New York: St. Martin's Press, 2000.

Duval, André. *Des sacrements au concile de Trente.* Paris: Editions du Cerf, 1985.

Ehlers, Benjamin. "Catholic Reform as Process: The Archbishop Juan de Ribera (1532–1611) and the Colegio de Corpus Christi, Valencia." *Archive for Reformation History* 95 (2004): 186–209.

———. "Christians and Muslims in Valencia: The Archbishop Juan de Ribera (1532–1611) and the Formation of a 'Communitas Christiana.'" Ph.D. diss., Johns Hopkins University, 1999.

Eire, Carlos M.N. *From Madrid to Purgatory: The Art and Craft of Dying in Sixteenth-Century Spain.* Cambridge: Cambridge University Press, 1995.

Elliott, Dyan. "Authorizing a Life: The Collaboration of Dorothea of Montau and John Marienwerder." In *Gendered Voices: Medieval Saints and Their Interpreters,* edited by Catherine M. Mooney, 168–91. Philadelphia: University of Pennsylvania Press, 1999.

———. "Dominae or Dominatae? Female Mysticism and the Trauma of Textuality." In *Women, Marriage, and Family in Medieval Christendom: Essays in Memory of Michael M. Sheehan, CSB,* edited by Constance M. Rousseau and Joel D. Rosenthal, 47–77. Kalamazoo, Mich.: Medieval Institute Publications, 1998.

Erba, Andrea. "Il 'caso' di Paola Antonia Negri nel Cinquecento italiano." In *Women and Men in Spiritual Culture, XIV–XVII Centuries: A Meeting of South and North,* edited by Elisja Schulte van Kessel, 193–211. The Hague: Netherlands Government Printing Office, 1986.

Evangelisti, Silvia. "'We Do Not Have It, and We Do Not Want It': Women, Power, and Convent Reform in Florence." *Sixteenth Century Journal* 34, no. 3 (2003): 677–700.

Foz y Foz, Pilar. "Los monasterios de la enseñanza y la educación de la mujer en España e Iberoamérica." In *I Congreso Internacional del Monacato Femenino en España, Portugal y América, 1492–1992,* 1:67–84. León: Universidad de León, 1993.

Gerardo de S. Juan de la Cruz. "María Díaz, llamada 'La esposa del Santísimo Sacramento.'" *El Monte Carmelo* 17 (1915): 166–70.

González Marmolejo, Jorge René. "Clérigos solicitantes, perversos de la confesión." In *De la santidad a la perversión, O de porqué no se cumpla la ley de Dios en la sociedad novohispana,* edited by Sergio Ortega, 239–52. Mexico City: Grijalbo, 1985.

Greer, Allan. "Colonial Saints: Gender, Race, and Hagiography in New France," *William and Mary Quarterly,* 3d ser., 57 (2000): 323–48.

———. "Iroquois Virgin: The Story of Catherine Tekakwitha in New France and New Spain." In *Colonial Saints: Discovering the Holy in the Americas, 1500–1800,* edited by Allan Greer and Jodi Bilinkoff, 235–50. New York: Routledge, 2003.

———. *Mohawk Saint: Catherine Tekakwitha and the Jesuits.* New York: Oxford University Press, 2004.

Greer, Allan, and Jodi Bilinkoff, eds. *Colonial Saints: Discovering the Holy in the Americas, 1500–1800.* New York: Routledge, 2003.

Guitton, Georges. *Perfect Friend: The Life of Blessed Claude de la Colombière, SJ, 1641–1682.* Translated by William J. Young. St. Louis: Herder, 1956.

Haliczer, Stephen. *Sexuality in the Confessional: A Sacrament Profaned.* New York: Oxford University Press, 1996.

Hampe Martínez, Teodoro. *Santidad e identidad criolla: estudio del proceso de canonización de Santa Rosa.* Cuzco: Centro de Estudios Regionales Andinos "Bartolomé de las Casas," 1998.

Harline, Craig. "Actives and Contemplatives: The Female Religious of the Low Countries before and after Trent." *Catholic Historical Review* 81, no. 4 (1995): 541–67.

Heffernan, Thomas J. *Sacred Biography: Saints and Their Biographers in the Middle Ages.* New York: Oxford University Press, 1988.

Heller, Thomas C., Morton Sosna, and David E. Wellbery. *Reconstructing Individualism: Autonomy, Individuality, and the Self in Western Thought.* Stanford: Stanford University Press, 1986.

Henderson, John. "Penitence and the Laity in Fifteenth-Century Florence." In *Christianity and the*

Renaissance: Image and Religious Imagination in the Quattrocento, edited by Timothy Verdon and John Henderson, 229–49. Syracuse: Syracuse University Press, 1990.

Herpoel, Sonja. "L'analphabétisme contre le pouvoir: le témoignage d'Isabel de Jesús." *Bulletin Hispanique* 91 (1989): 395–408.

———. "Los auditorios de Isabel de Jesús," In *Estudios sobre escritoras hispánicas en honor de Georgina Sabat-Rivers*, edited by Lou Charnon-Deutsch, 128–41. Madrid: Castalia, 1992.

———. *A la zaga de Santa Teresa: Autobiografías por mandato*. Amsterdam: Rodopi, 1999.

Homza, Lu Ann. *Religious Authority in the Spanish Renaissance*. Baltimore: Johns Hopkins University Press, 2000.

Hsia, R. Po-Chia. *The World of Catholic Renewal, 1540–1770*. Cambridge: Cambridge University Press, 1998.

Huerga, Alvaro. *Santa Catalina de Siena en la historia de la espiritualidad hispana*. Rome, 1969.

Ibsen, Kristine. *Women's Spiritual Autobiography in Colonial Spanish America*. Gainesville: University Press of Florida, 1999.

Jansen, Katherine L. *The Making of the Magdalen: Preaching and Popular Devotion in the Later Middle Ages*. Princeton: Princeton University Press, 2000.

Jonas, Raymond. *France and the Cult of the Sacred Heart: An Epic Tale for Modern Times*. Berkeley: University of California Press, 2000.

Kagan, Richard L. "Clio and the Crown: Writing History in Habsburg Spain." In *Spain, Europe and the Atlantic World: Essays in Honour of John H. Elliott*, edited by Richard L. Kagan and Geoffrey Parker, 73–99. Cambridge: Cambridge University Press, 1995.

Kieckhefer, Richard. *Unquiet Souls: Fourteenth-Century Saints and Their Religious Milieu*. Chicago: University of Chicago Press, 1984.

Kleinberg, Aviad. *Prophets in Their Own Country: Living Saints and the Making of Sainthood in the Later Middle Ages*. Chicago: University of Chicago Press, 1992.

Kostroun, Daniella J. "Undermining Obedience in Absolutist France: The Case of the Port Royal Nuns, 1609–1709." Ph.D. diss., Duke University, 2000.

Lagos, María Inés. "Confessing to the Father: Marks of Gender and Class in Ursula Suárez's *Relación*." *Modern Languages Notes* 110 (1995): 353–84.

Laningham, Susan D. "Gender, Body, and Authority in a Spanish Convent: The Life and Trials of María Vela y Cueto, 1561–1621." Ph.D. diss., University of Arkansas,2001.

Lavrin, Asunción. "La vida femenina como experiencia religiosa: biografía y hagiografía en Hispanoamérica colonial." *Colonial Latin American Review* 2 (1993): 27–51.

Lavrin, Asunción, and Rosalva Loreto López, eds. *Monjas y beatas: La escritura femenina en la espiritualidad barroca novohispana, siglos XVII y XVIII*. Puebla: Universidad de la Américas-Puebla, 2002.

Lebrun, François. "A corps perdu: Les biographies spirituelles féminines du XVIIe siècle." *Le temps de la réflexion* 7 (1986): 389–408.

———. "Mutations de la notion de martyre au XVIIe siècle d'après les biographies spirituelles féminines." In *Sainteté et martyre dans les religions du Livre*, edited by Jacques Marx, 77–90. Brussels: Université de Bruxelles, 1989.

———. "The Two Reformations: Communal Devotion and Personal Piety." In *A History of Private Life*, edited by Roger Chartier, translated by Arthur Goldhammer, 69–109. Cambridge, Mass: Harvard University Press, 1989; orig. publ. 1986.

Lehfeldt, Elizabeth A. "Discipline, Vocation, and Patronage: Spanish Religious Women in a Tridentine Microclimate." *Sixteenth Century Journal* 30, no. 4 (1999): 1009–30.

Lowe, K. J. P. *Nuns' Chronicles and Convent Culture in Renaissance and Counter-Reformation Italy*. Cambridge: Cambridge University Press, 2003.

Lualdi, Katharine Jackson, and Anne T. Thayer, eds. *Penitence in the Age of Reformations*. Aldershot, U.K.: Ashgate, 2000.

Luti, Mary. "'A Marriage Well Arranged': Teresa of Avila and Fray Jerónimo Gracián de la Madre de Dios." *Studia Mystica* 12 (1989): 32–46.

Maggi, Armando. *Uttering the Word: The Mystical Performances of Maria Maddalena de' Pazzi, a Renaissance Visionary*. Albany: State University of New York Press, 1998.

Maher, Michael. "Confession and Consolation: The Society of Jesus and its Promotion of the General Confession." In *Penitence in the Age of Reformations*, edited by Katharine Jackson Lualdi and Anne T. Thayer, 184–200. Aldershot, U.K.: Ashgate, 2000.

Mali, Anya. *Mystic in the New World: Marie de l'Incarnation (1599–1672)*. Leiden: Brill, 1996.

Márquez Villanueva, Francisco. "La vocación literaria de Santa Teresa." *Nueva Revista de Filología Hispánica* 32 (1983): 355–79.

Marshall, Donald. "Frequent and Daily Communion in the Catholic Church of Spain in the Sixteenth and Seventeenth Centuries." Ph.D. diss., Harvard University, 1952.

Martin, Henri-Jean. *Livre, pouvoirs et société a Paris au XVII siècle*. 2 vols. Geneva: Droz, 1999.

Mayer, Thomas F., and D. R. Woolf, eds. *The Rhetorics of Life-Writing in Early Modern Europe: Forms of Biography from Cassandra Fedele to Louis XIV*. Ann Arbor: University of Michigan Press, 1995.

McGinness, Frederick J. *Right Thinking and Sacred Oratory in Counter-Reformation Rome*. Princeton: Princeton University Press, 1995.

———. "'Roma Sancta' and the Saint: Eucharist, Chastity, and the Logic of Catholic Reform." *Historical Reflections/Reflexions Historiques* 15 (1988): 96–116.

McKnight, Kathryn Joy. *The Mystic of Tunja: The Writings of Madre Castillo, 1671–1742*. Amherst: University of Massachusetts Press, 1997.

McNamara, Jo Ann Kay. *Sisters in Arms: Catholic Nuns Through Two Millennia*. Cambridge, Mass.: Harvard University Press, 1996.

Mooney, Catherine M., ed. *Gendered Voices: Medieval Saints and Their Interpreters*. Philadelphia: University of Pennsylvania Press, 1999.

———. "Voice, Gender, and the Portrayal of Sanctity." In *Gendered Voices: Medieval Saints and Their Interpreters*, 1–15. Philadelphia: University of Pennsylvania Press., 1999.

Morgan, Ronald J. "'Just like Rosa': History and Metaphor in the *Life* of a Seventeenth-Century Peruvian Saint." *Biography* 21 (1998): 275–310.

———. *Spanish American Saints and the Rhetoric of Identity, 1600–1810*. Tucson: University of Arizona Press, 2002.

Morujão, Isabel. *Contributo para uma bibliografia cronológica da literatura monástica feminina portuguesa dos séculos XVII e XVIII*. Lisbon: Universidade Católica Portuguesa, 1995.

Mullett, Michael A. *The Catholic Reformation*. London: Routledge, 1999.

Murray, Alexander. "Confession as a Historical Source in the Thirteenth Century." In *The Writing of History in the Middle Ages: Essays Presented to Richard William Southern*, edited by R. H. C. Davis and J. M. Wallace-Hadrill, 275–322. Oxford: Oxford University Press, 1981.

Myers, Kathleen Ann. "The Mystic Triad in Colonial Mexican Nuns' Discourse: Divine Author, Visionary Scribe, and Clerical Mediator." *Colonial Latin American Historical Review* 6 (1997): 479–524.

———. *Neither Saints Nor Sinners: Writing the Lives of Women in Spanish America*. New York: Oxford University Press, 2003.

———. "'Redeemer of America': Rosa de Lima (1586–1617), the Dynamics of Identity and Canonization." In *Colonial Saints: Discovering the Holy in the Americas, 1500–1800*, edited by Allan Greer and Jodi Bilinkoff, 251–75. New York: Routledge, 2003.

————. "Sor Juana y su mundo: La influencia mediativa del clero en las 'Vidas' de religiosos y monjas." *Revista de Literatura* 61 (1999): 35–59.

Myers, W. David. *"Poor Sinning Folk": Confession and Conscience in Counter-Reformation Germany*. Ithaca: Cornell University Press, 1996.

Norman, Corrie. "The Social History of Preaching: Italy." In *Preachers and People in the Reformation and Early Modern Period*, edited by Larissa Taylor, 125–91. Leiden: Brill, 2001.

Oury, Guy-Marie. *Dom Claude Martin: Le fils de Marie de l'Incarnation*. Solesmes: Abbey de Solesmes, 1983.

————. *L'Itineraire Mystique de Catherine de Saint-Augustin*. Solesmes: Abbey de Solesmes, 1985.

Paolin, Giovanna. "Confessione e confessori al femminile: monache e direttori spirituali in ambito veneto tra '600 e '700." In *Finzione e santità tra medievo ed età moderna*, edited by Gabriella Zarri, 366–88. Turin: Rosenberg and Sellier, 1991.

Perry, Mary Elizabeth. *Gender and Disorder in Early Modern Seville*. Princeton: Princeton University Press, 1990.

Pons Fuster, Francisco. *Místicos, beatas y alumbrados: Ribera y la espiritualidad valenciana del s.XVII*. Valencia: Institució Valenciana D'Estudis i Investigació, 1991.

Poutrin, Isabelle. "Juana Rodríguez, una autora mística olvidada (Burgos, siglo XVII)." In *Estudios sobre escritoras hispánicas en honor de Georgina Sabat-Rivers*, edited by Lou Charnon-Deutsch, 268–84. Madrid: Castalia, 1992.

————. *Le voile et la plume: Autobiographie et sainteté féminine dans l'Espagne moderne*. Madrid: Casa de Velázquez, 1995.

Prosperi, Adriano. "Dalle 'divine madri' ai 'padri spirituali.'" In *Women and Men in Spiritual Culture, XIV–XVII Centuries: A Meeting of North and South*, edited by Elisja Schulte van Kessel, 71–90. The Hague: Netherlands Government Printing Office, 1986.

————. "Spiritual Letters," in *Women and Faith: Catholic Religious Life in Italy from Late Antiquity to the Present*, edited by Lucetta Scaraffia and Gabriella Zarri, 113–28. Cambridge, Mass.: Harvard University Press, 1999; orig. publ. 1994.

Ramos Medina, Manuel. *Místicas y Descalzas: Fundaciones Femeninas Carmelitas en la Nueva España*. Mexico City: CONDUMEX, 1997.

Randolph, Adrian. "Regarding Women in Sacred Space." In *Picturing Women in Renaissance and Baroque Italy*, edited by Geraldine A. Johnson and Sara F. Matthews Grieco. 17–41. Cambridge: Cambridge University Press, 1997.

Ranft, Patrica. "A Key to Counter Reformation Women's Activism: The Confessor-Spiritual Director." *Journal of Feminist Studies in Religion* 10 (1994): 9–23.

————. *A Woman's Way: The Forgotten History of Women Spiritual Directors*. New York: Palgrave, 2000.

Rapley, Elizabeth. *The Dévotes: Women and Church in Seventeenth-Century France*. Montreal and Kingston: McGill-Queen's University Press, 1990.

————. *A Social History of the Cloister: Daily Life in the Teaching Monasteries of the Old Regime*. Montreal and Kingston: McGill-Queen's University Press, 2001.

"Reportorio dei testi a stampa." In *Donna, disciplina, creanza cristiana dal XV al XVII secolo*, edited by Gabriella Zarri, 407–797. Rome: Edizioni di Storia e Letteratura, 1986.

Rhodes, Elizabeth. "What's in a Name: On Teresa of Avila's *Book*." In *The Mystical Gesture, Essays on Medieval and Early Modern Spiritual Culture in Honor of Mary E. Giles*, edited by Robert Boenig, 79–106. Aldershot, U.K.: Ashgate, 2000.

Rosa, Mario. *Settecento religioso: Politica della ragione e religione del cuore*. Venice: Marsilio, 1999.

Rossi, Rosa. *Teresa de Avila: Biografía de una escritora*. Barcelona: Icaria, 1984; orig. publ. 1983.

Rubial García, Antonio. *La santidad controvertida: Hagiografía y conciencia criolla alrededor de los venerables no canonizados de Nueva España*. Mexico City: Fondo de Cultura Económica, 1999.

Rubin, Miri. *Corpus Christi: The Eucharist in Late Medieval Culture.* Cambridge: Cambridge University Press, 1991.

Sampson Vera Tudela, Elisa. *Colonial Angels: Narratives of Gender and Spirituality in Mexico, 1580–1750.* Austin: University of Texas Press, 2000.

Sánchez Lora, José Luis. *Mujeres, conventos y formas de la religiosidad barroca.* Madrid: FUE, 1988.

Sánchez Ortega, María-Helena. *Pecadoras de verano, arrepentidas en invierno: El camino de la conversión femenina.* Madrid: Alianza, 1995.

Sarrión Mora, Adelina. *Sexualidad y confesión: La solicitación ante el Tribunal del Santo Oficio (siglos XVI-XIX).* Madrid: Alianza, 1994.

Scaraffia, Lucetta, and Gabriella Zarri, eds. *Women and Faith: Catholic Religious Life in Italy from Late Antiquity to the Present.* Cambridge, Mass.: Harvard University Press, 1999; orig. publ. 1994.

Scattigno, Anna. "'Carissimo figliulo in Cristo.' Direzione spirituale e mediazone sociale nell'epistolario di Caterina de' Ricci (1542–1590)." In *Ragnatele di rapporti: patronage e reti di relazione nella storia delle donne,* edited by Lucia Ferrante, Maura Palazzi, and Gianna Pomata, 219–39. Turin: Rosenberg and Sellier, 1988.

———. "Maria Maddalena de' Pazzi tra esperienza e modello." In *Donna, disciplina, creanza cristiana dal XV al XVII secolo,* edited by Gabriella Zarri, 85–101. Rome: Edizioni di Storia e Letteratura, 1996.

Schutte, Anne Jacobson. *Aspiring Saints: Pretense of Holiness, Inquisition, and Gender in the Republic of Venice, 1618–1750.* Baltimore: Johns Hopkins University Press, 2001.

Scott, Karen. "Catherine of Siena, 'Apostola.'" *Church History* 61 (1992): 34–46.

———. "Mystical Death, Bodily Death: Catherine of Siena and Raymond of Capua on the Mystic's Encounter with God." In *Gendered Voices: Medieval Saints and Their Interpreters,* edited by Catherine M. Mooney, 136–67. Philadelphia: University of Pennsylvania Press, 1999.

———. "Urban Spaces, Women's Networks, and the Lay Apostolate of Catherine Benincasa." In *Creative Women in Medieval and Early Modern Italy: A Religious and Artistic Renaissance,* edited by E. Ann Matter and John Coakley, 105–19. Philadelphia: University of Pennsylvania Press, 1994.

Seguin, Colleen. "Ambiguous Liaisons: Women's Relationships with Their Confessors in Early Modern England." *Archive for Reformation History* 95 (2004): 156–85.

Sheppard, Lancelot C. *Barbe Acarie: Wife and Mystic.* New York: David McKay, 1953.

Simón Díaz, José. "Hagiografías individuales publicadas en español de 1480 a 1700." *Hispania Sacra* 30, nos. 59–60 (1977): 421–80.

Slade, Carole. *St. Teresa of Avila: Author of a Heroic Life.* Berkeley: University of California Press, 1995.

Sluhovsky, Moshe. "The Devil in the Convent." *American Historical Review* 107, no. 5 (2002): 1379–1411.

Soergel, Philip M. *Wondrous in His Saints: Counter-Reformation Propaganda in Bavaria.* Berkeley: University of California Press, 1993.

Stargardt, Ute. "Male Clerical Authority in the Spiritual (Auto)biographies of Medieval Holy Women." In *Women as Protaganists and Poets in the German Middle Ages: An Anthology of Feminist Approaches to Middle High German Literature,* edited by Albrecht Classen, 209–38. Goppingen: Kummerle Verlag, 1991.

Strasser, Ulrike. "Bones of Contention: Cloistered Nuns, Decorated Relics, and the Contest over Women's Place in the Public Sphere of Counter-Reformation Munich." *Archive for Reformation History* 90 (1999): 255–88.

Surtz, Ronald E. *Writing Women in Late Medieval and Early Modern Spain: The Mothers of Saint Teresa of Avila.* Philadelphia: University of Pennsylvania Press, 1995.

Swanson, R. N. "Angels Incarnate: Clergy and Masculinity from Gregorian Reform to the Refor-mation." In *Masculinity in Medieval Europe,* edited by D. M. Hadley, 169–77. London: Long-man, 1999.

Taylor, Larissa, ed. *Preachers and People in the Reformation and Early Modern Period.* Leiden: Brill, 2001.

———. *Soldiers of Christ: Preaching in Late Medieval and Reformation France.* Toronto: University of Toronto Press, 2002; orig. publ. 1992.

Tentler, Thomas N. *Sin and Confession on the Eve of the Reformation.* Princeton: Princeton Uni-versity Press, 1977.

Thayer, Anne T. *Penitence, Preaching and the Coming of the Reformation.* Aldershot, U.K.: Ash-gate, 2002.

Tobin, Frank. "Henry Suso and Elsbeth Stagel: Was the *Vita* a Cooperative Effort?" In *Gendered Voices: Medieval Saints and Their Interpreters,* edited by Catherine M. Mooney, 118–35. Phila-delphia: University of Pennsylvania Press, 1999.

Valone, Carolyn. "Roman Matrons as Patrons: Various Views of the Cloister Wall." In *The Cran-nied Wall: Women, Religion, and the Arts in Early Modern Europe,* edited by Craig A. Monson, 49–72. Ann Arbor: University of Michigan Press, 1992.

Van Deusen, Nancy E. "Circuits of Knowledge among Lay and Religious Women in Early Sev-enteenth-Century Peru." Paper presented at the Twelfth Berkshire Conference on the History of Women, Storrs, Conn., June, 2002.

Van Kessel, Elisja Schulte, ed. *Women and Men in Spiritual Culture, XIV–XVII Centuries: A Meet-ing of South and North.* The Hague: Netherlands Government Printing Office, 1986.

Van Kley, Dale. *The Jansenists and the Expulsion of the Jesuits from France, 1757–1765.* New Haven: Yale University Press, 1975.

Van Wyhe, Cordula. "Cloistered Court Ladies: Teresian Routes to Sanctity in Seventeenth-Cen-tury Flanders." Paper presented at the international conference "Female Monasticism in Early Modern Europe," Wolfson College, Cambridge University, July 2003.

Vauchez, André. *The Laity in the Middle Ages: Religious Belief and Devotional Practices.* Translated by Margery J. Schneider. Notre Dame: University of Notre Dame Press, 1993; orig. publ. 1987.

———. *Sainthood in the Later Middle Ages.* Translated by Jean Birrell. Cambridge: Cambridge Uni-versity Press, 1997; orig. publ. 1988.

Velasco, Sherry M. *Demons, Nausea, and Resistance in the Autobiography of Isabel de Jesús (1611–1682).* Albuquerque: University of New Mexico Press, 1996.

Von Hügel, Friedrich. *The Mystical Element of Religion as Studied in Saint Catherine of Genoa and Her Friends.* 2 vols. London: J. M. Dent, 1908, 1923.

Walker, Claire. *Gender and Politics in Early Modern Europe: English Convents in France and the Low Countries.* Houndmills, U.K.: Palgrave Macmillan, 2003.

Weber, Alison. "Between Ecstasy and Exorcism: Religious Negotiation in Sixteenth-Century Spain." *Journal of Medieval and Renaissance Studies* 23 (1993): 221–34.

———. "On the Margins of Ecstasy: María de San José as (Auto)Biographer." *Journal of the Insti-tute of Romance Studies* 4 (1996): 251–68.

———. "The Partial Feminism of Ana de San Bartolomé." In *Recovering Spain's Feminist Tradi-tion,* edited by Lisa Vollendorf, 69–87. New York: Modern Languages Association, 2001.

———. "Spiritual Administration: Gender and Discernment in the Carmelite Reform." *Sixteenth Century Journal* 31, no. 1 (2000): 123–46.

———. *Teresa of Avila and the Rhetoric of Femininity.* Princeton: Princeton University Press, 1990.

———. "The Three Lives of the *Vida:* The Uses of Convent Autobiography." In *Women, Texts and Authority in the Early Modern Spanish World,* edited by Marta V. Vicente and Luis R. Corteguera, 107–25. Aldershot, U.K.: Ashgate, 2003.

Weinstein, Donald. "The Prophet as Physician of Souls: Savonarola's Manual for Confessors." In *Society and Individual in Renaissance Florence*, edited by William J. Connell, 241–60. Berkeley: University of California Press, 2002.

Weinstein, Donald, and Rudolph M. Bell. *Saints and Society: The Two Worlds of Western Christendom, 1000–1700*. Chicago: University of Chicago Press, 1982.

Woodford, Charlotte. *Nuns as Historians in Early Modern Germany*. Oxford: Oxford University Press, 2002.

Woodward, Kenneth L. *Making Saints: How the Catholic Church Determines Who Becomes a Saint, Who Doesn't, and Why*. New York: Simon and Schuster, 1990.

Wright, Wendy. *Bond of Perfection: Jeanne de Chantal and François de Sales*. New York: Paulist Press, 1985.

———. "Inside My Body Is the Body of God: Margaret Mary Alacoque and the Tradition of Embodied Mysticism." in *The Mystical Gesture: Essays on Medieval and Early Modern Spiritual Culture in Honor of Mary E. Giles*, edited by Robert Boenig, 185–92. Aldershot, U.K.: Ashgate, 2000.

Zarco Cuevas, Julián. *España y la comunión frecuente y diaria en los siglos XVI y XVII*. El Escorial: La Ciudad de Dios, 1913.

Zarri, Gabriella, ed. *Donna, disciplina, crean̄za cristiana dal XV al XVII secolo*. Rome: Edizioni di Storia e Letteratura, 1996.

———. "From Prophecy to Discipline, 1450–1650." In *Women and Faith: Catholic Religious Life in Italy from Late Antiquity to the Present*, edited by Lucetta Scaraffia and Gabriella Zarri, 83–112. Cambridge, Mass.: Harvard University Press, 1999; orig. publ. 1994.

———. "Living Saints: A Typology of Female Sanctity in the Early Sixteenth Century." In *Women and Religion in Medieval and Renaissance Italy*, edited by Daniel Bornstein and Roberto Rusconi, 219–303. Chicago: University of Chicago Press, 1996; orig. essay publ. 1980.

INDEX

Numbers in italics refer to figures.